INTERNATIONAL BUILDING CODES AND GUIDELINES
FOR INTERIOR DESIGN

INTERNATIONAL BUILDING CODES AND GUIDELINES
FOR INTERIOR DESIGN

LISA M. TUCKER, PhD, LEED, AIA, ASID, CID, IDEC

Virginia Polytechnic Institute and State University (Virginia Tech)

FAIRCHILD BOOKS
NEW YORK · LONDON · OXFORD · NEW DELHI · SYDNEY

FAIRCHILD BOOKS
Bloomsbury Publishing Inc
1385 Broadway, New York, NY 10018, USA
50 Bedford Square, London, WC1B 3DP, UK

BLOOMSBURY, FAIRCHILD BOOKS and the Fairchild Books logo are trademarks of
Bloomsbury Publishing Plc

First published in the United States of America 2019

Cover design by Toby Way
Cover image: Dubai metro station interior details,
UAE © Francisco Cabeza-Lopez/Getty Images

Library of Congress Cataloging-in-Publication Data
Names: Tucker, Lisa M., author.
Title: International building codes and guidelines for interior design / Lisa M. Tucker, PhD,
    LEED, AIA, ASID, CID, IDEC, Virginia Polytechnic Institute and State University (Virginia
    Tech).
Description: New York, NY, USA : Fairchild Books, Bloomsbury Publishing Inc., 2019. | Includes
    bibliographical references and index.
Identifiers: LCCN 2018003366 (print) | LCCN 2018004932 (ebook) | ISBN 9781501324390
    (epdf) | ISBN 9781501324383 (pbk.) | ISBN 9781501324390 (pdf)
Subjects: LCSH: Buildings—Standards. | Interior architecture—Standards. | Interior decoration.
    | Building laws.
Classification: LCC TH420 (ebook) | LCC TH420 .T83 2019 (print) | DDC 729.02/18—dc23
LC record available at https://lccn.loc.gov/2018003366

ISBN: PB: 978-1-5013-2438-3
         ePDF: 978-1-5013-2439-0

Typeset by Lachina
Printed and bound in China

To find out more about our authors and books visit
www.fairchildbooks.com and sign up for our newsletter.

Brief contents

Contents

Background, Scope, and Administration

35   Part two

The Process of Applying the Code

Preface

Although there are several codes guidebooks available for both interiors and architecture, none of them walks a designer through the process of how to use the codes. That is the purpose and rationale behind this book. Designers use a process that is not linear but is roughly divided into project phases: programming, schematic design, design development, construction documents, and finally, construction administration. At each stage beginning with programming and taken through construction documents, the codes are applied in different ways and refined throughout the development of a project design.

The chapters in this book are organized around project-sector types, including hospitality, healthcare, mixed use, residential, and corporate office. It is then broken down into the phases of a project. The book begins with an overview of building codes and the history of codes. It takes project types through the design phases, includes a chapter on programming, discusses the code and guidelines research that happens at the beginning before design, and then covers the post-occupancy evaluation (POE). Although POEs are not often done, they are integral to

improving design work in the future. The last chapter contains a series of checklists that I have developed over the years to track the integration of codes during the phases of the design process.

Multiple projects are used to demonstrate a variety of design concepts and how various designers have worked through the code, The Americans with Disabilities Act (ADA), and various guidelines that might apply. Special attention has been given to including both LEED and WELL Building Standards. Historic preservation guidelines, FGI Guidelines for Healthcare, and universal design principles are also included. The conceptual approach is to illustrate how the multitude of regulatory requirements can be used to support a design concept.

This book would not have been possible without the many talented designers I have been privileged to work with over the years. I want to give special thanks to Meagan Kelley who helped me with the images in this book, of which there are many. I thank her for her hard work and determination to stick with what was often a messy project. Thanks Meagan!

Chapter 1: Intro
Chapter 2: History Background
Chapter 3: Scope and Administration/Enforcement

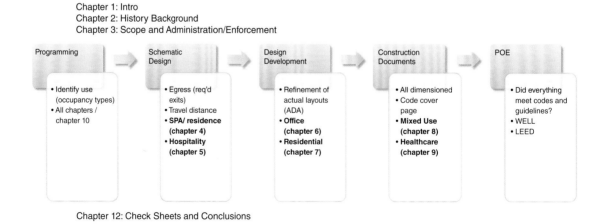

Chapter 12: Check Sheets and Conclusions

Part one

Background, Scope, and Administration

1

An Overview of Building Codes and the Design Process

Learning Objectives:

After reading this chapter and doing the exercises, students will be able to

- Understand an overview of the use of building codes and guidelines at each stage of the design process
- Be familiar with the structure of this book and how and where to find necessary information

Introduction

This chapter reviews each step of the design process and how building codes, accessibility guidelines, green building rating systems, the WELL Building Standard, and other industry specific guidelines impact each phase of the project design. Each specific project included in this book has a variety of goals and, depending of the use group, will require the use of several different codes and standards. Building codes are legal requirements consisting of a system of rules with which a building must comply. Guidelines, on the other hand, are general rules or principles that represent best practices. Standards, such as LEED (Leadership in Energy and Environmental Design), WELL, Green Globes, and the Living Building Challenge, are optional and are usually adopted by the designer and client based on the desire to create a building that goes above and beyond standard operating procedure as prescribed by the baseline building codes. The Americans with Disabilities Act (ADA) is a federal law that must be followed, whereas law does not mandate universal design. The International Building Code references ICC A117.1 Standard for Accessible and Usable Buildings and Facilities.

Book Organization

In large part, the organization of this book follows the design process. Each chapter will follow a specific design project type through the steps of using the applicable codes and standards, as well as additional guidelines such as LEED, the WELL Building Standard, and other sources of information related to the project type. The chapters are arranged by complexity, starting with the more basic projects and evolving into more complex issues and types. By layering in additional requirements, each chapter supports the development of an integrated design process using codes, guidelines, and standards. Through repetition, the process becomes familiar and integrated. Later chapters will contain at least one case study and will describe the process of integrating codes, guidelines, and standards for a specific project type. Chapter 12 contains a series of checklists that can be used during each phase of a project to meet the applicable codes and guidelines in a holistic manner. Figure 1.1 shows what has come to be known as the **MacLeamy curve** (2004) even though MacLeamy's work was based on earlier work by Boyd Paulson and others. The curve overlays effort expended at different points in the project design versus potential costs and compares traditional building delivery methods with **integrated project delivery** to demonstrate why integrated project delivery saves time and money and is the more efficient model. This is also the model adopted and required by both LEED and WELL.

Figure 1.1
MacLeamy curve for integrated project delivery

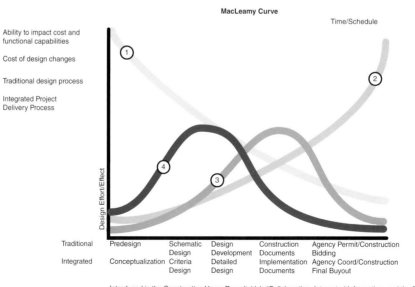

Introduced in the Construction Users Roundtable's "Collaboration, Integrated Information, and the Project Lifecycle in Building Design and Construction and Operation" (WP-1202, August 2004), the "MacLeamy Curve" illustrates the advantages of Integrated Project Delivery

Programming

During the **programming** stage of a project, the design team works with the owner and users of a building to determine the needs of the project. As a part of this early phase of the project, any special considerations, such as whether to design to meet LEED criteria or the WELL Building Standard should be a part of the discussion. The basic use group or groups is one of the first things to be determined, as this will lead to a variety of different code requirements. The use of the building will provide the direction for other considerations, such as which green building guidelines to use, which other standards might apply, and specific sections of the International Building Code (IBC) that are pertinent. For some project types, other industry specific guidelines might also apply—for example, historic preservation standards or healthcare design guidelines.

Integrated Project Delivery

For sustainability guidelines, such as the LEED Green Building Rating System v.4 and the Living Building Challenge 3.1 and the WELL Building Standard v.1, it is critical that all members of the design team be included as early as possible. An integrated design team will typically include the architect, engineers, owner, interior designer, landscape architect, and either a **LEED Accredited Professional** or **WELL Accredited Professional** or both. In order to be successful, the team (designers, contractor, consultants, and owner) should work together throughout all phases of the design project. The 2018 **International Green Construction Code (IgCC)** will be published in 2018, combining the International Code Council's (ICC) IgCC and ASHRAE's (American Society of Heating, Refrigeration and Air Conditioning Engineers) Standard 189.1. The ICC and ASHRAE have partnered to develop and publish one green code that will likely be adopted in many jurisdictions.

LEED Green Building Rating System

The LEED Green Building Rating System
(Leadership in Energy and Environmental Design) is the most widely used green building rating system in the world. It is organized around eight key areas: Location and Transportation, Sustainable Sites, Water Efficiency, Energy and Atmosphere, Materials and Resources, Indoor Environmental Quality, Innovation, and Regional Priority. The four main types of the LEED Green Building Rating Systems are Building Design and Construction, Interior Design and Construction, Building Operations and Maintenance, and Neighborhood Development. Since different building types have different needs and requirements, specific facility types comprise each of these four primary certifications, including retail, schools, healthcare, hospitality, commercial interiors, data centers, homes and multifamily low-rise, multifamily high-rise, and warehouses and distribution centers. LEED certification levels include certified, Silver, Gold, and Platinum (Figure 1.2).

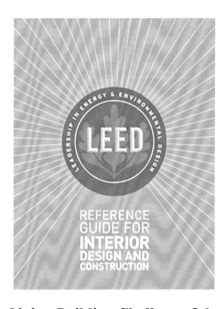

Figure 1.2
LEED guidelines cover

The Living Building Challenge 3.1

The Living Building Challenge 3.1 consists of seven petals or areas: Place, Water, Energy, Health and Happiness, Materials, Equity and Beauty. A project meeting all twenty imperatives is **Living Certified**. **Petal Certification** requires that at least three of the seven petals are met, and **Net Zero Energy Certification** demonstrates that 100 percent of the building's energy needs are produced with onsite renewable energy. A unique aspect of the Living Building Challenge is that a project must meet all requirements for a year before becoming certified (Figure 1.3).

Green Globes

Like LEED, **Green Globes** is a third-party green building rating system. It was originally developed by Energy and Environment Canada (ECD) in 2000 and was adapted by the Green Building Initiative in 2004 for the United States. Table 1.1 compares Green Globes and the LEED rating systems. A detailed study completed by faculty at the University of Minnesota (2006) comparing the two systems can be found at http://www.nlcpr. com/Green_Building_Rating_UofM.pdf.

The Canadian government has been using Green Globes for new construction for years, and the US General Services Administration (GSA) recommended its use beginning in 2013. The Green Globes assessment is designed to be completed in-house by the project team and uses a questionnaire to obtain required information. Final document submission requirements include **construction documents** and specifications, life-cycle cost information, energy modeling, and meeting records indicating green building plans for the project.

Figure 1.3
Living Building
Challenge cover

Table 1.1 Comparison of Green Globes and LEED

	Green Globes	LEED
Uses ANSI-approved consensus development process	Yes	No
Nationally accepted program	Yes	Yes
Program delivery	Online interactive questionnaires	Online submission of templates
Total program points	1,000	110
Partial credits and recognizes that some criteria may be "not applicable"	Yes	Limited
Prerequisites	No	Yes
Uses life-cycle assessment and multiple attribute evaluations	Yes	No
Forest certifications accepted	FSC, SFI, ATFS, CSA	FSC

The WELL Building Standard 1.0

The WELL Building Standard is the first standard that addresses human well-being in the built environment. It uses seven concepts to guide design for the improved health and well-being of human occupants: Air, Water, Nourishment, Light, Comfort, Fitness, and Mind. The WELL Building Standard was developed by **Delos** and is administered by the International WELL Building Institute. Certification is for a three-year period for three project types: Core and Shell, Existing and New Interiors, and Existing and New Buildings. Certification levels include Silver, Gold, and Platinum. Core and Shell projects are not eligible for recertification (Figure 1.4).

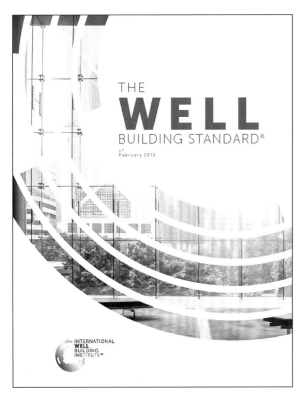

Figure 1.4
WELL Building
Standard cover

Schematic Design

During the **schematic design** phase, the design team will establish an overall form and floor plan and a conceptual approach for the project. Overall egress considerations will impact the circulation of the spatial model. Although many things will change during the design process and in future phases, the overall egress component of the design needs to be established early in the process to insure that the required number and placement of exits, as well as corridor widths, vertical circulation, and other major components, are in place to meet the needs of the project and that they are in compliance with building codes and accessibility guidelines.

Making sure these are correct at the beginning will save time and money, as well as aggravation, later in the design process. As with all design stages of the project, it is important to get client approval of the schematic design prior to moving on to the next stage (Figure 1.5).

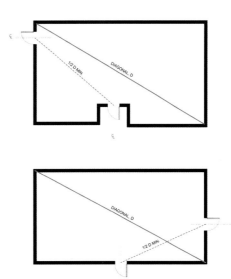

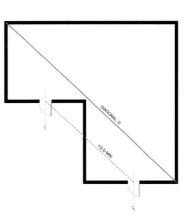

Figure 1.5
Space-planning
code diagram
showing required
exit distances

Design Development

Once a final direction is chosen at the completion of the schematic design phase, the project team will move into **design development**. During this stage of the project, the team will be making actual material, finish, furniture, and equipment selections. Ideally, these will reflect both the design concept as well as any project goals regarding sustainability and other applicable guidelines. All selections must also comply with all applicable codes and guidelines. Like programming and schematic design, the owner needs to approve all decisions prior to creating the construction documents for the project.

Space-Planning Considerations

Maintaining adequate clearances and a clear egress path is essential for building code compliance. The need for integrated accessibility will inform the size of key spaces, such as restrooms.

Three-Dimensional Considerations

ADA impacts several three-dimensional characteristics of the design, including countertop and other work-surface heights, wall sconce placement and other projections, water fountains, bathroom design, and signage (Figures 1.6, 1.7, 1.8).

WELL Building Standard

Designing a space that meets various aspects of the WELL Building Standard can impact the placement of stairs and their proximity to the lobby and elevators (fitness), water fountain placement (water), and fixture and furniture placement (lighting).

Ergonomics

The WELL Standard also incorporates ergonomic considerations for the design. By integrating active furnishings (treadmill desks, bicycle desks) and adjustable-height workstations, the WELL Building Standard supports a more active lifestyle by building occupants (Table 1.2).

Finishes

Finishes must first meet the requirements of the code based on their fire-rating class. Additional considerations include durability concerns, ADA requirements with regard to slip resistance, and WELL Building Standards related to volatile organic compounds (VOCs) and materials content, many of which overlap or go beyond those found in the LEED Green Building Rating System standards and the Living Building Challenge requirements (Table 1.3).

Figure 1.6
ADA elevation/3D diagram showing how ADA impacts 3D design

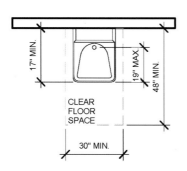

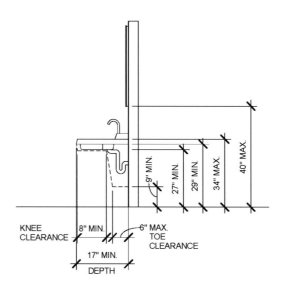

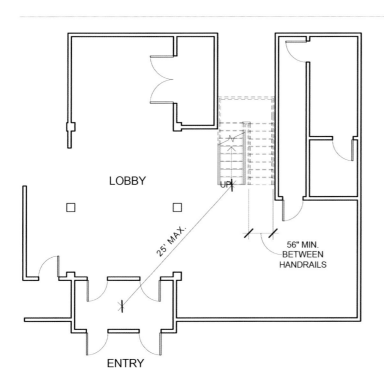

LOBBY

25' MAX.

UP

56" MIN.
BETWEEN
HANDRAILS

ENTRY

STAIRS

- Clearly visible from main entry

- Open/accessible during all regular business hours

- At least two of the following:
    Art
    Music
    Daylight/Skylight
    Views
    Light min. 20 fc (215 lux)

Figure 1.7
Stair placement
requirements
based on the
WELL Building
Standard

KEYBOARD & MONITOR HEIGHT	SEATED ELBOW RANGE	STANDING ELBOW HEIGHT RANGE	SEATED EYE HEIGHT RANGE	STANDING EYE HEIGHT RANGE
5' 0"	21.9"	36.5"	42"	55.7"
5' 6"	24.4"	40.1"	45.6"	61.2"
6' 0"	30.5"	45.4"	52.1"	68.6"

Figure 1.8
Adjustable-height
desk (as required
in the WELL
Building Standard)

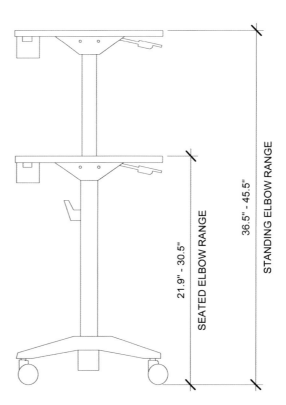

21.9" - 30.5"
SEATED ELBOW RANGE

36.5" - 45.5"
STANDING ELBOW RANGE

Table 1.2 Monitor and Keyboard Height Variations for Sitting and Standing Based on Height*

Height	Seated elbow height	Standing elbow height	Seated eye height	Standing eye height
5'-0"	21.9"	36.5"	42"	55.7"
5'-1"	22.3"	37.1"	42.5"	56.6"
5'-2"	22.6"	37.8"	43"	57.6"
5'-3"	22.6"	38.2"	43.4"	58.6"
5'-4"	23"	38.8"	44"	59.4"
5'-5"	23.8"	39.6"	44.9"	60.4"
5'-6"	24.4"	40.1"	45.6"	61.2"
5'-7"	25.3"	40.7"	46.5"	62.2"
5'-8"	26.4"	41.9"	47.8"	63.6"
5'-9"	27"	42.5"	48.5"	64.4"
5'-10"	27.8"	43.3"	49.4"	65.4"
5'-11"	28.6"	43.5"	49.8"	66.1"
6'-0"	29.3"	44.2"	50.7"	67"
6'-1"	30.5"	45.4"	52.1"	68.6"

(*subject to variations based on actual person)
Source: Ergoprize.com

Table 1.3 VOC Requirements from LEED, Living Building Challenge, and WELL Building Standard

WELL Building Standard

Air Feature Level Matrix

01 Air Quality Standards
   1: Standards for Volatile Substances
   2: Standards for Particulate Matter and Inorganic Gases
   3: Radon

02 Smoking Ban
   1: Indoor Smoking Ban
   2: Outdoor Smoking Ban

03 Ventilation Effectiveness
   1: Ventilation Design
   2: Demand Controlled Ventilation

04 VOC Reduction
   1: Interior Paints and Coatings
   2: Interior Adhesives and Sealants
   3: Flooring
   4: Insulation
   5: Furniture and Furnishings

05 Air Filtration
   1: Filter Accommodation
   2: Particle Filtration
   3: Air Filtration Maintenance

06 Microbe and Mold Control
   1: Cooling Coil Mold Reduction
   2: Mold Inspections

07 Construction Pollutant Management
   1: Duct Protection
   2: Filter Replacement
   3: VOC Absorption Management
   4: Dust Containment and Removal

08 Healthy Entrance
   1: Permanent Entryway Walk-Off System
   2: Entryway Air Seal

09 Cleaning Protocol
   1: Cleaning Plan for Occupied Spaces

10 Pesticide Management
   1: Pesticide Use

11 Fundamental Material Safety
   1: Asbestos and Lead Restriction
   2: Lead Abatement
   3: Asbestos Abatement
   4: Polychlorinated Biphenyl Abatement
   5: Mercury Limitation

Additional areas controlled and monitored: cleaning equipment, combustion minimization, toxic material reduction, ventilation, air filtration, and pest control.

Source: WELL Building Standard v.1

Table 1.3 VOC Requirements from LEED, Living Building Challenge, and Well Building Standard *(continued)*

LEED v.4 ID + C	Living Building Challenge
Indoor Environmental Quality	**Health and Happiness**
Minimum Indoor Air Quality Performance (Prerequisite) Environmental Tobacco Control (Prerequisite) Enhanced Indoor Air Quality Strategies Low Emitting Materials • Indoor paints and coatings applied on site • Interior adhesives and sealants applied on site • Flooring • Composite wood • Ceilings, walls, thermal, and acoustic insulation • Furniture Construction Indoor Air Quality Management Plan Indoor Air Quality Assessment	Healthy Interior Environment • Compliance with ASHRAE 62 • Smoking prohibited • Results of IAQ (Indoor Air Quality) test before and nine months after occupancy Compliance with CDPH (California Department of Health) Standard Method v1.1-2010 for all interior building products that have the potential to emit VOCs Dedicated exhaust systems for kitchens, bathrooms, and janitorial spaces An entry approach that reduces particulates tracked in through shoes An outline of a cleaning protocol that complies with EPA Design for Environment label
Source: LEED v.4 ID + C	
	Materials
	Red List • Products cannot contain Red List materials or chemicals Responsible Industry • All timber must be FSC 100% • Stone must meet Natural Stone Council (NSC) 373 Standard • Must use one "Declare" product for every 500 square meters
	Source: Living Building Challenge 3.1

Construction Documents

The final phase of the document preparation for construction includes the completion of drawings and specifications consistent with all applicable codes and guidelines as well as other standards used for the project.

Construction Administration

During **construction administration**, the design team representative is charged with making sure everything being built is consistent with the design intent, including all applicable standards, codes, and guidelines.

Post-Occupancy Evaluation

Upon completion of the construction, a design team representative typically does a building walk-through to create a punch list of any items that need to be addressed prior to final completion. Once the space has been occupied, it is important to test the design solution to see if it is working the way it was intended. A **post-occupancy evaluation** typically involves surveying and interviewing the client and occupants.

The WELL Standard has a provision whereby building occupants must be surveyed within thirty days and that all results are made available to building occupants, the building owner, and the **International WELL Building Institute (IWBI)**. Questions in the survey include inquiries about building acoustics, lighting, thermal comfort, and other building features (Table 1.4).

Table 1.4 Typical Survey Questions for WELL Building Standard Based on the Occupant Indoor Environment Quality (IEQ) Survey from the Center for the Built Environment (CBE) at UC Berkeley

IEQ Research Topics

CBE projects related to IEQ in buildings include:

- *Advanced Human Thermal Comfort Model*
  A tool for predicting human comfort resulting from HVAC, building, and façade design decisions.
- *Acoustical Analysis in Office Environments Using POE Surveys*
  CBE mined Occupant IEQ Survey data to investigate occupant satisfaction in a variety of office configurations.
- *Acoustical Field Study in a UFAD Building*
  Verifying acoustical performance of as-built partitions and acoustical construction.
- *Occupant IEQ Survey and Building Benchmarking Database*
  Occupant surveys are an invaluable source of information regarding occupant satisfaction and workplace effectiveness.
- *Occupant Satisfaction with IEQ in Green and LEED-Certified Buildings*
  The LEED system is transforming the building industry, but little is known about occupant satisfaction in these buildings.
- *Occupant Perspectives on Outdoor Noise in Office Buildings*
  Testing perceived barriers to adoption of naturally ventilated and mixed mode buildings.
- *Personal Comfort Systems*
  Providing individual control of thermal comfort for occupant satisfaction and reduced energy consumption.
- *Speech Privacy in Office Environments*
  Validation of a method to predict speech privacy in a diversity of office environments.
- *Using Task Ambient Conditioning Systems to Improve Comfort and Energy Performance*
  New space conditioning systems provide individual occupant control and may increase comfort and productivity while reducing overall building energy.
- *The Impact of Team Space Design on Collaboration*
  Assessing individual and group worker effectiveness in today's new workplace paradigm.
- *Thermal Comfort in Non-Uniform Spaces*
  Using the Advanced Thermal Comfort Model to study comfort implications of emerging green building technologies.
- *CBE Thermal Comfort Tool*
  Creating a free online tool for evaluating comfort according to ASHRAE Standard 55.
- *The Impact of Ventilation on Productivity*
  Comparing worker productivity to physical conditions in the workplace environment.
- *Using Wireless Power for Personal Comfort Devices*
  Developing the next generation of personal comfort devices.
- *Symposium on the High Performance Workplace*
  A discussion of directions for creating effective, healthy, and productive environments.

Source: CBE Website, https://www.cbe.berkeley.edu/research/research_ieq.htm

Building Codes

The primary baseline building code used in the United States is the **International Building Code (IBC)** produced by the **International Codes Council (ICC)**. The IBC covers all building types and construction except that which is covered by the **International Residential Code (IRC)**. The ICC has created a family of codes that include the International Fire Code (IFC), the International Mechanical Code (IMC), the International Plumbing Code (IPC), the International Private Sewage Disposal Code (IPSDC), the International Fuel Gas Code (IFGC), the International Energy Conservation Code (IECC), the International Existing Building Code (IEBC), the International Code Council Performance Code (ICCPC), the International Zoning Code (IZC), the International Property Maintenance Code (OPMC), and the International Urban-Wildland Interface Code (IUWIC).

The IgCC

The IgCC is a green building code that includes minimum mandatory requirements. Unlike other building codes by the ICC, the IgCC allows for jurisdictional choice as to how to comply with its requirements. IgCC is designed to overlay and interact with all the other ICC baseline codes, including the IBC. The purpose of the IgCC is to integrate minimum mandatory requirements that meet best practices for green design and sustainability. The jurisdiction choosing to follow the IgCC makes a series of choices as to how it will comply with this overlay code. This includes the selection of project electives, from which a jurisdiction must choose between one and fourteen. Several organizations were cooperating sponsors of the IgCC, these were the American Institute of Architects (AIA), ASTM International, ASHRAE, US Green Building Council (USGBC), and Illuminating Engineering Society (IES). In 2016, ASHRAE and ICC partnered and agreed to merge the ASHRAE 189.1 Green Standard and IgCC to publish one joint green code in 2018.

Conclusions

Building codes, standards, and guidelines provide a rich context within which the design can provide a safe and healthy interior environment that contributes to the welfare of the building occupants. When viewed as a contributory factor, these regulations and guidelines can help the design team create the best possible solution for a project.

Key Terms

construction administration
construction documents
Delos
design development
Green Globes
integrated project delivery
International Building Code (IBC)
International Codes Council (ICC)

IgCC
International Residential Code (IRC)
International WELL Building Institute (IWBI)
LEED (Leadership in Energy and Environmental Design)
LEED Accredited Professional
Living Building Challenge 3.1
Living Certified
MacLeamy curve
Net Zero Energy Certification
Petal Certified
post-occupancy evaluation
programming
schematic design
WELL Accredited Professional
WELL Building Standard

Assignments

1. Look at each of the following websites to familiarize yourself with the content provided for each of the following: WELL Building Standard, LEED Rating Systems, Living Building Challenge Rating System.
    a. https://Wellonline.Wellcertified.com/
    b. http://www.usgbc.org/leed
    c. http://living-future.org/lbc
2. Compare and contrast what you have already learned about the design process with any new information you have just read about the integrated design process. What are the advantages of each approach? What are the potential problems with each?
3. Contact your local building inspector and find out what codes and regulations have been adopted in your locale.
4. Visit the ICC website to learn more about the organization, their codes and standards, and support services at www.iccsafe.org.

Background for Codes and Guidelines

Learning Objectives:

After reading this chapter and doing the exercises, students will be able to

- Describe the history of the development of building codes
- Describe the importance of building codes and standards
- Describe the purpose of building codes and how they came to exist
- Understand the relationship between the International Building Code and the International Green Construction Code
- Identify standards referenced in the International Building Code

History of Building Codes

Building codes have been around since Hammurabi, circa 1754 BCE. In the **Code of Hammurabi**, an ancient Babylonian text from Mesopotamia, six provisions referenced buildings and builders. Specifically, if a builder built a house that killed the owner, the builder, too, would be killed. Similarly, if a slave died as a result of shoddy construction, the builder had to give the slave's owner a new slave; if a child died, the builder's own child would be killed.

While the Code of Hammurabi seems overly punitive by today's standards, it does reflect the desire to make buildings safe for occupants. Following the burning of Rome in 64 CE, the Roman Empire developed construction standards in response to the poor construction of vernacular buildings. These new standards addressed construction, the space between buildings, and even sanitation issues (see Figures 2.1 and 2.2 and Table 2.1).

Figure 2.1
Bas relief of Hammurabi

Table 2.1 Hammurabi's Code

Section	Code
228	If a builder constructed a house for someone, that person would pay the builder two shekels of silver per sar (36 square meters)
229	A builder will be slain if he builds a house that is weak and falls down and kills its owner
230	If the householder's child is killed, the builder's child will be killed
231	If the householder's slave is killed, the builder must give a slave for the slave
232	If goods are destroyed, then the builder must replace all that is lost, and he will rebuild the house from his own material
233	If the work was not done properly, the builder will pay to make the construction correct

Shekel: ancient measure of weight or currency

1 Sar = 36 square meters = 1 garden plot = 60 gin

Source: "Babylonian Weights and Measures," http://www.daviddfriedman.com/Academic/Course_Pages/Legal%20Systems%202017/Hammurabi/babylon_wts_and_measures.html

Figure 2.2
Painting of the Burning of Rome: The above image is *The Fire of Rome, 18 July 64 AD*, an oil painting by Hubert Robert (1733–1808). This painting is now located in the Musee des Beaux-Arts Andre Malraux. Le Havre, France.

Figure 2.3
Great Fire of London

Similar issues were addressed following the Great Fire of London. The typical medieval city had tightly placed buildings; no sanitation system, resulting in raw sewage in the city; and timber construction that led to both fire and contamination concerns. Following the fire in 1666, Parliament debated for two years before passing the "London Building Act," which provided regulations for most of London. Unfortunately, much of the city was rebuilt during the two years of debate, using the same flawed practices that had led to the fire (Figure 2.3).

When the Chicago Fire broke out in 1871, there were roughly 60,000 buildings in the city, and approximately half of these were constructed of wood. The fire, which raged for two days, resulted in the loss of 17,000 buildings and the deaths of between 200 and 300 people; it also left roughly 100,000 people homeless. Despite this, there was still resistance to tightened building controls in the United States (Figure 2.4).

In 1903, more than 600 people died inside the "fireproof" Iroquois Theater (also located in Chicago), which boasted many fireproof materials. The massive loss of life led to many of the assembly codes that govern buildings containing large entertainment venues. Investigators found that twenty-seven of the thirty exits were either blocked or contained mechanisms that made them hard to open as people panicked while attempting to escape.

The 1906 San Francisco Earthquake resulted in widespread ruin. The parts of the city not destroyed directly as a result of the earthquake were lost to the ensuing fires. Following the extensive devastation, the scientific community finally committed to creating a building code. The primary focus of the building codes were to keep a building standing long enough to safely evacuate people in the event of catastrophe (Figure 2.5).

The 1911 Triangle shirtwaist factory fire in New York City is often cited as one of the most horrific fires in industrial history, resulting in the death of 146 workers. The Asch Building had only one operational elevator (of four), one of two exit stairs was locked from the outside, and the other opened inward. Because of the lack of exits, the workers in the building were unable to make it out during the eighteen minutes in which the building was consumed by fire. The resulting tragedy led to building codes that protected worker safety in the event of a fire. The American Society of Safety Engineers (originally called the United Association of Casualty Inspectors) was founded in October 1911 in New York City in response to the fire.

In 1930, a fire at another fireproof building, the Ohio Penitentiary, led to the loss of 322 lives. Oily rags and wood scaffolding provided fuel for the fire. These conditions resulted in new regulations mandating smoke alarms, sprinkler systems, and noncombustible materials in spaces made for the containment of human beings.

A fire in 1942 at one of Boston's most popular night clubs, the Cocoanut Grove, led to the deaths of 492 people, in only twelve minutes, when guests became trapped by a revolving door at the main entrance. This tragedy led to the establishment of new National Fire Protection Association (NFPA) guidelines regulating stair enclosures, interior finishes, lighting, and loose furniture in similar settings to make sure exits are not obstructed.

Seventy-nine years later to the day after the Triangle Fire (March 25, 1990), another tragic fire in New York City resulted in the loss of eighty-seven lives. The Happy Land Social Club, located in the Bronx, was an unlicensed club that had been cited previously for building code violations, including a lack of exits, sprinkler system, and fire alarms. In this case, intentional arson was the cause of the fire.

Fire is not the only tragedy that has caused a review of existing building codes in the United States. In 1992, for example, Hurricane Andrew devastated Florida and Louisiana. Ninety percent of the homes in Dade County, Florida, had roof damage as a result of the hurricane, and 117,000 homes were either destroyed or damaged by high winds (Figure 2.6).

Over time, building codes have developed to protect building occupants in several ways, usually in response to a catastrophic event, such as the Great Fire of London, the 1871 Chicago Fire, the San Francisco Earthquake of 1906, and more recently Hurricane Andrew (1992) (Table 2.2).

Figure 2.4
Chicago Fire 1871, Currier and Ives

Figure 2.5
San Francisco Earthquake 1906

Figure 2.6
Hurricane Andrew

Table 2.2 Historic Disasters and Resulting Building Codes

Disaster	Resulting Change or New Code
1903 Iroquois Theater Fire	Maximum seating capacity Exit signage Exit doors Sprinklers
1911 Triangle Shirtwaist Factory Fire	Sprinklers additional standards High-rise exits requirements
1930 Ohio Penitentiary Fire	Codes for jails and prisons were added to NFPA 101 Life Safety Code
1942 Cocoanut Grove Fire	Requirements for suppression systems added to Life Safety Code (see also the Rhythm Club Fire of 1940)
1946 Winecoff Hotel Fire, Atlanta	Requirements for inclusions of fire-suppression and fire-alarm systems in hotels
1949 St. Anthony Hospital Fire	Need for national codes in hospitals and healthcare facilities
1958 Our Lady of Angels school fire, Illinois	Automatic fire-alarm requirement, firewalls, and emergency lighting added; addition of sprinklers in school buildings
1977 Beverly Hills Supper Club, Southgate, Kentucky	Sprinklers in nightclubs and other places of assembly with over 300 people
1980 casino fires—MGM Grand and Dupont Plaza	All had to be retrofitted with positive alarm sequencing and legislations requiring sprinklers in US hotels and motels
2003 Station Night Club, Rhode Island	New standards for night clubs

Source: Siemens, "Commercial and Fire Codes," http://w3.usa.siemens.com/buildingtechnologies/us/en/fire-products-and-systems/fire-protection-products/fire-detection/smoke-detection-knowledge-center/pages/fires-that-changed-fire-codes.aspx

The International Building Codes

The International Code Council (ICC) was first established in 1994 as a nonprofit organization with the purpose of developing a single comprehensive set of building codes. The group combined previous codes groups **Building Officials and Code Administrators International (BOCA)**, **International Conference of Building Officials (ICBO)**, and the **Southern Building Code Congress International (SBCCI)**. The ICC releases both the **International Building Code (IBC)** and the **International Residential Code (IRC)**, as well as energy codes, plumbing codes, mechanical code, fire code, and the **International Green Construction Code (IgCC)** and other codes in the family of ICC Codes. ICC Codes are updated and published every three years to stay up to the latest research and technology. The most current editions of the ICC Codes at the time of printing of this book are the 2018 editions, on which this book is based.

The International Energy Conservation Code (IECC)

The International Energy 2016 Conservation Code allows for three commercial building compliance paths: ASHRAE 90.1-2016 or one of two prescriptive approaches to building energy performance. Within this series of approaches, lighting and power requirements apply when a new lighting system is installed in a new building, addition, or tenant build out; when an existing system is altered; when an occupancy change increases energy use; or when a change in occupancy requires less lighting power density (LPD) than in the LPD tables. (There are exceptions made for historic buildings, dwelling units, and walk-in coolers and freezers.)

The electrical power and lighting system requirements include required controls and wattage efficiency limits, interior and exterior power allowances, exterior controls and lamp efficiencies, electrical metering, and both motor and vertical and horizontal transportation equipment.

The International Existing Building Code

The International Existing Building Code (IEBC) allows for alternative ways of approaching existing building alterations, renovations, additions, and change of occupancy since many times they do not meet current building codes for new construction. Three paths allow the designer to work within the IEBC to meet current requirements: using a prescriptive compliance method (Chapter 5), using a work area compliance method (Chapters 6 through 12), or using a performance compliance method (Chapter 13).

The International Green Construction Code

The IgCC model code addresses sustainability of a building and its site through all the phases of a project. The IgCC code is designed to work in conjunction with the other ICC codes and as an additional overlay to the IBC. It integrates ASHRAE Standards 189.1 as an alternate compliance path as well as the National Green Building Standard ICC-700 and the International Energy Conservation Code. In the 2018 edition of IgCC, ASHRAE 189.1 will make up the entire body of the requirements except for the administrative provisions. The 2018 edition is published as a result of partnership between ICC and ASHRAE.

The purpose of the IgCC is to reduce the impact of the built environment on the natural environment through the conservation of materials, energy, natural resources, and water. The IgCC works with all buildings—existing and new—except those falling under the IRC, R-3 or R-2 or R-4 under four stories. The goal is for the IgCC to be adopted on a mandatory basis; it is not a rating system, such as LEED, nor is it intended to replace such rating systems.

As a layer on the IBC, the IgCC allows jurisdictions to add up to twenty additional environmental criteria, including storm-water management, a natural resources inventory, landscape irrigation, management of vegetation, building-site waste management, transportation impact, heat-island mitigation, and site lighting. It requires recycling areas and for 55 percent of materials to be recycled, recyclable, bio-based, or indigenous.

The IgCC provides two compliance paths: prescriptive based and performance based, using the Zero Energy Performance Index. Water efficiency is required for plumbing fixtures, appliances, cooling towers, and car washes; metering monitors water use. Rain water collection, gray-water reuse, reclaimed water systems, and alternative water sources are all encouraged. The IgCC has currently been adopted by the states of Rhode Island, Maryland, and Oregon, as well as cities in Arizona, Florida, Washington, and New Hampshire (Figure 2.7).

Figure 2.7
Cover
International
Green
Construction Code

History of the Americans with Disabilities Act

Although the current Americans with Disabilities Act dates to 1990, the history of this legislation dates to much earlier. The first major policy shift took place in 1973, with the passage of Section 504 of the Rehabilitation Act. This was the first time that antidiscrimination was applied to people with disabilities as a class of people or minority group. The ADA was first introduced in Congress in 1988. In 1989, the **Americans with Disabilities Act (ADA)** was first introduced during the 101st Congress by Senators Harkin and Durrenberger and Representatives Coelho and Fish. The ADA was signed into law on July 26, 1990. In 2008, a series of amendments were added to ADA, and in 2010, the updated ADA regulations, with Titles II and III and revised transportation regulations, were released (Figure 2.8), with Title I updates added in 2013. ICC also publishes Standard A117.1 Accessible and Usable Building and Facilities that is referenced in the IBC; the latest edition of the ICC A117.1 is the 2017 edition.

NFPA Electrical and Fire Safety Codes

The National Fire Protection Association (NFPA) provides codes and standards for electrical, life safety, and fire alarms and signaling for new and existing buildings. These standards cover fire sprinkler systems, fire alarms, electrical systems, and other fire safety standards (Figure 2.9).

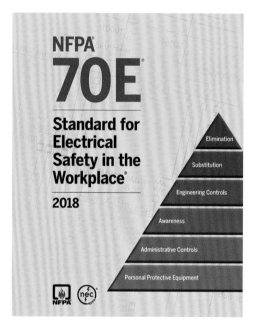

Figure 2.9
Cover Standard for Electrical Safety in the Workplace

Figure 2.8
Cover ADA, 2010 revisions

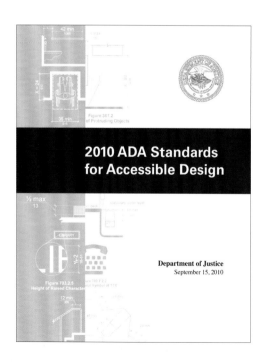

Other Standards

In addition to federal regulations (ADA) and building codes, the ICC references several pertinent standards that apply to building construction.

- **American Concrete Institute (ACI)**
- **American Society of Heating, Refrigerating, and Air Conditioning Engineers (ASHRAE)**
- **American National Standards Institute (ANSI)**
- **American Society for Testing and Materials (ASTM International)**

Deciding Which Code to Use

Each jurisdiction goes through a formal procedure of adopting the building codes they will apply. At this time, additional provisions or changes can also be made. For example, in Virginia, code officials adopt the IBC and make revisions to it for the state. The Uniform Statewide Building Code includes four parts: the Construction Code, the Rehabilitation Code, the Maintenance Code, and Errata to the Virginia Building and Fire Regulations (http://www.dhcd.virginia.gov/index. php/va-building-codes/building-and-fire-codes/ regulations/uniform-statewide-building-code-usbc.html). This process is fairly typical across the United States.

Guidelines

Guidelines are not mandatory unless required by the jurisdiction. They provide guidance for how to improve a building's performance in either sustainability or overall occupant health. For example, ICC has published four guidelines: ICC G1-2010 Guideline for Replicable Buildings, ICC G2-2010 Guideline for Acoustics, ICC G3-2011 Global Guideline for Practical Public Toilet Design, and ICC G4-2012 Guideline for Commissioning.

LEED

The LEED Green Building Rating Systems are in version 4.0 and have been developed for both building design and construction and commercial interiors. There are also guidelines for neighborhood development, homes and building operations, and maintenance.

Living Building Challenge 3.1

The Living Building Challenge is not as widely known or used as LEED. It takes a more proactive approach to sustainability and incorporated Net-Zero concepts, as well as an overall approach based on a completely new approach to buildings, as opposed to working within the existing parameters as LEED does. LEED seeks to transform the built environment within existing systems, while the Living Building Challenge provides a new approach.

Green Globes

Like LEED, Green Globes is a green building rating system. Originally developed in Canada and later adopted in the United States, Green Globes allocates points in the areas of project management, site, energy, water, resources, emission and effluents, and indoor environment. There are four possible tiers in the rating, Tier 1 achieving 35 to 54 percent of the points; Tier 2, 55 to 69 percent; Tier 3, 70 to 84 percent; and Tier 4 with 85 percent or more of the points achieved.

WELL Building Standard

The WELL Building Standard is the first of its kind and seeks to have buildings that support human health. The rating system, developed by Delos under the directive of the Clinton Global Initiative works in conjunction with both LEED and the Living Building Challenge; it is organized around seven Concepts: Air, Water, Nourishment, Light, Fitness, Comfort, and Mind. The individual features are either performance based or prescriptive. Buildings must meet all preconditions and must be reevaluated every three years for compliance. Buildings meeting all preconditions and 40 percent of optimization credits are Gold certified, while those meeting all preconditions and 80 percent of optimization credits are Platinum certified.

Industry Specific Guidelines

Each industry has become increasingly more specialized as buildings and building systems have become more complex. Examples of this include buildings for healthcare, education, retail, hospitality, and historic buildings.

Healthcare

Healthcare design is specialization that is both highly regulated and highly complex. LEED has a Green Rating System supplement specifically for healthcare. Additional guidelines for healthcare include the **Facility Guidelines Institute (FGI)** *Guidelines for the Design and Construction of Hospitals and Outpatient Facilities* (Figure 2.10). According to the American Institute of Architects (AIA) Academy of Architecture for Health, architects should follow changes to the IBC, FGI guidelines, and NFPA 99: Health Care Facilities Code. The Centers for Disease Control (CDC) has written guidelines for the containment and treatment of infectious diseases, such as the Ebola virus.

Figure 2.10
Cover FGI
Guidelines

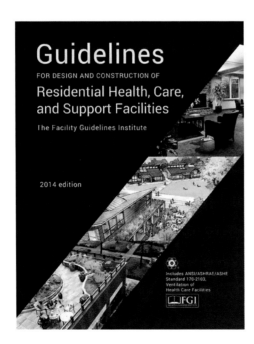

Education

The Collaborative for High Performance Schools (CHPS) focuses on student performance through improvements in the built environment. The CHPS Best Practices Manual outlines how a design team can meet the demands for a high performance school in six volumes.

> Volume I: Planning for High Performance Schools
>
> Volume II: Design for High Performance Schools
>
> Volume III: Criteria for High Performance Schools
>
> Volume IV: Maintenance and Operations of High Performance Schools
>
> Volume V: Commissioning of High Performance Schools
>
> Volume VI: High Performance Relocatable Classrooms

In addition to the manuals, the CHPS website provides several other resources for design teams, including a searchable database, product resources, and technical resources.

Hospitality

The primary resource for hospitality design is the NEWH (Network of Executive Women in Hospitality). Today, the organization simply calls itself NEWH: The Hospitality Industry Network and includes an extensive membership of all people in the industry. The organization provides information on sustainability for hospitality design, including several resources for this. Additional references for hospitality design include *Hospitality Design* magazine and *Boutique Design* magazine, with extensive product inks, the LEED Guidelines for Hospitality (both ID+C and BD+C), and several individual corporate sets of guidelines for designers, such as the Wyndham Hotels and Resorts guidelines.

Historic Preservation

Synergies between historic preservation and sustainability have been explored in recent decades. One advantage of historic buildings is the simplicity of the materials used for construction. They tend to be locally obtained or fabricated and rely heavily on natural components, such as wood, stone, clay, and brick. This makes the materials inherently sustainable and meets locally sourced objectives. In addition, these materials often contribute to good indoor air quality. The primary toxins found in historic buildings are lead, asbestos, and combustion-related by-products related to early methods of heating.

The guidelines for historic buildings in the United States are the **Secretary of the Interior's Guidelines for the Treatment of Historic Properties** (Figure 2.11). The standards are divided into approach types: reconstruction, rehabilitation, restoration, and preservation. In addition to the ten standards, the Department of the Interior has produced forty-seven Preservation Briefs on specific materials and components of historic buildings. The use of historic preservation guidelines is required for properties listed on the **National Register of Historic Places**, and the state-level historic preservation officer should review all work to make sure it complies with the Secretary's Standards. Failure to do so can result in removal from historic registers (state and national). When applying for state or federal tax credits, use of the Secretary's Standards is also required to make sure work is compliant with recommended guidelines prior to achieving a tax credit. The International Code Council (ICC) publishes the International Existing Building Code (IEBC) that contains one chapter on historic buildings.

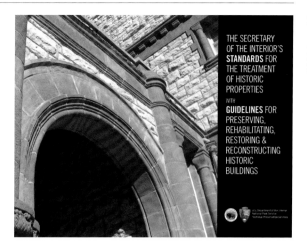

Figure 2.11
Secretary of the Interior's Standard for Historic Preservation Cover

Conclusions

Understanding codes, standards, and guidelines can be confusing, particularly when they disagree. As a general rule, the more restrictive requirement should be followed when two different codes or guidelines seem to conflict. Further, not all of these are required unless they have been adopted by the local jurisdiction within which the project is being constructed. It is important to consult with a local building official when in doubt.

Table 2.3 summarizes all the codes, guidelines, and standards mentioned in this chapter and describes whether they are required or recommended best practices.

American Society of Heating, Refrigerating, and Air Conditioning Engineers (ASHRAE)
Americans with Disabilities Act (ADA)
Building Officials and Code Administrators (BOCA)
Code of Hammurabi
Facility Guidelines Institute (FGI)
International Building Code (IBC)
International Code Council (ICC)
International Conference of Building Officials (ICBO)
International Existing Building Code (IEBC)
International Green Construction Code (IgCC)
International Residential Code (IRC)
National Fire Protection Association (NFPA) Electrical and Fire Safety Codes
National Register of Historic Places
Secretary of the Interior's Guidelines for the Treatment of Historic Properties
Southern Building Code Congress, International (SBCCI)

Key Terms

American Concrete Institute (ACI)
American National Standards Institute (ANSI)
American Society for Testing and Materials (ASTM International)

Assignment

1. Visit the following websites to see the resources available to design teams:

    a. http://www.usgbc.org/projects/hospitality—-new-construction

    b. http://www.chps.net/dev/Drupal

    c. https://www.nps.gov/tps/standards.htm

    d. www.iccsafe.org

Table 2.3 Codes, Standards, and Guidelines

Code, Standard, or Guideline	Which Is It?	Who Wrote It?	Is It Required?
International Building Code	Code	International Code Council	Yes*
International Energy Conservation Code	Code	International Code Council	Yes*
International Existing Building Code	Code	International Code Council	Yes*
International Green Construction Code	Code	International Code Council	Maybe**
Americans with Disabilities Act	Federal Law	Federal	Yes
NFPA Electrical and Fire Safety Codes	Standard	National Fire Protection Association	Yes
LEED v.4	Guideline	USGBC	Maybe**
Living Building Challenge 3.0	Guideline	Living Future Institute	No
Green Globes	Guideline	ECD Energy and Environmental Canada	Maybe**
WELL Building Standard 1.0	Guideline	Delos	No
Guidelines for the Design and Construction of Hospitals and Outpatient Facilities	Guidelines	Facility Guidelines Institute	Yes****
Center for High Performance School Guidelines	Guideline	Collaborative for High Performance Schools	No
Secretary's Standards for Historic Preservation	National Standard	National Park Service	Yes***

*Year based on local jurisdiction and which one has been adopted

**If adopted locally

***If on the National Register or applying for Historic Tax Credits

****Most states require

Sources

Crimmins, Jerry (1993, March 17), "Iroquois Theater Fire of 1903 Is Still the Worst of Chicago's Deadly Blazes," *Chicago Tribune*. Available online: http://articles.chicagotribune.com/1993-03-17/news/9303170288_1_worst-fires-early-morning-fire-terrible-fires

Horne, Charles, F. (1915), *The Code of Hammurabi: Introduction*. Available online: http://avalon.law.yale.edu/ancient/hammint.asp

"International Green Construction Code" (2012), IgCC. Available online: http://www.iccsafe.org/codes-tech-support/international-green-construction-code-igcc/international-green-construction-code/

Johns, Claude H. W. (1910–1911), "Babylonian Law—The Code of Hammurabi," *Encyclopedia Britannica*, eleventh edition. Available online: http://avalon.law.yale.edu/ancient/hammpre.asp

Mayerson, Arlene (1992), "The History of the Americans with Disabilities Act: A Movement Perspective," DREDF. Available online: http://dredf.org/news/publications/the-history-of-the-ada/

Ohio History Central (n.d.), *Ohio Penitentiary Fire*. Available online: http://www.ohiohistorycentral.org/w/Ohio_Penitentiary_Fire?rec=558

"Trial by Fire." (2016), Strike First Corporation. Available online: http://www.strikefirstusa.com/2016/07/trial-fire-5-fires-ultimately-improved-world/

3

Building Codes and Standards: Application and Administration

Learning Objectives:

After reading this chapter and doing the exercises, students will be able to

- Provide an overview of the process of building code administration
- Understand the difference between a maintenance document and a building code
- Describe the process used in obtaining LEED Certification for a building
- Describe the process used in obtaining WELL Building Certification for a building
- Describe the process used in meeting the Secretary of the Interior's Standards for historic projects

Introduction

Each state jurisdiction has legislation enabling the use and administration of the building codes. As such, each state decides when to adopt a code and which version and amendments will be made to each code adopted.

Code Administration

The building code applies to all new buildings and existing buildings that are being renovated, moved, enlarged, or altered. It is not a **maintenance code** like the Life Safety Code and is not monitored over time requiring periodic inspections. The purpose of the code is to provide for a minimum level of safety, public health, and welfare by requiring a means of egress, adequate light, sanitation, and ventilation, as well as structural stability. In the ICC complete building safety system, the International Existing Building Code is developed for administration of renovation and repairs to existing buildings, and the International Fire Code has provisions for design as well as maintenance of building and fire safety systems. Throughout the building code, other codes are referenced, including the International Gas Code, the International Mechanical Code, the International Plumbing Code, the International Property Maintenance Code, the International Fire Code, the International Energy Conservation Code, and the International Existing Building Code.

Conflicts

When a conflict emerges between a general code and a specific requirement, the specific requirement should be met. Further, no aspects of the building code should be seen as a way to nullify any existing laws, local, state, or federal. All other referenced standards are considered to be a part of the code. When a conflict exits between the building code and a referenced standard the building code provisions prevail.

Administration of the Code

The **building official** is in charge of the **Department of Building Safety**. The building official is responsible for appointing others within the jurisdiction as needed to enforce the building code. The building official is responsible for reviewing all applications and construction documents for reconstruction, rehabilitation, repair, alteration, additions, and new buildings and for issuing **building permits**. In addition to reviewing applications, the building official also makes inspections or may accept reports from approved inspectors to ensure compliance with the code. Building permits are required for any new construction and for changes to existing buildings. The code accounts for thirteen exemptions for work not requiring a building permit (see Table 3.1).

Table 3.1 Exemptions to Getting a Building Permit

1. One-story detached accessory structures (such as a tool or storage shed) not greater than 120 square feet
2. Fences not over 7 feet high
3. Oil derricks
4. Retaining walls not over 4 feet high
5. Water tanks supported directly on grade and not over 5,000 gallons capacity
6. Sidewalks and driveways not more than 30 inches above adjacent grade
7. Painting, papering, tiling, carpeting, cabinets, countertops, and similar finish work
8. Temporary motion picture, television, and theater stage sets and scenery
9. Prefabricated swimming pools accessory to R-3 less than 24 inches deep and not greater than 5,000 gallons
10. Shade cloth structures for nursery or agricultural purposes
11. Swings and other playground equipment accessory to one- and two-family dwellings
12. Window awnings in R-3 and U occupancies
13. Nonfixed movable fixtures, cases, racks, counters, and partitions not over 5 feet 9 inches

Building Permits

To obtain a building permit, the applicant must provide seven items. The work for which the application is being requested must be included, and the application must also include a description of the land where the work is to be done (site plan and legal description, including street address). Other information required includes the proposed use, construction documents, the value of the proposed work, the applicant's signature, and other data and information required by the building official. The permit becomes invalid if work has not commenced within 180 days of issuance of the permit or if the work is stopped for 180 days, although extensions are possible. The building permit must be placed in a visible location at the job site until the work is completed.

Once the work is completed and floor load signs have been posted as required, a **certificate of occupancy** can be issued. A building cannot be occupied until a certificate of occupancy is issued. The certificate of occupancy includes the building permit number, the address of the structure, the name and address of the owner or owner's agent, a description of the portion of the structure for which the permit is issued, a statement that the structure has been inspected in compliance for occupancy, the name of the building official, the edition of the code used, the use and occupancy, the type of construction, the design occupant load, if an automatic sprinkler is provided, and any special stipulations and conditions.

Submittal Documents

Two sets of **construction documents**, accompanied by a geotechnical report and any other special inspections and the application, are required for a complete submittal. Construction documents must be completed by a qualified design professional and need to include the location; nature and extent of the work, showing how it conforms to the building code, including fire protection system shop drawings; means of egress information; exterior wall envelope information; a site plan; and design flood elevations, where applicable. Many jurisdictions allow electronic submittals of permit application, building plans, and construction documents and perform plan review, communicate with permit applicant, and do other related tasks electronically.

Design Professional

The **registered design professional in responsible charge** is engaged by the building owner to coordinate and review certain aspects of the process for compatibility with the building code. The design professional in charge is responsible for submitting documents prepared by others, deferred submittal documents, phased submittal documents, and special inspection reports. A **registered design professional** is an individual who is licensed by the state or jurisdiction in which the project is completed.

Inspections

The building official makes several inspections during the construction of a building, including a footing and foundation inspection; a concrete and under-floor inspection; a lowest floor elevation inspection; a frame inspection; a lath, gypsum board, and gypsum panel product inspection; a fire- and smoke-resistant penetrations inspection; energy efficiency inspections; and other inspections as required by specific codes and laws.

Violations

The building official can serve a violation notice to a person responsible for the construction of alteration, repair, or removal of a structure without a permit and may pursue legal counsel of the jurisdiction to correct any violations. A person who violates this code or fails to comply is subject to penalties under the law. If the building official finds work not in compliance with the code, they may issue a **stop work order** that terminates all work on the site.

Americans with Disabilities Act 2010 Standards for Public Accommodations and Commercial Facilities Standard Title III

Beginning March 15, 2012, all state and local governments must meet the 2010 standards, including both Title III, 28 CFR 35.151 and 2004 **ADAAG** (ADA Accessibility Guidelines) 36 CFR part 1191 Appendices B and D. TITLE III 28 CFR part 35.151 covers changes to new construction and alterations to a variety of facility types, including assembly areas, medical care facilities, detention and correctional facilities, and facilities with dwelling units for sale. The ADA covers all newly designed and constructed facilities, as well as altered portions of existing buildings. Residential dwelling units are not required to be in compliance with ADA. There is also an exception for qualified historic buildings. Areas used only by employees do not have to be fully accessible, although they should provide accessible elements when possible. The IBC references ICC A117.1 Standard for Accessible Building and Facilities, the latest edition of which is the 2017 edition. ICC A117.1 is compatible with the ADAAG and most jurisdictions adopting the IBC also use the ICC A117.1, except states where a state specific accessibility standard has been adopted (Figure 3.1).

LEED v.4 Green Building Certification

Buildings can become LEED certified in one of several ways: Building Design and Construction, Interior Design and Construction, Building Operations and Maintenance, Neighborhood Development, and Homes. The Green Business Certification Inc. (GCBI) oversees the LEED Building certification program on behalf of the United States Green Building Council (USGBC), and LEED is currently in version 4.0. Project teams work collaboratively from the programming phase through construction to achieve all LEED **prerequisites** (required for certification) and additional LEED credits to obtain the desired level of certification. All LEED certifications (except Homes) are on a hundred-point system. With additional points for Innovation (six) and Regional Priority (four) up to 110 points are possible (Tables 3.2, 3.3).

Table 3.2 LEED Certification

All prerequisites must be met in order to be certified.

Certified	40–49 points
Silver	50–59 points
Gold	60–79 points
Platinum	80+ points

Points are achieved in Location and Transportation, Sustainable Sites, Water Efficiency, Energy and Atmosphere, Materials and Resources, Indoor Environmental Quality, Innovation, and Regional Priority.

Figure 3.1
Diagram showing ADA + ADAAG 2010

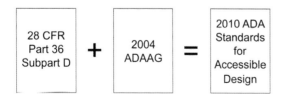

Table 3.3 LEED Points Breakdown

Project Name:							
Date:							
			LEED v4 for BD+C: New Construction and Major Renovation				
			Project Checklist				
Y	**?**	**N**					
			Credit	Integrative Process	1		
0	**0**	**0**	**Location and Transportation**		**16**		
			Credit	LEED for Neighborhood Development Location	16		
			Credit	Sensitive Land Protection	1		
			Credit	High Priority Site	2		
			Credit	Surrounding Density and Diverse Uses	5		
			Credit	Access to Quality Transit	5		
			Credit	Bicycle Facilities	1		
			Credit	Reduced Parking Footprint	1		
			Credit	Green Vehicles	1		
0	**0**	**0**	**Sustainable Sites**		**10**		
Y			Prereq	Construction Activity Pollution Prevention	Required		
			Credit	Site Assessment	1		
			Credit	Site Development—Protect or Restore Habitat	2		
			Credit	Open Space	1		
			Credit	Rainwater Management	3		
			Credit	Heat Island Reduction	2		
			Credit	Light Pollution Reduction	1		
0	**0**	**0**	**Water Efficiency**		**11**		
Y			Prereq	Outdoor Water Use Reduction	Required		
Y			Prereq	Indoor Water Use Reduction	Required		
Y			Prereq	Building-Level Water Metering	Required		
			Credit	Outdoor Water Use Reduction	2		
			Credit	Indoor Water Use Reduction	6		
			Credit	Cooling Tower Water Use	2		
			Credit	Water Metering	1		

Table 3.3 LEED Points Breakdown (*continued*)

0	**0**	**0**		**Energy and Atmosphere**		**33**		
Y			Prereq	Fundamental Commissioning and Verification		Required		
Y			Prereq	Minimum Energy Performance		Required		
Y			Prereq	Building-Level Energy Metering		Required		
Y			Prereq	Fundamental Refrigerant Management		Required		
			Credit	Enhanced Commissioning		6		
			Credit	Optimize Energy Performance		18		
			Credit	Advanced Energy Metering		1		
			Credit	Demand Response		2		
			Credit	Renewable Energy Production		3		
			Credit	Enhanced Refrigerant Management		1		
			Credit	Green Power and Carbon Offsets		2		
0	**0**	**0**		**Materials and Resources**		**13**		
Y			Prereq	Storage and Collection of Recyclables		Required		
Y			Prereq	Construction and Demolition Waste Management Planning		Required		
			Credit	Building Life-Cycle Impact Reduction		5		
			Credit	Building Product Disclosure and Optimization—Environmental Product Declarations		2		
			Credit	Building Product Disclosure and Optimization—Sourcing of Raw Materials		2		
			Credit	Building Product Disclosure and Optimization—Material Ingredients		2		
			Credit	Construction and Demolition Waste Management		2		
0	**0**	**0**		**Indoor Environmental Quality**		**16**		
Y			Prereq	Minimum Indoor Air Quality Performance		Required		
Y			Prereq	Environmental Tobacco Smoke Control		Required		
			Credit	Enhanced Indoor Air Quality Strategies		2		
			Credit	Low-Emitting Materials		3		
			Credit	Construction Indoor Air Quality Management Plan		1		
			Credit	Indoor Air Quality Assessment		2		
			Credit	Thermal Comfort		1		
			Credit	Interior Lighting		2		
			Credit	Daylight		3		
			Credit	Quality Views		1		
			Credit	Acoustic Performance		1		

Table 3.3 LEED Points Breakdown (*continued*)

0	0	0	**Innovation**		**6**	
			Credit	Innovation	5	
			Credit	LEED Accredited Professional	1	
0	0	0	**Regional Priority**		**4**	
			Credit	Regional Priority: Specific Credit	1	
			Credit	Regional Priority: Specific Credit	1	
			Credit	Regional Priority: Specific Credit	1	
			Credit	Regional Priority: Specific Credit	1	
0	0	0	TOTALS	Possible Points	110	
	Certified: 40 to 49 points, **Silver:** 50 to 59 points, **Gold:** 60 to 79 points, **Platinum:** 80 to 110					

WELL Building Certification

While there are many synergies between the LEED Green Building Rating Systems and the WELL Building Certification, they are two separate and distinct building ratings. The focus of LEED is on building sustainability, and WELL focuses on the health of building occupants. The WELL Building Standard is also administered by GBCI and, like LEED, requires that all prerequisites—called **preconditions** under WELL—be met in order for a project to be certified. Unlike LEED, WELL Building certification is only good for three years (LEED is a one-time certification). New and Existing Buildings, New and Existing Interiors, and Core and Shell Compliance comprise the three types of WELL Building certifications available. All project types can be recertified every three years except Core and Shell, which is a one-time certification (Table 3.4).

Like LEED, different levels of certification are possible. For basic certification—Silver—all preconditions must be met. For Gold, in addition to the preconditions, 40 percent of optimization credits are required; for Platinum certification, 80 percent of optimization credits must be achieved. For Core and Shell Compliance, all preconditions and at least one Optimization from each Concept must be achieved. The categories in the WELL Building Standard are called **Concepts** and the points are called **Optimizations**.

The WELL Building checklist in Table 3.5 outlines all Concepts (Air, Water, Nourishment, Light, Fitness, Comfort, and Mind) and provides the items beneath each Concept, accompanied by a short description of each item. The verification type is also listed on the right-hand side. Examples include a letter of assurance (from the designer or owner), a visual inspection by a WELL site visitor, architectural drawings, or a performance test by a third-party inspector. In some cases, a written policy document or innovation proposal will meet the verification requirement.

Table 3.4 WELL Building Certification

All prerequisites must be met in order to be certified.

Typology	Preconditions	Optimization	Total
New and Existing Building Certification	41	61	102
New and Existing Interiors Certification	36	64	100
Core and Shell Compliance	26	30	56

Table 3.5 WELL Building Standard v.1

Instructions

Introduction

The WELL Building Standard® is organized into seven categories of wellness called Concepts: Air, Water, Nourishment, Light, Fitness, Comfort and Mind. Each Concept is comprised of multiple features, which are intended to address specific aspects of occupant health, comfort or knowledge. Each feature is divided into parts, which are often tailored to a specific building type. Within each part are one or more requirements, which dictate specific parameters that must be met.

Satisfying a feature requires that all applicable parts of that feature are met. The applicability of a part is determined by the project space type and scope. Tables indicating the applicability of each feature and part based on the project type and scope are included in the introduction to WELL and each WELL pilot standard.

WELL features are categorized as either Preconditions or Optimizations. Preconditions are necessary for all levels of WELL Certification. Optimizations are additional features, a certain percentage of which must be attained depending on the level of achievement that is pursued (Table 1).

Worksheets

The Project Checklist allows teams to track whether a project intends to pursue a particular feature towards certification. The selections on the Project Checklist are reflected automatically on the Certification Matrix, indicating the estimated target level of certification.

Project Checklist Layout
Concepts, Features & Parts: Identifies each feature and the details of each part requirement, sorted by Concept
Optimizations & Preconditions Symbols: Signifies the applicability of a feature based on the definitions of Precondition and Optimizations as described above
Verification Type: Specifies what verification method will be used to determine adherence to that part
Pursuing (Yes, No, Maybe, N/A, Pending PV): States whether a project intends to pursue or not pursue the parts of a feature. N/A can be used when a part requirement is not applicable to the project site or is considered outside of the project scope. Pending PV shows in the Certification Matrix as a Yes and is uneditable for required Preconditions
Notes: Allows project teams to make notes about their response or implementation of that part
Project Info: Allows teams to track ongoing edit versions

Certification Matrix Layout
Concepts, Features & Parts: Tracks pursuing responses from Project Checklist
Summary: Totals the responses for Yes, Maybe and No by Precondition and Optimization applicability
Requirements: Identifies the minimum totals for each level of certification
Results: Lists the outcome of applying the totals against the requirements
Performance Verification Asterisk: Informs that these Yes counts are subject to onsite testing for achievement

Table 1. Certification and Compliance requirements

STANDARD VERSION	LEVEL OF ACHIEVEMENT	PRECONDITIONS THAT MUST BE ACHIEVED
WELL Building Standard v1	Core and Shell Compliance	all applicable preconditions
	Silver Certification	all applicable preconditions
	Gold Certification	all applicable preconditions
	Platinum Certification	all applicable preconditions
WELL Pilot Standards	Silver Certification	all applicable preconditions
	Gold Certification	all applicable preconditions
	Platinum Certification	all applicable preconditions

For more information on the certification process, please consult the Certification Guidebook.
http://www.wellcertified.com/sites/default/files/resources/WELL-Certification-Guidebook.pdf

Table 3.5 WELL Building Standard v.1 *(continued)*

Project Checklist

WELL Building Standard v1: New and Existing Buildings

Project:
Location:
Updated By:
Date:

P Precondition (required)
O Optimization (optional)

		Verification Type	Pursuing
			--> Yes
P Feature 01. Air quality standards			
Part 1. Standards For Volatile Substances	The following conditions are met: a. Formaldehyde levels less than 27 ppb. b. Total volatile organic compounds less than 500 µg/m³.	Performance Test	Pending PV
Part 2. Standards For Particulate Matter And Inorganic Gases	The following conditions are met: a. Carbon monoxide less than 9 ppm. b. PM2.5 less than 15 µg/m³. c. PM10 less than 50 µg/m³. d. Ozone less than 51 ppb.	Performance Test	Pending PV
Part 3. Radon	The following conditions are met in projects with regularly occupied spaces at or below grade: a. Radon less than 4 pCi/L in the lowest occupied level of the project.	Performance Test	Pending PV
P Feature 02. Smoking Ban			
Part 1. Indoor Smoking Ban	Building policy or local code reflects the following: a. Smoking and the use of e-cigarettes is prohibited inside the building.	Policy Document	
Part 2. Outdoor Smoking Ban	Signage is present to indicate: a. A smoking ban within 7.5 m [25 ft] (or the maximum extent allowable by local codes) of all entrances, operable windows and building air intakes. b. A smoking ban on all decks, patios, balconies, rooftops and other regularly occupied exterior building spaces. c. The hazards of smoking, in all areas beyond 7.5m of the building entrances (if smoking is permitted in this areas). These signs are to be placed along all walkways with a distance of not more than 30 m [100 ft] between signs.	Visual Inspection	Pending PV
P Feature 03. Ventilation Effectiveness			
Part 1. Ventilation Design	One of the following requirements is met for all spaces: a. Ventilation rates comply with all requirements set in ASHRAE 62.1-2013 (Ventilation Rate Procedure or IAQ Procedure). b. Projects comply with all requirements set in any procedure in ASHRAE 62.1-2013 (including the Natural Ventilation Procedure) and demonstrate that ambient air quality withi 1.6 km [1 mi] of the building is compliant with either the U.S. EPA's NAAQS or passes the Air Quality Standards in the WELL Building Standard for at least 95% of all hours in the previous year.	Letter of Assurance	
Part 2. Demand Controlled Ventilation	For all spaces with an actual or expected occupant density greater than 25 people per 93 m² [1,000 ft²], one of the following requirements is met: a. A demand controlled ventilation system regulates the ventilation rate of outdoor air to keep carbon dioxide levels in the space below 800 ppm. b. Projects that have met the Operable windows feature demonstrate that natural ventilation is sufficient to keep carbon dioxide levels below 800 ppm at intended occupancies.	Letter of Assurance	
Part 3. System Balancing	After the HVAC system is installed, the following requirement is met: a. After substantial completion and prior to occupancy, the HVAC system undergoes testing and balancing.	Commissioning Report	
P Feature 04. VOC Reduction			
Part 1. Interior Paints And Coatings	The VOC limits of newly applied paints and coatings meet one of the following requirements: a. 100% of installed products meet California Air Resources Board (CARB) 2007, Suggested Control Measure (SCM) for Architectural Coatings, or South Coast Air Quality Management District (SCAQMD) Rule 1113, effective June 3, 2011 for VOC content. b. At minimum 90%, by volume, meet the California Department of Public Health (CDPH) Standard Method v1.1-2010 for VOC emissions. c. Applicable national VOC control regulations or conduct testing of VOC content in accordance with ASTM D2369-10; ISO 11890, part 1; ASTM D6886-03; or ISO 11890-2.	Letter of Assurance	
Part 2. Interior Adhesives And Sealants	The VOC limits of newly applied adhesives and sealants meet one of the following requirements: a. 100% of installed products meet South Coast Air Quality Management District (SCAQMD) Rule 1168, July 1 2005 for VOC content. b. At minimum 90%, by volume, meet the California Department of Public Health (CDPH) Standard Method v1.1-2010 for VOC emissions. c. Applicable national VOC control regulations or conduct testing of VOC content in accordance with ASTM D2369-10; ISO 11890, part 1; ASTM D6886-03; or ISO 11890-2.	Letter of Assurance	
Part 3. Flooring	The VOC content of all newly installed flooring must meet all limits set by the following, as applicable: a. California Department of Public Health (CDPH) Standard Method v1.1-2010.	Letter of Assurance	
Part 4. Insulation	The VOC content of all newly installed thermal and acoustic insulation in ceilings and walls must meet all limits set by the following, as applicable: a. California Department of Public Health (CDPH) Standard Method v1.1-2010.	Letter of Assurance	
Part 5. Furniture And Furnishings	The VOC content of at least 95% (by cost) of all newly purchased furniture and furnishings within the project scope must meet all limits set by the following, as applicable: a. ANSI/BIFMA e3-2011 Furniture Sustainability Standard sections 7.6.1 and 7.6.2, tested in accordance with ANSI/BIFMA Standard Method M7.1-2011.	Letter of Assurance	

Historic Building Standards

The Secretary of the Interior's Standards apply to buildings that are either on the National Register of Historic Places or might be eligible for the National Register. Compliance with the standards allows a building owner to be eligible for historic tax credits. Depending on the project type and use, these might be federal or state tax credits. The standards ensure that work that is done will not compromise the integrity of the historic building. The Secretary's Standards for historic properties are divided into four approaches—preservation, rehabilitation, restoration, and reconstruction, with both standards and guidelines for each.

Historic Standards for Rehabilitation

(retrieved from https://www.nps.gov/tps/standards/rehabilitation/rehab/stand.htm 1/21/18)

1. A property will be used as it was historically or be given a new use that requires minimal change to its distinctive materials, features, spaces, and spatial relationships.
2. The historic character of a property will be retained and preserved. The removal of distinctive materials or alteration of features, spaces, and spatial relationships that characterize a property will be avoided.
3. Each property will be recognized as a physical record of its time, place, and use. Changes that create a false sense of historical development, such as adding conjectural features or elements from other historic properties, will not be undertaken.
4. Changes to a property that have acquired historic significance in their own right will be retained and preserved.
5. Distinctive materials, features, finishes, and construction techniques or examples of craftsmanship that characterize a property will be preserved.
6. Deteriorated historic features will be repaired rather than replaced. Where the severity of deterioration requires replacement of a distinctive feature, the new feature will match the old in design, color, texture, and, where possible, materials. Replacement of missing features will be substantiated by documentary and physical evidence.
7. Chemical or physical treatments, if appropriate, will be undertaken using the gentlest means possible. Treatments that cause damage to historic materials will not be used.
8. Archeological resources will be protected and preserved in place. If such resources must be disturbed, mitigation measures will be undertaken.
9. New additions, exterior alterations, or related new construction will not destroy historic materials, features, and spatial relationships that characterize the property. The new work shall be differentiated from the old and will be compatible with the historic materials, features, size, scale and proportion, and massing to protect the integrity of the property and its environment.
10. New additions and adjacent or related new construction will be undertaken in a such a manner that, if removed in the future, the essential form and integrity of the historic property and its environment would be unimpaired.

In addition to the standards, there are guidelines for application and technical briefs available to project teams on the National Park Service's website.

The International Existing Building Code also contains a chapter on historic buildings and addresses the renovation, repair, and additions to historic buildings.

Conclusions

Building codes and ADA are required by law, and all commercial buildings must meet the requirements of both. Single-family residential buildings must meet the International Residential Code but not ADA. Guidelines such as LEED and the WELL Building Standard are voluntary unless required by a local, state, or federal agency. When a project is listed on the National Register of Historic Places, the Secretary's Standards can be required. In all cases, they are recommended on significant historic buildings as an appropriate way to do new work on a historic building.

Key Terms

ADAAG
building official
building permits
certificate of occupancy
Concepts
construction documents
Department of Building Safety
maintenance code
Optimizations
prerequisites
preconditions
registered design professional in responsible charge
registered design professional
stop work order

Assignments

1. Are historic tax credits available in your state? On which type of projects? How might these work in conjunction with federal tax credits?

2. Where might you find a listing of the historic buildings in your locale?

3. What synergies exist between the various standards and guidelines?

4. Why is it important to understand which codes are applicable to a given project?

5. Contact your local building official or research online the building department in your locale and find out what version of the IBC, IEBC, and so on are currently being used in your area. Which have been adopted? What amendments have been made? Which drawings are required to get a building permit?

6. Invite a building inspector to a class project critique to talk about the life-safety and code issues he/she sees in the student projects.

Part two

The Process of Applying the Code

Programming

Learning Objectives:

After reading this chapter and doing the exercises, students will be able to

- Identify the occupancy categories for the design project
- Determine egress requirements based on square footages
- Outline basic plumbing fixture requirements based on occupancy
- Determine material types required based on occupancy
- Define the difference between a code and a standard
- Have a basic understanding of industry specific regulations
- Determine the appropriate codes, standards, and guidelines that apply to the project during the programming phase
- Determine the construction type for the project
- Decide if the building must be sprinklered
- Establish overall applicable building codes, ADA requirements, standards, and guidelines for the project

Introduction

The programming phase of the project is where the team gathers all the necessary information to be able to design the project. This can include interviews, surveys, observations, and physical examination of existing spaces, as well as researching codes and guidelines. This chapter provides an overview of the types of information that a design team must gather during the programming phase of a project with regard to codes, guidelines, and standards.

Codes Process

As will become evident in the coming chapters, there is a preliminary building code assessment during programming and then additional code work resulting in revisions during schematic design with refinement during design development.

Building Construction Type

As an interior designer, the building construction is usually provided. Construction is classified into five types: Type I, II, III, IV, and V. Types I and II are of materials considered noncombustible. These include materials such as concrete and brick. The primary difference between Types I and II is that Type II can have a combustible roof material. Type III construction consists of noncombustible exterior walls with potentially combustible interior walls—or any material permitted by code. Heavy timber construction is classified as Type IV, while Type V covers all other permissible materials of the building code for exterior and interior construction (Table 4.1).

The projects discussed in the coming chapters include examples of all of the above types of construction (Figure 4.1).

Table 4.1 Construction Types

Type	Exterior/Roof	Interior	Combustible/ noncombustible
I	Concrete and steel walls and roof Note: Type IA requires higher fire-resistance rating than Type IB		noncombustible
II	Concrete and steel walls Note: Type IIA requires a 1-hour resistance rating for all building elements; Type IIB does not	Combustible asphalt waterproofing with combustible felt paper	noncombustible
III	Brick and joist masonry bearing walls with wood structural framework floor and roof Note: Type IIIA requires 1-hour fire resistance for all building elements except exterior bearing walls, which are 2-hour; Type IIIB requires 2-hour for exterior bearing walls only	Fire-retardant wood framing	Combustible
IV	Brick and joist masonry bearing walls with wood structural framework floor and roof	Heavy timber interior wood without plaster coating	Combustible
V (typically single-family home)	Wood construction 2 x 4 or 2 x 6 wood floor trusses and wood roof framing Note: Type VA requires 1-hour fire resistance for all building elements except nonbearing walls; Type VB requires no fire resistance for any building element	Wood framed 2 x 4 or 2 x 6	Combustible

CONSTRUCTION TYPE

Figure 4.1
Construction
types illustrated

I   II   III   IV   V

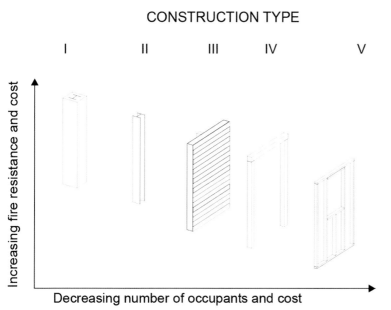

Increasing fire resistance and cost

Decreasing number of occupants and cost

Occupancy Type

There are ten basic occupancy classifications:

Assembly

A-1:

Motion picture theaters

Symphony and concert halls

Television and radio studios admitting an audience

Theaters

A-2:

Banquet halls

Casinos (gaming areas)

Nightclubs

Restaurants, cafeterias, and similar dining facilities

Taverns and bars

A-3:

Amusement arcades

Art galleries

Bowling alleys

Community halls

Courtrooms

Dance halls (not including drink or food consumption)

Exhibition halls

Funeral parlors

Greenhouses for conservation and exhibition of plants that provide public access

Indoor swimming pools (without spectator seating)

Indoor tennis courts (without spectator seating)

Lecture halls

Libraries

Museums

Places of religious worship

Pool and billiard parlors

Waiting areas in transportation terminals

A-4:

Arenas

Skating rinks

Swimming pools

Tennis courts

A-5:

Amusement park structures

Bleachers

Grandstands

Stadiums

Business

B

Airport traffic-control towers

Ambulatory care facilities

Animal hospitals, kennels, and ponds

Banks

Barber and beauty shops

Car washes

Civil administration

Clinic: outpatient

Dry-cleaning and laundries: pick-up and delivery stations and self-service

Educational occupancies above twelfth grade

Electronic data processing

Food processing establishments and commercial kitchens not associated with restaurants, cafeterias, and similar dining facilities not more than 2,500 square feet in area

Laboratories: testing and research

Motor vehicle showrooms

Post offices

Print shops

Professional services (architects, attorneys, dentists, physicians, engineers, etc.)

Radio and televisions stations

Telephone exchanges

Training and skill development not in a school or academic program (this shall include, but not be limited to, tutoring centers, martial arts studios, gymnastics, and similar uses, regardless of the ages served, and where not classified as a Group A occupancy)

Educational

E

Day care facilities

Educational facilities for six or more students through the 12th grade

Factory

F-1

Aircraft (manufacturing, not to include repair)

Appliances

Athletic equipment

Automobiles and other motor vehicles

Bakeries

Beverages: over 16 percent alcohol content)

Bicycles

Boats

Brooms and brushes

Business machines

Cameras and photo equipment

Canvas or similar fabric

Carpets and rugs

Clothing

Construction and agricultural machinery

Disinfectants

Dry-cleaning and dyeing

Electric generation plants

Electronics

Engines (including rehabilitating)

Food processing establishments and commercial kitchens not associated with restaurants, cafeterias, and similar dining facilities not more than 2,500 square feet in area

Furniture

Hemp products

Jute products

Laundries

Leather products

Machinery

Metals

Millwork (sash and door)

Motion picture and television filming (without spectators)

Musical equipment

Optical goods

Paper mills or products

Photographic equipment

Plastic products

Printing or publishing

Recreational vehicles

Refuse incineration

Shoes

Soaps and detergents

Textiles

Tobacco

Trailers

Upholstering

Wood: distillation

Woodworking (cabinet)

F-2

Beverages: up to and including 16 percent alcohol content

Brick and masonry

Ceramic products

Foundries

Glass products

Gypsum

Ice

Metal products (fabrication and assembly)

Hazardous

Institutional

I-1

Alcohol and drug centers

Assisted-living facilities

Congregate care facilities

Group homes

Halfway houses

Residential board and care facilities

Social rehabilitation facilities

I-2

Foster care facilities

Detoxification facilities

Hospitals

Nursing homes

Psychiatric hospitals

I-3

Correctional centers

Detention centers

Jails

Prerelease centers

Prisons

Reformatories

I-4

Adult day care

Child day care

Mercantile

M

Department stores

Drug stores

Greenhouses for display and sale of plants that provide public access

Markets

Motor fuel-dispensing facilities

Retail or wholesale stores

Sales rooms

Residential

R-1

Boarding houses (transient) greater than ten occupants

Congregate living facilities greater than ten occupants

Hotels (transient)

Motels (transient)

R-2

Apartment houses

Congregate living facilities (nontransient) greater than sixteen occupants

    Boarding house (nontransient)

    Convents

Dormitories

Fraternities and sororities

Monasteries

Hotels (nontransient)

Live/work units

Motels (nontransient)

Vacation timeshare properties

R-3

Buildings with less than or equal to two dwelling units

Care facilities with less than or equal to five persons

Boarding houses (transient) with less than or equal to ten occupants

Congregate living facilities (nontransient) with less than or equal to sixteen occupants

Boarding houses (nontransient)

Convents

Dormitories

Fraternities and sororities

Monasteries

Congregate living facilities (transient) with less than or equal to ten occupants

Lodging houses with less than or equal to five guest rooms and ten or fewer occupants

R-4

Alcohol and drug centers

Assisted-living facilities

Congregate care facilities

Group homes

Halfway houses

Residential board and care facilities

Social rehabilitation facilities

Storage

S-1

Aerosols, Level 2 and Level 3

Aircraft hanger

Bags: cloth, burlap, or paper

Bamboos and rattan

Baskets

Belting: canvas and leather

Books and paper in rolls or packs

Boots and shoes

Buttons, including cloth covered, pearl, or bone

Cardboard and cardboard boxes

Clothing, woolen wearing apparel

Cordage

Dry boat storage (indoor)

Furniture

Furs

Glues, mucilage, pastes, and size

Grains

Horns and combs, other than celluloid

Leather

Linoleum

Lumber

Motor vehicle repair garages

Photo engravings

Resilient flooring

Self-service storage facility

Silks

Soaps

Sugar

Tires, bulk storage of

Tobacco, cigars, cigarettes, and snuff

Upholstery and mattresses

S-2

Asbestos

Beverages up to and including 16 percent alcohol in metal, glass, or ceramic containers

Cement in bags

Chalk and crayons

Dairy products in nonwaxed coated paper containers

Dry cell batteries

Electrical coils

Electric motors

Food products

Foods in noncombustible containers

Fresh fruits and vegetables in nonplastic trays or containers

Frozen foods

Glass

Glass bottles, empty or filled with noncombustible liquids

Gypsum board

Inert pigments

Ivory

Meats

Metal cabinets

Metal desks with plastic tops and trim

Metal parts

Metals

Mirrors

Oil-filled and other types of distribution transformers

Parking garages, open or enclosed

Porcelain and pottery

Stoves

Talc and soapstones

Washers and dryers

Utility

U

Agricultural buildings

Barns

Carports

Communication equipment structures with a gross floor area of less than 1,500 square feet

Fences more than 6 feet high

Grain silos, accessory to a residential occupancy

Livestock shelters

Private garages

Retaining walls

Sheds

Stables

Tanks

Towers

The first decision that must be made about a project is which occupancy group or groups it will fall into. All other calculations are related to this use group.

Occupant Load

Based on the use and function of a space, an occupant load factor can be determined using Table 1004.5 (see Table 4.2).

Factors are either gross or net. Using a **gross factor** simply means the square footage is divided by the factor. With a **net factor**, removing spaces that are not regularly occupied, such as a closet, wall divider, and fireplace, reduces the overall square footage. The occupant load should be

---

IBC 2018 TABLE 1004.5: MAXIMUM FLOOR AREA ALLOWANCES PER OCCUPANT

The primary changes to the table are its number and links to other sections in the code. For example, Assembly with fixed seats links to Section 1004.4 in the 2015 IBC but to Section 1004.6 in the 2018 IBC.

The function "Business areas" has had a change in the occupancy load factor. In the IBC 2015, the factor was 100 gross. In the 2018 IBC, the factor has been changed to 150 gross and adds "Concentrated business use areas" to the function of the space, as well as a reference to Section 1004.8 and the occupant load factor column.

Industrial areas in IBC 2015 has been corrected in the 2018 IBC. In the 2015 table, inpatient, outpatient, and sleeping areas were mistakenly placed under Industrial. This has been corrected and placed under Institutional areas in the IBC 2018. Industrial areas now has a factor of 100 gross in the 2018 IBC. The factors for inpatient, outpatient, and sleeping rooms have remained the same.

Locker rooms have been added in the 2018 IBC. The factor for locker rooms is 50 gross.

The Mercantile function has been changed to omit basement and grade floor areas that were in the IBC 2015 but are no longer in the IBC 2018 table.

(Formerly IBC 2015 Table 1004.1.2)

Table 4.2 IBC 2018 Table 1004.5: Maximum Floor Area Allowances per Occupant

MEANS OF EGRESS

TABLE 1004.5
MAXIMUM FLOOR AREA ALLOWANCES PER OCCUPANT

FUNCTION OF SPACE	OCCUPANT LOAD FACTOR[a]
Accessory storage areas, mechanical equipment room	300 gross
Agricultural building	300 gross
Aircraft hangars	500 gross
Airport terminal	
Baggage claim	20 gross
Baggage handling	300 gross
Concourse	100 gross
Waiting areas	15 gross
Assembly	
Gaming floors (keno, slots, etc.)	11 gross
Exhibit gallery and museum	30 net
Assembly with fixed seats	See Section 1004.6
Assembly without fixed seats	
Concentrated (chairs only—not fixed)	7 net
Standing space	5 net
Unconcentrated (tables and chairs)	15 net
Bowling centers, allow 5 persons for each lane including 15 feet of runway, and for additional areas	7 net
Business areas	150 gross
Concentrated business use areas	See Section 1004.8
Courtrooms—other than fixed seating areas	40 net
Day care	35 net
Dormitories	50 gross
Educational	
Classroom area	20 net
Shops and other vocational room areas	50 net
Exercise rooms	50 gross
Group H-5 fabrication and manufacturing areas	200 gross
Industrial areas	100 gross
Institutional areas	
Inpatient treatment areas	240 gross
Outpatient areas	100 gross
Sleeping areas	120 gross
Kitchens, commercial	200 gross
Library	
Reading rooms	50 net
Stack area	100 gross
Locker rooms	50 gross
Mall buildings—covered and open	See Section 402.8.2
Mercantile	60 gross
Storage, stock, shipping areas	300 gross
Parking garages	200 gross
Residential	200 gross
Skating rinks, swimming pools	
Rink and pool	50 gross
Decks	15 gross
Stages and platforms	15 net
Warehouses	500 gross

For SI: 1 foot = 304.8 mm, 1 square foot = 0.0929 m^2.

a. Floor area in square feet per occupant.

calculated initially to provide guidance on the number of exits required and after finalizing the floor plan to ensure accuracy of corridor widths required, door swings and widths, and other key components constituting the path of egress.

An example of an occupant load calculation of each type is as follows:

Gross Calculation:

Use Group: Business

Square Footage: 4,000 square feet

Factor from Table 1004.5: 150 gross

Divide 4,000 by 150; that means you can have up to twenty-six occupants in this space.

Net Calculation:

Use Group: Educational classroom

Square Footage: Total 1,000 square feet, 240 of which is a closet

Factor from Table 1004.5: 20 net

First subtract closet from total: 1,000 − 240 = 760 square feet

Then divide by the factor: 760 square feet / 20 = 38 occupants permitted

Egress

Number

Once the occupant load is determined, the number of exits can also be determined using Table 1006.3.2. Although Table 1006.3.2 indicates that both examples above require two exits per story, Table 1006.3.3(2) clarifies that for both

Table 4.3 IBC 2018 Table 1006.3.2: Minimum Number of Exits or Access to Exits per Story

TABLE 1006.3.2
MINIMUM NUMBER OF EXITS OR
ACCESS TO EXITS PER STORY

OCCUPANT LOAD PER STORY	MINIMUM NUMBER OF EXITS OR ACCESS TO EXITS FROM STORY
1-500	2
501-1,000	3
More than 1,000	4

IBC 2018 TABLE 1006.3.2: MINIMUM NUMBER OF EXITS OR ACCESS TO EXITS PER STORY

The IBC 2018 table, Minimum Number of Exits or Access to Exits per Story, is now Table 1006.3.2. The content of the table has not changed.

(Formerly IBC 2015 Table 1006.3.1)

occupancies B and E, with fewer than forty-nine occupants and a common path of travel no more than 75 feet, a single exit would be permitted if located on the first story above or below grade (Table 4.3).

Travel Distance

Similarly, the maximum length of the distance to an exist is found in Table 1006.3.3(2) for one exit or Table 1017.2, which includes information for both sprinklered and non-sprinklered buildings (Tables 4.4, 4.5).

Table 4.4 IBC 2018 Table 1006.3.3(2): Stories with One Exit or Access to One Exit for Other Occupancies Table

TABLE 1006.3.3(2)
STORIES WITH ONE EXIT OR ACCESS TO ONE EXIT FOR OTHER OCCUPANCIES

STORY	OCCUPANCY	MAXIMUM OCCUPANT LOAD PER STORY	MAXIMUM COMMON PATH OF EGRESS TRAVEL DISTANCE (feet)
First story above or below grade plane	A, B[b], E F[b], M, U	49	75
	H-2, H-3	3	25
	H-4, H-5, I, R-1, R-2[a, c]	10	75
	S[b, d]	29	75
Second story above grade plane	B, F, M, S[d]	29	75
Third story above grade plane and higher	NP	NA	NA

For SI: 1 foot = 304.8 mm.

NP = Not Permitted.

NA = Not Applicable.

a. Buildings classified as Group R-2 equipped throughout with an automatic sprinkler system in accordance with Section 903.3.1.1 or 903.3.1.2 and provided with emergency escape and rescue openings in accordance with Section 1030.

b. Group B, F and S occupancies in buildings equipped throughout with an automatic sprinkler system in accordance with Section 903.3.1.1 shall have a maximum exit access travel distance of 100 feet.

c. This table is used for R-2 occupancies consisting of sleeping units. For R-2 occupancies consisting of dwelling units, use Table 1006.3.3(1).

d. The length of exit access travel distance in a Group S-2 open parking garage shall be not more than 100 feet.

Table 4.5 IBC 2018 Table 1017.2: Exit Access Travel Distance

TABLE 1017.2
EXIT ACCESS TRAVEL DISTANCE[a]

OCCUPANCY	WITHOUT SPRINKLER SYSTEM (feet)	WITH SPRINKLER SYSTEM (feet)
A, E, F-1, M, R, S-1	200[e]	250[b]
I-1	Not Permitted	250[b]
B	200	300[c]
F-2, S-2, U	300	400[c]
H-1	Not Permitted	75[d]
H-2	Not Permitted	100[d]
H-3	Not Permitted	150[d]
H-4	Not Permitted	175[d]
H-5	Not Permitted	200[c]
I-2, I-3	Not Permitted	200[c]
I-4	150	200[c]

For SI: 1 foot = 304.8 mm.

a. See the following sections for modifications to exit access travel distance requirements:
  Section 402.8: For the distance limitation in malls.
  Section 404.9: For the distance limitation through an atrium space.
  Section 407.4: For the distance limitation in Group I-2.
  Sections 408.6.1 and 408.8.1: For the distance limitations in Group I-3.
  Section 411.3: For the distance limitation in special amusement buildings.
  Section 412.6: For the distance limitations in aircraft manufacturing facilities.
  Section 1006.2.2.2: For the distance limitation in refrigeration machinery rooms.
  Section 1006.2.2.3: For the distance limitation in refrigerated rooms and spaces.
  Section 1006.3.3: For buildings with one exit.
  Section 1017.2.2: For increased distance limitation in Groups F-1 and S-1.
  Section 1029.7: For increased limitation in assembly seating.
  Section 3103.4: For temporary structures.
  Section 3104.9: For pedestrian walkways.
b. Buildings equipped throughout with an automatic sprinkler system in accordance with Section 903.3.1.1 or 903.3.1.2. See Section 903 for occupancies where automatic sprinkler systems are permitted in accordance with Section 903.3.1.2.
c. Buildings equipped throughout with an automatic sprinkler system in accordance with Section 903.3.1.1.
d. Group H occupancies equipped throughout with an automatic sprinkler system in accordance with Section 903.2.5.1.
e. Group R-3 and R-4 buildings equipped throughout with an automatic sprinkler system in accordance with Section 903.3.1.3. See Section 903.2.8 for occupancies where automatic sprinkler systems are permitted in accordance with Section 903.3.1.3.

Common Path of Travel

The **common path of travel** is the route a person would take to get to a point where two egress routes are possible. This distance should be added to the egress route distance for the maximum travel distance to an exit. **Travel distance** includes the complete path of travel to an exit including the common path of travel (Figure 4.2).

Plumbing

Based on the use and number of building occupants, the number of plumbing fixtures can be assessed in accordance with Table 2902.1 (see Table 4.6).

ADA guidelines should be followed for specific information on making the restrooms and water fountains accessible. These would also apply to any kitchens included in a project.

Materials

The class ratings required for various occupancy types are found in Chapter 8 of the IBC, Table 803.13. Class A are the most restrictive and Class C the least restrictive types of finishes (see Table 4.7).

Sustainability Ratings

In addition to code requirements, finish materials contribute to indoor air quality and sustainability standards. The materials components might include recycled content (either postindustrial or postconsumer), they may have been obtained within a 500-mile radius, or they might have

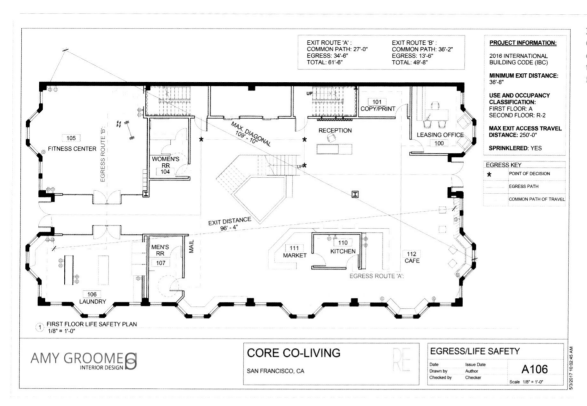

EXIT ROUTE 'A' :
COMMON PATH: 27'-0"
EGRESS: 34'-6"
TOTAL: 61'-6"

EXIT ROUTE 'B' :
COMMON PATH: 36'-2"
EGRESS: 13'-6"
TOTAL: 49'-8"

PROJECT INFORMATION:

2016 INTERNATIONAL
BUILDING CODE (IBC)

MINIMUM EXIT DISTANCE:
36'-8"

USE AND OCCUPANCY
CLASSIFICATION:
FIRST FLOOR: A
SECOND FLOOR: R-2

MAX EXIT ACCESS TRAVEL
DISTANCE: 250'-0"

SPRINKLERED: YES

EGRESS KEY
*   POINT OF DECISION
_____ EGRESS PATH
_____ COMMON PATH OF TRAVEL

101 COPY/PRINT
RECEPTION
LEASING OFFICE 100
105 FITNESS CENTER
WOMEN'S RR 104
MAX DIAGONAL 109'- 10"
EXIT DISTANCE 96' - 4"
MEN'S RR 107
MAIL
111 MARKET
110 KITCHEN
112 CAFE
EGRESS ROUTE 'A':
106 LAUNDRY
EGRESS ROUTE 'B':

1 FIRST FLOOR LIFE SAFETY PLAN
   1/8" = 1'-0"

AMY GROOME
INTERIOR DESIGN

CORE CO-LIVING
SAN FRANCISCO, CA

EGRESS/LIFE SAFETY

Date   Issue Date
Drawn by   Author
Checked by   Checker

A106

Scale 1/8" = 1'-0"

Figure 4.2
Common path
of travel and
travel distance
illustrated

come from a rapidly renewable source. All these contribute to their inherent sustainability. Additionally, products that have no or low volatile organic compounds provide better indoor air quality, thus contributing to both LEED and WELL Building certification.

Building Certifications

Whether a project team plans to pursue a building certification or multiple types of certifications should be determined from the outset of the project as this will impact programming for the project.

LEED Green Building Rating Systems, Green Globes, and the Living Building Challenge

Deciding whether to pursue a green building standard must be done at the earliest point in a project. Either the owner or the designer may want to pursue this, and it is an important decision that should be made during the programming stage.

A key component of the LEED Green Building Rating Systems, as well as other green building

systems, is the need for the project team to work collaboratively at all phases of the project. During programming, the strategy for meeting all prerequisites as well as targeting which points to pursue should be undertaken by the team members. Having a well-established plan from the beginning makes success more likely.

WELL Building Certification

As with LEED and other green building systems, the project team should decide whether they plan to embrace the WELL Building Standard during programming. Several of the WELL requirements impact the design of the building, including important components such as where and how stairs are integrated into a multistory building.

Historic Building Standards

For buildings listed on the National Register of Historic Places (and those eligible to be listed), the Secretary of the Interior's Standards for Historic Preservation provide guidance for new design work. Levels of intervention are divided into four approaches: preservation, reconstruction, rehabilitation, and restoration. A historic building consultant will make sure that design decisions are made that do not compromise important historic fabric of the building.

IBC 2018 TABLE 2902.1: MINIMUM NUMBER OF REQUIRED PLUMBING FIXTURES

Table 2902.1 has retained the same number. Assembly has been adjusted to remove the occupancy column that contained A-1, A-2, A-3, A-4, and A-5 from the table. A category for "casino gaming areas" has been added with pertinent plumbing requirements.

As with Assembly, the occupancy column has been removed for Factory (F-1 and F-2) and for Institutional (I-1, I-2, I-3, and I-4). Under Institutional, a new row item has been added for "Custodial care facilities," with the pertinent plumbing requirements. Under Institutional a new row item has been added for "Medical care recipients in hospitals and nursing homes," with the pertinent plumbing requirements. (This replaces "Hospitals, ambulatory nursing home care recipient" in the IBC 2015.) "Employees other than residential care" in the IBC 2015 has been replaced by "Employees in hospitals and nursing homes" in the IBC 2018. "Visitors other than residential care" in the IBC 2015 has been replaced with "Visitors in hospitals and nursing homes" in the IBC 2018. Beneath reformatories, "Employees" in the IBC 2015 has been replaced by "Employees in reformatories, detention centers, and correctional centers" in the IBC 2018. The occupancy column has been removed for the Residential classification, eliminating the column with R-1, R-2, R-3, and R-4 in the IBC 2018. The occupancy column has been removed for the Storage classification, eliminating the column with S-1 and S-2 in the IBC 2018.

(Formerly IBC 2015 Table 2902.1)

Table 4.6 IBC 2018 Table 2902.1: Minimum Number of Required Plumbing Fixtures

[P] TABLE 2902.1
MINIMUM NUMBER OF REQUIRED PLUMBING FIXTURES[a]
(See Sections 2902.1.1 and 2902.2)

No.	CLASSIFICATION	DESCRIPTION	WATER CLOSETS (URINALS SEE SECTION 424.2 OF THE *INTERNATIONAL PLUMBING CODE*)		LAVATORIES		BATHTUBS/ SHOWERS	DRINKING FOUNTAINS (SEE SECTION 410 OF THE *INTERNATIONAL PLUMBING CODE*)	OTHER
			Male	Female	Male	Female			
1	Assembly	Theaters and other buildings for the performing arts and motion pictures[d]	1 per 125	1 per 65	1 per 200		—	1 per 500	1 service sink
		Nightclubs, bars, taverns, dance halls and buildings for similar purposes[d]	1 per 40	1 per 40	1 per 75		—	1 per 500	1 service sink
		Restaurants, banquet halls and food courts[d]	1 per 75	1 per 75	1 per 200		—	1 per 500	1 service sink
		Casino gaming areas	1 per 100 for the first 400 and 1 per 250 for the remainder exceeding 400	1 per 50 for the first 400 and 1 per 150 for the remainder exceeding 400	1 per 250 for the first 750 and 1 per 500 for the remainder exceeding 750		—	1 per 1,000	1 service sink

(continued)

Table 4.6 IBC 2018 Table 2902.1: Minimum Number of Required Plumbing Fixtures *(continued)*

PLUMBING SYSTEMS

[P] TABLE 2902.1—(continued)
MINIMUM NUMBER OF REQUIRED PLUMBING FIXTURES[a]
(See Sections 2902.1.1 and 2902.2)

No.	CLASSIFICATION	DESCRIPTION	WATER CLOSETS (URINALS SEE SECTION 424.2 OF THE *INTERNATIONAL PLUMBING CODE*)		LAVATORIES		BATHTUBS/ SHOWERS	DRINKING FOUNTAINS (SEE SECTION 410 OF THE *INTERNATIONAL PLUMBING CODE*)	OTHER
			Male	Female	Male	Female			
1	Assembly	Auditoriums without permanent seating, art galleries, exhibition halls, museums, lecture halls, libraries, arcades and gymnasiums[d]	1 per 125	1 per 65	1 per 200		—	1 per 500	1 service sink
		Passenger terminals and transportation facilities[d]	1 per 500	1 per 500	1 per 750		—	1 per 1,000	1 service sink
		Places of worship and other religious services[d]	1 per 150	1 per 75	1 per 200		—	1 per 1,000	1 service sink
		Coliseums, arenas, skating rinks, pools and tennis courts for indoor sporting events and activities	1 per 75 for the first 1,500 and 1 per 120 for the remainder exceeding 1,500	1 per 40 for the first 1,520 and 1 per 60 for the remainder exceeding 1,520	1 per 200	1 per 150	—	1 per 1,000	1 service sink
		Stadiums, amusement parks, bleachers and grandstands for outdoor sporting events and activities[f]	1 per 75 for the first 1,500 and 1 per 120 for the remainder exceeding 1,500	1 per 40 for the first 1,520 and 1 per 60 for the remainder exceeding 1,520	1 per 200	1 per 150	—	1 per 1,000	1 service sink
2	Business	Buildings for the transaction of business, professional services, other services involving merchandise, office buildings, banks, light industrial, ambulatory care and similar uses	1 per 25 for the first 50 and 1 per 50 for the remainder exceeding 50		1 per 40 for the first 80 and 1 per 80 for the remainder exceeding 80		—	1 per 100	1 service sink[e]
3	Educational	Educational facilities	1 per 50		1 per 50		—	1 per 100	1 service sink
4	Factory and industrial	Structures in which occupants are engaged in work fabricating, assembly or processing of products or materials	1 per 100		1 per 100		—	1 per 400	1 service sink
5	Institutional	Custodial care facilities	1 per 10		1 per 10		1 per 8	1 per 100	1 service sink
		Medical care recipients in hospitals and nursing homes[b]	1 per room[c]		1 per room[c]		1 per 15	1 per 100	1 service sink
		Employees in hospitals and nursing homes[b]	1 per 25		1 per 35		—	1 per 100	—
		Visitors in hospitals and nursing homes	1 per 75		1 per 100		—	1 per 500	—
		Prisons[b]	1 per cell		1 per cell		1 per 15	1 per 100	1 service sink

(continued)

Table 4.6 IBC 2018 Table 2902.1: Minimum Number of Required Plumbing Fixtures *(continued)*

PLUMBING SYSTEMS

[P] TABLE 2902.1—continued
MINIMUM NUMBER OF REQUIRED PLUMBING FIXTURES[a]
(See Sections 2902.1.1 and 2902.2)

No.	CLASSIFICATION	DESCRIPTION	WATER CLOSETS (URINALS SEE SECTION 424.2 OF THE *INTERNATIONAL PLUMBING CODE*)		LAVATORIES		BATHTUBS OR SHOWERS	DRINKING FOUNTAINS (SEE SECTION 410 OF THE *INTERNATIONAL PLUMBING CODE*)	OTHER
			Male	Female	Male	Female			
5	Institutional	Reformatories, detention centers and correctional centers[b]	1 per 15		1 per 15		1 per 15	1 per 100	1 service sink
		Employees in reformitories, detention centers and correctional centers[b]	1 per 25		1 per 35		—	1 per 100	—
		Adult day care and child day care	1 per 15		1 per 15		1	1 per 100	1 service sink
6	Mercantile	Retail stores, service stations, shops, salesrooms, markets and shopping centers	1 per 500		1 per 750		—	1 per 1,000	1 service sink[e]
7	Residential	Hotels, motels, boarding houses (transient)	1 per sleeping unit		1 per sleeping unit		1 per sleeping unit	—	1 service sink
		Dormitories, fraternities, sororities and boarding houses (not transient)	1 per 10		1 per 10		1 per 8	1 per 100	1 service sink
		Apartment house	1 per dwelling unit		1 per dwelling unit		1 per dwelling unit	—	1 kitchen sink per dwelling unit; 1 automatic clothes washer connection per 20 dwelling units
		One- and two-family dwellings and lodging houses with five or fewer guestrooms	1 per dwelling unit		1 per 10		1 per dwelling unit	—	1 kitchen sink per dwelling unit; 1 automatic clothes washer connection per dwelling unit
		Congregate living facilities with 16 or fewer persons	1 per 10		1 per 10		1 per 8	1 per 100	1 service sink
8	Storage	Structures for the storage of goods, warehouses, storehouses and freight depots, low and moderate hazard	1 per 100		1 per 100		—	1 per 1,000	1 service sink

a. The fixtures shown are based on one fixture being the minimum required for the number of persons indicated or any fraction of the number of persons indicated. The number of occupants shall be determined by this code.

b. Toilet facilities for employees shall be separate from facilities for inmates or care recipients.

c. A single-occupant toilet room with one water closet and one lavatory serving not more than two adjacent patient sleeping units shall be permitted, provided that each patient sleeping unit has direct access to the toilet room and provisions for privacy for the toilet room user are provided.

d. The occupant load for seasonal outdoor seating and entertainment areas shall be included when determining the minimum number of facilities required.

e. For business and mercantile classifications with an occupant load of 15 or fewer, a service sink shall not be required.

f. The required number and type of plumbing fixtures for outdoor swimming pools shall be in accordance with Section 609 of the *International Swimming Pool and Spa Code*.

Table 4.7 IBC 2018 Table 803.13: Interior Wall and Ceiling Finish Requirement

TABLE 803.13
INTERIOR WALL AND CEILING FINISH REQUIREMENTS BY OCCUPANCY[k]

GROUP	SPRINKLERED[l]			NONSPRINKLERED		
	Interior exit stairways and ramps and exit passageways[a, b]	Corridors and enclosure for exit access stairways and ramps	Rooms and enclosed spaces[c]	Interior exit stairways and ramps and exit passageways[a, b]	Corridors and enclosure for exit access stairways and ramps	Rooms and enclosed spaces[c]
A-1 & A-2	B	B	C	A	A[d]	B[e]
A-3[f], A-4, A-5	B	B	C	A	A[d]	C
B, E, M, R-1	B	C[m]	C	A	B	C
R-4	B	C	C	A	B	B
F	C	C	C	B	C	C
H	B	B	C[g]	A	A	B
I-1	B	C	C	A	B	B
I-2	B	B	B[h, i]	A	A	B
I-3	A	A[j]	C	A	A	B
I-4	B	B	B[h, i]	A	A	B
R-2	C	C	C	B	B	C
R-3	C	C	C	C	C	C
S	C	C	C	B	B	C
U	No restrictions			No restrictions		

For SI: 1 inch = 25.4 mm, 1 square foot = 0.0929 m^2.

a. Class C interior finish materials shall be permitted for wainscotting or paneling of not more than 1,000 square feet of applied surface area in the grade lobby where applied directly to a noncombustible base or over furring strips applied to a noncombustible base and fireblocked as required by Section 803.15.1.

b. In other than Group I-3 occupancies in buildings less than three stories above grade plane, Class B interior finish for nonsprinklered buildings and Class C interior finish for sprinklered buildings shall be permitted in interior exit stairways and ramps.

c. Requirements for rooms and enclosed spaces shall be based on spaces enclosed by partitions. Where a fire-resistance rating is required for structural elements, the enclosing partitions shall extend from the floor to the ceiling. Partitions that do not comply with this shall be considered to be enclosing spaces and the rooms or spaces on both sides shall be considered to be one room or space. In determining the applicable requirements for rooms and enclosed spaces, the specific occupancy thereof shall be the governing factor regardless of the group classification of the building or structure.

d. Lobby areas in Group A-1, A-2 and A-3 occupancies shall be not less than Class B materials.

e. Class C interior finish materials shall be permitted in places of assembly with an occupant load of 300 persons or less.

f. For places of religious worship, wood used for ornamental purposes, trusses, paneling or chancel furnishing shall be permitted.

g. Class B material is required where the building exceeds two stories.

h. Class C interior finish materials shall be permitted in administrative spaces.

i. Class C interior finish materials shall be permitted in rooms with a capacity of four persons or less.

j. Class B materials shall be permitted as wainscotting extending not more than 48 inches above the finished floor in corridors and exit access stairways and ramps.

k. Finish materials as provided for in other sections of this code.

l. Applies when protected by an automatic sprinkler system installed in accordance with Section 903.3.1.1 or 903.3.1.2.

m. Corridors in ambulatory care facilities shall be provided with Class A or B materials.

IBC 2018 TABLE 803.13: INTERIOR WALL AND CEILING FINISH REQUIREMENT

Table 803.11 in the IBC 2015 had been replaced by Table 803.13 in the IBC 2018. Note that "m" has been added in the 2018 IBC, stating that corridors in ambulatory care facilities shall be provided with Class A or B materials.

(Formerly Interior Wall and Ceiling Finish Requirement IBC 2015 Table 803.11)

Conclusions

The programming phase of the project is the time to make all of the big decisions about building code use groups and the use of additional standards and approaches, such as whether to invoke the Secretary's Standards, whether to try to obtain LEED certification, Green Globes, the Living Building Challenge, and/or WELL Building Certification. Deciding on these key components will shape future aspects of the design process throughout the project design.

Key Terms

common path of travel
gross factor
net factor
occupant load factor
travel distance
occupancy group

Assignment

1. Using your most recent studio design project, follow the process outlined in this chapter. Assess what you might have done differently in the design you created if you had followed this process first.

5

Case Study: Mixed-Use Spa and Residence

Learning Objectives:

After reading this chapter and doing the exercises, students will be able to

- Identify the occupancy type, determine the construction type, calculate preliminary occupant loads, and determine the required number of exits
- Evaluate travel distance, number of exits required, and common path of travel
- Determine ADA clearances at all doors and fixtures
- Calculate the number of plumbing fixtures needed for a specific use
- Identify appropriate strategies for fire separation between use groups

Introduction

This chapter takes a combination spa/residential project, consisting of approximately 4,600 square feet, through the codes application process as a part of the schematic design. Using a spa facility dedicated for patients diagnosed with multiple sclerosis (MS) and a residence for the live-in physicians of the facility, the chapter identifies minimum code requirements and then discusses the nature of building codes as a minimum requirement versus good and appropriate design responses for this type of client.

Scope of the Project

As a part of the 2015 Bienenstock/ASID design competition, this project for a spa and residence building was located in a 4,600 square foot building (1,000 square feet designated for a residential component) constructed in a small suburban community. The one-story, four-sided brick building has an entrance on the north side into the spa with two more entries recommended—one for the residence and the other as a second egress door for the spa. The spa is for MS patients and includes an exercise area, a pool, two massage rooms, two offices, and a reception/lobby area. Public bathrooms include shower facilities and dressing rooms. The entire building is equipped with automatic fire sprinklers throughout.

BIENENSTOCK PROJECT OUTLINE

Building Location & Description

Location: The building is located outside of a large city, in a smaller suburban community with a population of 4,220. The surrounding area is mainly residential and office space within walking distance of the center of the community. The site for the building is in a park-like setting at the base of a mountain.

Description: The building is a new free-standing building with a private parking lot located on a secondary street. The four-sided brick building has an entrance location on the north side of the building with a "zero step" threshold. Four columns define the entrance. Heating, ventilating, and air conditioning (HVAC) units are located on the roof. Supply and return air ducts are flexible. This distribution ductwork can be installed in each space when the layout is completed. The building has a sprinkler system. Building support walls are located on the floor plan as indicated.

The interior walls are gypsum wallboard. See additional wall information on the drawings. The maximum ceiling height is 11 feet high. The ceiling may be lowered to a minimum height of 9 feet in the day spa and to 8 feet in the residence. Windows are 4 feet high by 3 feet wide and are located 2 feet, 10 inches AFF to the bottom of the frame. With one floor, new building construction, plumbing must be located within a 10 foot radius of an existing exterior wall or 20 foot radius from the columns located in the center of the plan. Skylights may be added.

Specific Program Requirements by Area

Day Spa

Entry/Lobby, Receptionist Station, and Bookkeeper's Office: Maximum of 400 square feet.

Entry/Lobby

1. Direct access to receptionist
2. Seating for three people and space for a wheelchair
3. Occasional tables
4. Space to hang twenty coats
5. Literature display rack

Receptionist Station

1. 8'-0" transaction counter
2. 8' x 30" work surface
3. Desk chair
4. 24 lineal feet of lateral files
5. Locking cabinet for supplies and retail stock
6. Retail product display case to hold candles, incense, and cooling products (hats, scarves, vests, pads, and bandanas). Must be visible from Entry/Lobby, accessed by the receptionist

Bookkeeper's Office

1. Office must be secured
2. Desk with a return
3. Chair
4. 30 lineal feet of filing

Day Spa

1. Swimming pool, 8' x 15', in an enclosed space, but visible from the floor exercise area
2. Floor exercise area: floor space for twenty yoga mats, twenty resistance bands, two stair master machines (approx. 4' W x 6' L), and barbell rack (44" W x 18" D)
3. Open room accommodation to store the above items when not in use
4. Two massage rooms—each approx. 12' x 15', containing a massage bed approx. 4' W x 6' L, with cabinet for linen storage and table for oils, lotions, etc.
5. 12' x 12' room with desk/chair, guest chair for private consultation by therapist, and space for literature storage
6. Area to sit/rest/cool down/reflect/view the outdoors after exercising

Barrier-Free Bathrooms/Dressing Rooms

Women's Room

1. One toilet stall
2. One shower stall
3. One dressing cubicle with a bench
4. Two lavatories, one must be barrier-free
5. Grab bars appropriately located
6. Bathroom accessories appropriately located
7. Four small secured lockers to store clothing and personal items

Men's Room

1. One toilet stall
2. One urinal
3. One shower stall
4. One dressing cubicle with a bench
5. Two lavatories, one must be barrier-free
6. Grab bars appropriately located
7. Bathroom accessories appropriately located
8. Four small secured lockers to store clothing and personal items

Residential Space

Pat and Chris Helf, the doctor and physical therapist team, will be living in this residential space of approximately 1,000 square feet. They are low key and want the space to reflect the natural environment surrounding this facility. They request the use of materials that reflect nature and are considered green/

environmentally friendly. They would like a spacious living/dining area, a bedroom with adjoining bath and closet. They occasionally will have one or two overnight personal guests that will use the second bedroom and half bath. They will also use the second bedroom for their personal bills/emails/correspondence. Due to the nature of the facility, the entire residential area is to be designed with universal/barrier-free components. There needs to be a separate entrance from the exterior and an entrance from the day spa area.

Living Room/Dining Room

1. One sofa and a pair of comfortable reading chairs
2. Appropriate end or cocktail or sofa table for lamps and storage
3. Supply one conversation area
4. Medium size (you determine the size) flat-screen television to be inconspicuously wall mounted
5. Dining table to seat six
6. A china cabinet for storage and display
7. Green plants

Kitchen

1. Configuration of U, L, or parallel
2. Gas stove
3. Wall oven
4. Wall-mounted microwave
5. Two dishwasher drawers
6. Side-by-side refrigerator/freezer
7. Double sink
8. Varying heights of countertops

Half Bath

1. Minimum of 30 square feet
2. Sink
3. Toilet

Master Bedroom

1. Queen-sized bed with two nightstands
2. Closet with built in drawers for flat clothing storage
3. Easy chair with table
4. Television mounted on a wall so that it may be watched from bed or easy chair
5. Window required, see code

Master Bath

1. Sink, shower, and toilet in bath
2. Provide a minimum of four lineal feet of counter space
3. Linen closet

Guest Bedroom/Den

1. Double-sized sleeper sofa
2. Appropriate end table(s) for lamps and storage
3. Personal computer and printer
4. Management task chair
5. Desk
6. Storage closet for clothes and a minimum of 5 lineal feet of lateral filing cabinet storage
7. Minimum of 4 lineal feet of shelving for books/display

Applying the Code

In order to apply the proper building code, some basic building data are required, including the overall area and height of the building. In addition to this, whether the building is sprinklered and the materials of construction should be identified. Under recent building codes, buildings containing residential occupancies are required to be equipped with automatic fire sprinklers throughout.

Programming Phase

During the programming stage of the project, the basic use groups, building construction type, and any applicable zoning information is established. This is also the time when the design team, in conjunction with the owner, determines whether the project will try to meet sustainable design rating systems, such as LEED, Green Globes, or the Living Building Challenge, as well as whether to use the WELL Building Standard. All of these types of approaches require an integrated project delivery and for all members of the design team to be on board from the beginning of the project.

Schematic Design Phase

Once project design commences with the schematic design phase, the design team must determine the use group(s), building type, height and area, construction type, and the requirements for overall means of egress.

Use Group

As a mixed-use building, the first thing to be determined was the use and occupancy classifications for the project. These are Business (spa) and R-3 (residence). R-3 is the appropriate occupancy, since the occupants are permanent in nature, there are not more than two dwelling units, and the building contains a mixed occupancy. As a spa for people with MS, it is technically a business use but contains components of an ambulatory care facility. For example, an MS patient who is wheelchair bound might be in the pool or receiving a massage at the time of an emergency. In this instance, they would require assistance in exiting the facility. Due to the mixed use of the facility, the residence contained within the same facility is classified as R-3. As a mixed-use building, a one-hour fire separation is required between the two uses.

Building Type, Height, and Area

Although a single story is specified by the program requirements, the permissible height and size should still be assessed using Tables 504.3 and 504.4 (see Tables 5.1, 5.2). In this instance, as a mixed-use facility, the building must comply with the limitations of both uses.

Construction Classification

Types I and II are those construction assemblies composed of noncombustible materials. In Type III construction, the exterior walls are noncombustible, and the interior elements are any materials permitted by the building code. Type IV construction is heavy timber with noncombustible exterior walls and interior building elements of solid or laminated wood. Type V includes exterior walls, structural elements, and interior walls composed of materials permitted by the code. The construction type determines the allowable area in a building (Table 5.3). For this project, the construction type is Type II.

Based on Section 506.2.2, this mixed-occupancy one-story building shall be determined in accordance with Section 508.1 based on Equation 1 for each occupancy. However, in Section 508.1, provision 3, live-work units are not considered separate occupancies. A **live-work unit** is defined as a dwelling or sleeping unit where a significant portion of the space includes a nonresidential use that is operated by the tenant. In this project, if the tenant operates the spa, it would fall into this definition. According to Table 508.4, the required separation of occupancies in hours is one hour because the building is equipped with an automatic sprinkler system, and it is required to be sprinklered based on IBC Section 903.2.8 (Table 5.4).

Means of Egress

Once the construction classification and subsequent allowable height, floor numbers, and allowable floor space are determined, the means of egress out of the building are considered.

Maximum Floor Area Allowance per Occupant
The first step in figuring out the number and placement of exits is to determine the design occupant load of the building. This can be done using Table 1004.5. The occupant load factor is given in either net or gross. If the factor is a gross number, the square footage times the factor yields the number of occupants permitted. If a net factor is to be applied, the net square footage must first be established for the area under consideration.

Table 5.1 IBC 2018 Table 504.3: Allowable Building Height in Feet above Grade Plane

TABLE 504.3
ALLOWABLE BUILDING HEIGHT IN FEET ABOVE GRADE PLANE[a]

OCCUPANCY CLASSIFICATION	SEE FOOTNOTES	TYPE I A	TYPE I B	TYPE II A	TYPE II B	TYPE III A	TYPE III B	TYPE IV HT	TYPE V A	TYPE V B
A, B, E, F, M, S, U	NS[b]	UL	160	65	55	65	55	65	50	40
	S	UL	180	85	75	85	75	85	70	60
H-1, H-2, H-3, H-5	NS[c,d]	UL	160	65	55	65	55	65	50	40
	S	UL	160	65	55	65	55	65	50	40
H-4	NS[c,d]	UL	160	65	55	65	55	65	50	40
	S	UL	180	85	75	85	75	85	70	60
I-1 Condition 1, I-3	NS[d,e]	UL	160	65	55	65	55	65	50	40
	S	UL	180	85	75	85	75	85	70	60
I-1 Condition 2, I-2	NS[d,e,f]	UL	160	65	55	65	55	65	50	40
	S	UL	180	85	55	65	55	65	50	40
I-4	NS[d,g]	UL	160	65	55	65	55	65	50	40
	S	UL	180	85	75	85	75	85	70	60
R[h]	NS[d]	UL	160	65	55	65	55	65	50	40
	S13D	60	60	60	60	60	60	60	50	40
	S13R	60	60	60	60	60	60	60	60	60
	S	UL	180	85	75	85	75	85	70	60

For SI: 1 foot = 304.8 mm.

UL = Unlimited; NS = Buildings not equipped throughout with an automatic sprinkler system; S = Buildings equipped throughout with an automatic sprinkler system installed in accordance with Section 903.3.1.1; S13R = Buildings equipped throughout with an automatic sprinkler system installed in accordance with Section 903.3.1.2; S13D = Buildings equipped throughout with an automatic sprinkler system installed in accordance with Section 903.3.1.3.

a. See Chapters 4 and 5 for specific exceptions to the allowable height in this chapter.

b. See Section 903.2 for the minimum thresholds for protection by an automatic sprinkler system for specific occupancies.

c. New Group H occupancies are required to be protected by an automatic sprinkler system in accordance with Section 903.2.5.

d. The NS value is only for use in evaluation of existing building height in accordance with the *International Existing Building Code*.

e. New Group I-1 and I-3 occupancies are required to be protected by an automatic sprinkler system in accordance with Section 903.2.6. For new Group I-1 occupancies Condition 1, see Exception 1 of Section 903.2.6.

f. New and existing Group I-2 occupancies are required to be protected by an automatic sprinkler system in accordance with Section 903.2.6 and Section 1103.5 of the *International Fire Code*.

g. For new Group I-4 occupancies, see Exceptions 2 and 3 of Section 903.2.6.

h. New Group R occupancies are required to be protected by an automatic sprinkler system in accordance with Section 903.2.8.

IBC 2018 TABLE 504.3: ALLOWABLE BUILDING HEIGHT IN FEET ABOVE GRADE PLANE

Table 504.3 has retained the same number in the IRC 2018. A change is the addition of a new "footnote" under occupancy classification R. S13D has been added to the table below NS and above S13R in the IBC 2018. S13D is a building equipped throughout with an automatic sprinkler system in accordance with Section 903.3.1.3.

(Formerly Table 504.3 IBC 2015)

Table 5.2 IBC 2018 Table 504.4 Allowable Number of Stories above Grade Plane

GENERAL BUILDING HEIGHTS AND AREAS

TABLE 504.4
ALLOWABLE NUMBER OF STORIES ABOVE GRADE PLANE[a, b]

OCCUPANCY CLASSIFICATION	SEE FOOTNOTES	TYPE I		TYPE II		TYPE III		TYPE IV	TYPE V	
		A	B	A	B	A	B	HT	A	B
A-1	NS	UL	5	3	2	3	2	3	2	1
	S	UL	6	4	3	4	3	4	3	2
A-2	NS	UL	11	3	2	3	2	3	2	1
	S	UL	12	4	3	4	3	4	3	2
A-3	NS	UL	11	3	2	3	2	3	2	1
	S	UL	12	4	3	4	3	4	3	2
A-4	NS	UL	11	3	2	3	2	3	2	1
	S	UL	12	4	3	4	3	4	3	2
A-5	NS	UL	UL	UL	UL	UL	UL	UL	UL	UL
	S	UL	UL	UL	UL	UL	UL	UL	UL	UL
B	NS	UL	11	5	3	5	3	5	3	2
	S	UL	12	6	4	6	4	6	4	3
E	NS	UL	5	3	2	3	2	3	1	1
	S	UL	6	4	3	4	3	4	2	2
F-1	NS	UL	11	4	2	3	2	4	2	1
	S	UL	12	5	3	4	3	5	3	2
F-2	NS	UL	11	5	3	4	3	5	3	2
	S	UL	12	6	4	5	4	6	4	3
H-1	NS[c, d]	1	1	1	1	1	1	1	1	NP
	S									
H-2	NS[c, d]	UL	3	2	1	2	1	2	1	1
	S									
H-3	NS[c, d]	UL	6	4	2	4	2	4	2	1
	S									
H-4	NS[c, d]	UL	7	5	3	5	3	5	3	2
	S	UL	8	6	4	6	4	6	4	3
H-5	NS[c, d]	4	4	3	3	3	3	3	3	2
	S									
I-1 Condition 1	NS[d, e]	UL	9	4	3	4	3	4	3	2
	S	UL	10	5	4	5	4	5	4	3
I-1 Condition 2	NS[d, e]	UL	9	4	3	4	3	4	3	2
	S	UL	10	5						
I-2	NS[d, f]	UL	4	2	1	1	NP	1	1	NP
	S	UL	5	3						
I-3	NS[d, e]	UL	4	2	1	2	1	2	2	1
	S	UL	5	3	2	3	2	3	3	2
I-4	NS[d, g]	UL	5	3	2	3	2	3	1	1
	S	UL	6	4	3	4	3	4	2	2
M	NS	UL	11	4	2	4	2	4	3	1
	S	UL	12	5	3	5	3	5	4	2

(continued)

Table 5.2 IBC 2018 Table 504.4 Allowable Number of Stories above Grade Plane *(continued)*

TABLE 504.4—continued
ALLOWABLE NUMBER OF STORIES ABOVE GRADE PLANE[a, b]

OCCUPANCY CLASSIFICATION	SEE FOOTNOTES	TYPE I A	TYPE I B	TYPE II A	TYPE II B	TYPE III A	TYPE III B	TYPE IV HT	TYPE V A	TYPE V B
R-1[h]	NS[d]	UL	11	4	4	4	4	4	3	2
	S13R	4	4	4	4	4	4	4	4	3
	S	UL	12	5	5	5	5	5	4	3
R-2[h]	NS[d]	UL	11	4	4	4	4	4	3	2
	S13R	4	4	4	4	4	4	4	4	3
	S	UL	12	5	5	5	5	5	4	3
R-3[h]	NS[d]	UL	11	4	4	4	4	4	3	3
	S13D	4	4	4	4	4	4	4	3	3
	S13R	4	4	4	4	4	4	4	4	4
	S	UL	12	5	5	5	5	5	4	4
R-4[h]	NS[d]	UL	11	4	4	4	4	4	3	2
	S13D	4	4	4	4	4	4	4	3	2
	S13R	4	4	4	4	4	4	4	4	3
	S	UL	12	5	5	5	5	5	4	3
S-1	NS	UL	11	4	2	3	2	4	3	1
	S	UL	12	5	3	4	3	5	4	2
S-2	NS	UL	11	5	3	4	3	4	4	2
	S	UL	12	6	4	5	4	5	5	3
U	NS	UL	5	4	2	3	2	4	2	1
	S	UL	6	5	3	4	3	5	3	2

UL = Unlimited; NP = Not Permitted; NS = Buildings not equipped throughout with an automatic sprinkler system; S = Buildings equipped throughout with an automatic sprinkler system installed in accordance with Section 903.3.1.1; S13R = Buildings equipped throughout with an automatic sprinkler system installed in accordance with Section 903.3.1.2; S13D = Buildings equipped throughout with an automatic sprinkler system installed in accordance with Section 903.3.1.3.

a. See Chapters 4 and 5 for specific exceptions to the allowable height in this chapter.

b. See Section 903.2 for the minimum thresholds for protection by an automatic sprinkler system for specific occupancies.

c. New Group H occupancies are required to be protected by an automatic sprinkler system in accordance with Section 903.2.5.

d. The NS value is only for use in evaluation of existing building height in accordance with the *International Existing Building Code*.

e. New Group I-1 and I-3 occupancies are required to be protected by an automatic sprinkler system in accordance with Section 903.2.6. For new Group I-1 occupancies, Condition 1, see Exception 1 of Section 903.2.6.

f. New and existing Group I-2 occupancies are required to be protected by an automatic sprinkler system in accordance with Section 903.2.6 and 1103.5 of the *International Fire Code*.

g. For new Group I-4 occupancies, see Exceptions 2 and 3 of Section 903.2.6.

h. New Group R occupancies are required to be protected by an automatic sprinkler system in accordance with Section 903.2.8.

IBC 2018 TABLE 504.4: ALLOWABLE NUMBER OF STORIES ABOVE GRADE PLANE

Table 504.4 has retained the same number in the IRC 2018. A change is the addition of a new "footnote" under occupancy classification R-3 and R-4. S13D has been added to the table below NS and above S13R in both instances in the IBC 2018. S13D is a building equipped throughout with an automatic sprinkler system in accordance with Section 903.3.1.3.

(Formerly Table 504.4 IBC 2015)

Table 5.3 IBC 2018 Table 506.2: Allowable Area Factor

TABLE 506.2
ALLOWABLE AREA FACTOR (A_t = NS, S1, S13R, S13D or SM, as applicable) IN SQUARE FEET[a, b]

OCCUPANCY CLASSIFICATION	SEE FOOTNOTES	TYPE OF CONSTRUCTION								
		TYPE I		TYPE II		TYPE III		TYPE IV	TYPE V	
		A	B	A	B	A	B	HT	A	B
A-1	NS	UL	UL	15,500	8,500	14,000	8,500	15,000	11,500	5,500
	S1	UL	UL	62,000	34,000	56,000	34,000	60,000	46,000	22,000
	SM	UL	UL	46,500	25,500	42,000	25,500	45,000	34,500	16,500
A-2	NS	UL	UL	15,500	9,500	14,000	9,500	15,000	11,500	6,000
	S1	UL	UL	62,000	38,000	56,000	38,000	60,000	46,000	24,000
	SM	UL	UL	46,500	28,500	42,000	28,500	45,000	34,500	18,000
A-3	NS	UL	UL	15,500	9,500	14,000	9,500	15,000	11,500	6,000
	S1	UL	UL	62,000	38,000	56,000	38,000	60,000	46,000	24,000
	SM	UL	UL	46,500	28,500	42,000	28,500	45,000	34,500	18,000
A-4	NS	UL	UL	15,500	9,500	14,000	9,500	15,000	11,500	6,000
	S1	UL	UL	62,000	38,000	56,000	38,000	60,000	46,000	24,000
	SM	UL	UL	46,500	28,500	42,000	28,500	45,000	34,500	18,000
A-5	NS	UL	UL	UL	UL	UL	UL	UL	UL	UL
	S1									
	SM									
B	NS	UL	UL	37,500	23,000	28,500	19,000	36,000	18,000	9,000
	S1	UL	UL	150,000	92,000	114,000	76,000	144,000	72,000	36,000
	SM	UL	UL	112,500	69,000	85,500	57,000	108,000	54,000	27,000
E	NS	UL	UL	26,500	14,500	23,500	14,500	25,500	18,500	9,500
	S1	UL	UL	106,000	58,000	94,000	58,000	102,000	74,000	38,000
	SM	UL	UL	79,500	43,500	70,500	43,500	76,500	55,500	28,500
F-1	NS	UL	UL	25,000	15,500	19,000	12,000	33,500	14,000	8,500
	S1	UL	UL	100,000	62,000	76,000	48,000	134,000	56,000	34,000
	SM	UL	UL	75,000	46,500	57,000	36,000	100,500	42,000	25,500
F-2	NS	UL	UL	37,500	23,000	28,500	18,000	50,500	21,000	13,000
	S1	UL	UL	150,000	92,000	114,000	72,000	202,000	84,000	52,000
	SM	UL	UL	112,500	69,000	85,500	54,000	151,500	63,000	39,000
H-1	NS[c]	21,000	16,500	11,000	7,000	9,500	7,000	10,500	7,500	NP
	S1									
H-2	NS[c]	21,000	16,500	11,000	7,000	9,500	7,000	10,500	7,500	3,000
	S1									
	SM									
H-3	NS[c]	UL	60,000	26,500	14,000	17,500	13,000	25,500	10,000	5,000
	S1									
	SM									
H-4	NS[c, d]	UL	UL	37,500	17,500	28,500	17,500	36,000	18,000	6,500
	S1	UL	UL	150,000	70,000	114,000	70,000	144,000	72,000	26,000
	SM	UL	UL	112,500	52,500	85,500	52,500	108,000	54,000	19,500
H-5	NS[c, d]	UL	UL	37,500	23,000	28,500	19,000	36,000	18,000	9,000
	S1	UL	UL	150,000	92,000	114,000	76,000	144,000	72,000	36,000
	SM	UL	UL	112,500	69,000	85,500	57,000	108000	54,000	27,000

(continued)

Table 5.3 IBC 2018 Table 506.2: Allowable Area Factor *(continued)*

GENERAL BUILDING HEIGHTS AND AREAS

TABLE 506.2—continued
ALLOWABLE AREA FACTOR (A_t = NS, S1, S13R, S13D or SM, as applicable) IN SQUARE FEET[a, b]

OCCUPANCY CLASSIFICATION	SEE FOOTNOTES	TYPE OF CONSTRUCTION								
		TYPE I		TYPE II		TYPE III		TYPE IV	TYPE V	
		A	B	A	B	A	B	HT	A	B
I-1	NS[d, e]	UL	55,000	19,000	10,000	16,500	10,000	18,000	10,500	4,500
	S1	UL	220,000	76,000	40,000	66,000	40,000	72,000	42,000	18,000
	SM	UL	165,000	57,000	30,000	49,500	30,000	54,000	31,500	13,500
I-2	NS[d, f]	UL	UL	15,000	11,000	12,000	NP	12,000	9,500	NP
	S1	UL	UL	60,000	44,000	48,000	NP	48,000	38,000	NP
	SM	UL	UL	45,000	33,000	36,000	NP	36,000	28,500	NP
I-3	NS[d, e]	UL	UL	15,000	10,000	10,500	7,500	12,000	7,500	5,000
	S1	UL	UL	45,000	40,000	42,000	30,000	48,000	30,000	20,000
	SM	UL	UL	45,000	30,000	31,500	22,500	36,000	22,500	15,000
I-4	NS[d, g]	UL	60,500	26,500	13,000	23,500	13,000	25,500	18,500	9,000
	S1	UL	121,000	106,000	52,000	94,000	52,000	102,000	74,000	36,000
	SM	UL	181,500	79,500	39,000	70,500	39,000	76,500	55,500	27,000
M	NS	UL	UL	21,500	12,500	18,500	12,500	20,500	14,000	9,000
	S1	UL	UL	86,000	50,000	74,000	50,000	82,000	56,000	36,000
	SM	UL	UL	64,500	37,500	55,500	37,500	61,500	42,000	27,000
R-1[h]	NS[d]	UL	UL	24,000	16,000	24,000	16,000	20,500	12,000	7,000
	S13R									
	S1	UL	UL	96,000	64,000	96,000	64,000	82,000	48,000	28,000
	SM	UL	UL	72,000	48,000	72,000	48,000	61,500	36,000	21,000
R-2[h]	NS[d]	UL	UL	24,000	16,000	24,000	16,000	20,500	12,000	7,000
	S13R									
	S1	UL	UL	96,000	64,000	96,000	64,000	82,000	48,000	28,000
	SM	UL	UL	72,000	48,000	72,000	48,000	61,500	36,000	21,000
R-3[h]	NS[d]	UL	UL	UL	UL	UL	UL	UL	UL	UL
	S13D									
	S13R									
	S1									
	SM									
R-4[h]	NS[d]	UL	UL	24,000	16,000	24,000	16,000	20,500	12,000	7,000
	S13D									
	S13R									
	S1	UL	UL	96,000	64,000	96,000	64,000	82,000	48,000	28,000
	SM	UL	UL	72,000	48,000	72,000	48,000	61,500	36,000	21,000
S-1	NS	UL	48,000	26,000	17,500	26,000	17,500	25,500	14,000	9,000
	S1	UL	192,000	104,000	70,000	104,000	70,000	102,000	56,000	36,000
	SM	UL	144,000	78,000	52,500	78,000	52,500	76,500	42,000	27,000
S-2	NS	UL	79,000	39,000	26,000	39,000	26,000	38,500	21,000	13,500
	S1	UL	316,000	156,000	104,000	156,000	104,000	154,000	84,000	54,000
	SM	UL	237,000	117,000	78,000	117,000	78,000	115,500	63,000	40,500
U	NS[i]	UL	35,500	19,000	8,500	14,000	8,500	18,000	9,000	5,500
	S1	UL	142,000	76,000	34,000	56,000	34,000	72,000	36,000	22,000
	SM	UL	106,500	57,000	25,500	42,000	25,500	54,000	27,000	16,500

(continued)

Table 5.3 IBC 2018 Table 506.2: Allowable Area Factor *(continued)*

TABLE 506.2—continued
ALLOWABLE AREA FACTOR (A_t = NS, S1, S13R, S13D or SM, as applicable) IN SQUARE FEET[a, b]

For SI: 1 square foot = 0.0929 m[2].

UL = Unlimited; NP = Not Permitted; NS = Buildings not equipped throughout with an automatic sprinkler system; S1 = Buildings a maximum of one story above grade plane equipped throughout with an automatic sprinkler system installed in accordance with Section 903.3.1.1; SM = Buildings two or more stories above grade plane equipped throughout with an automatic sprinkler system installed in accordance with Section 903.3.1.1; S13R = Buildings equipped throughout with an automatic sprinkler system installed in accordance with Section 903.3.1.2; S13D = Buildings equipped throughout with an automatic sprinkler system installed in accordance with Section 903.3.1.3.

a. See Chapters 4 and 5 for specific exceptions to the allowable height in this chapter.

b. See Section 903.2 for the minimum thresholds for protection by an automatic sprinkler system for specific occupancies.

c. New Group H occupancies are required to be protected by an automatic sprinkler system in accordance with Section 903.2.5.

d. The NS value is only for use in evaluation of existing building area in accordance with the *International Existing Building Code*.

e. New Group I-1 and I-3 occupancies are required to be protected by an automatic sprinkler system in accordance with Section 903.2.6. For new Group I-1 occupancies, Condition 1, see Exception 1 of Section 903.2.6.

f. New and existing Group I-2 occupancies are required to be protected by an automatic sprinkler system in accordance with Section 903.2.6 and Section 1103.5 of the *International Fire Code*.

g. New Group I-4 occupancies see Exceptions 2 and 3 of Section 903.2.6.

h. New Group R occupancies are required to be protected by an automatic sprinkler system in accordance with Section 903.2.8.

i. The maximum allowable area for a single-story nonsprinklered Group U greenhouse is permitted to be 9,000 square feet, or the allowable area shall be permitted to comply with Table C102.1 of Appendix C.

IBC 2018 TABLE 506.2: ALLOWABLE AREA FACTOR

Table 506.2 has retained the same number in the IBC 2018. A change is the addition of a new "footnote" under occupancy classification R-3 and R-4. S13D has been added to the table below NS and above S13R in both instances in the IBC 2018. S13D is a building equipped throughout with an automatic sprinkler system in accordance with Section 903.3.1.3.

(Formerly Table 506.2 IBC 2015)

For maximum floor area allowances per occupant, please refer to Table 4.2 and its accompanying Box 4.1, which summarizes the primary changes to the table.

Applying this generally to the spa project, the facility overall is 4,600 square feet, with 1,000 square feet dedicated to the residence, resulting in the following design occupant load:

Residence 1,000 square feet / 200 gross per occupant = 5 occupants

Spa 3,600 square feet / 150 gross per occupant = 24 occupants

Total building occupants: 29

Means of Egress Sizing
Once an occupant load is established, the size of the means of egress must be considered. This includes both the number of required exits, the travel distance permitted, and the width of the egress path required. The minimum width is based on the more restrictive of two measures: one calculated based on occupant design load and the other an actual minimum width. The stairway means of egress factor is 0.3 inch (Section 1005.3.1).

Example: Spa egress 24 occupants x 0.3 inch = 7.2 inches minimum; however, the minimum possible width per stair for egress cannot be less 44 inches. So, in this case, the 44 inch width is the more restrictive and would apply.

Number of Exits and Travel Distance
The number of exits is first determined using Table 1006.2.1. For occupancy B, with forty-nine or fewer occupants, one exit is permitted with a maximum travel distance of 75 feet for an occupant load over thirty people in an unsprinklered building, and of 100 feet in a sprinklered building. For R-3, the building must be sprinklered and the maximum travel distance is 125 feet. According to IBC Section 903.2.8, this entire building, both the B and R-3 portions, are required to be equipped with an automatic sprinkler system (Table 5.5).

Table 5.4 IBC 2018 Table 508.4: Required Separation of Occupancies

TABLE 508.4
REQUIRED SEPARATION OF OCCUPANCIES (HOURS)[f]

OCCUPANCY	A, E		I-1[a], I-3, I-4		I-2		R[a]		F-2, S-2[b], U		B[e], F-1, M, S-1		H-1		H-2		H-3, H-4		H-5	
	S	NS	S	NS	S	NS	S	NS	S	NS	S	NS	S	NS	S	NS	S	NS	S	NS
A, E	N	N	1	2	2	NP	1	2	N	1	1	2	NP	NP	3	4	2	3	2	NP
I-1[a], I-3, I-4	—	—	N	N	2	NP	1	NP	1	2	1	2	NP	NP	3	NP	2	NP	2	NP
I-2	—	—	—	—	N	N	2	NP	2	NP	2	NP	NP	NP	3	NP	2	NP	2	NP
R[a]	—	—	—	—	—	—	N	N	1[c]	2[c]	1	2	NP	NP	3	NP	2	NP	2	NP
F-2, S-2[b], U	—	—	—	—	—	—	—	—	N	N	1	2	NP	NP	3	4	2	3	2	NP
B[e], F-1, M, S-1	—	—	—	—	—	—	—	—	—	—	N	N	NP	NP	2	3	1	2	1	NP
H-1	—	—	—	—	—	—	—	—	—	—	—	—	N	NP	NP	NP	NP	NP	NP	NP
H-2	—	—	—	—	—	—	—	—	—	—	—	—	—	—	N	NP	1	NP	1	NP
H-3, H-4	—	—	—	—	—	—	—	—	—	—	—	—	—	—	—	—	1[d]	NP	1	NP
H-5	—	—	—	—	—	—	—	—	—	—	—	—	—	—	—	—	—	—	N	NP

S = Buildings equipped throughout with an automatic sprinkler system installed in accordance with Section 903.3.1.1.
NS = Buildings not equipped throughout with an automatic sprinkler system installed in accordance with Section 903.3.1.1.
N = No separation requirement.
NP = Not Permitted.
a. See Section 420.
b. The required separation from areas used only for private or pleasure vehicles shall be reduced by 1 hour but not to less than 1 hour.
c. See Section 406.3.2.
d. Separation is not required between occupancies of the same classification.
e. See Section 422.2 for ambulatory care facilities.
f. Occupancy separations that serve to define fire area limits established in Chapter 9 for requiring fire protection systems shall also comply with Section 707.3.10 and Table 707.3.10 in accordance with Section 901.7.

IBC 2018 TABLE 508.4: REQUIRED SEPARATION OF OCCUPANCIES

Table 508.4 has retained the same number in the IRC 2018 and no changes have been made to the table except the addition of footnote f.

(Formerly IBC 2015 Table 508.4)

Egress Summary
Based on the IBC 2018, for this project, only one exit is required for the residence, and the travel distance is 125 feet. The travel distance to an exit in the spa is 100 feet due to the sprinklered condition of the building. It is important to keep in mind that MS patients might be wheelchair bound or otherwise physically impaired, and the building code outlines minimum design requirements for safety.

Exit and Exit Access Doorway Configuration
The placement of exits, when two or more are required, shall be placed a distance equal to at least half the diagonal apart. This can be decreased to one-third the diagonal when the building has an automatic sprinkler system.

Table 5.5 IBC 2018 Table 1006.2.1: Spaces with One Exit or Exit Access Doorway

TABLE 1006.2.1
SPACES WITH ONE EXIT OR EXIT ACCESS DOORWAY

OCCUPANCY	MAXIMUM OCCUPANT LOAD OF SPACE	MAXIMUM COMMON PATH OF EGRESS TRAVEL DISTANCE (feet)		
		Without Sprinkler System (feet)		With Sprinkler System (feet)
		Occupant Load		
		OL ≤ 30	OL > 30	
A[c], E, M	49	75	75	75[a]
B	49	100	75	100[a]
F	49	75	75	100[a]
H-1, H-2, H-3	3	NP	NP	25[b]
H-4, H-5	10	NP	NP	75[b]
I-1, I-2[d], I-4	10	NP	NP	75[a]
I-3	10	NP	NP	100[a]
R-1	10	NP	NP	75[a]
R-2	20	NP	NP	125[a]
R-3[e]	20	NP	NP	125[a, g]
R-4[e]	20	NP	NP	125[a, g]
S[f]	29	100	75	100[a]
U	49	100	75	75[a]

For SI: 1 foot = 304.8 mm.

NP = Not Permitted.

a. Buildings equipped throughout with an automatic sprinkler system in accordance with Section 903.3.1.1 or 903.3.1.2. See Section 903 for occupancies where automatic sprinkler systems are permitted in accordance with Section 903.3.1.2.

b. Group H occupancies equipped throughout with an automatic sprinkler system in accordance with Section 903.2.5.

c. For a room or space used for assembly purposes having fixed seating, see Section 1029.8.

d. For the travel distance limitations in Group I-2, see Section 407.4.

e. The common path of egress travel distance shall only apply in a Group R-3 occupancy located in a mixed occupancy building.

f. The length of common path of egress travel distance in a Group S-2 open parking garage shall be not more than 100 feet.

g. For the travel distance limitations in Groups R-3 and R-4 equipped throughout with an automatic sprinkler system in accordance with Section 903.3.1.3, see Section 1006.2.2.6.

IBC 2018 TABLE 1006.2.1

IBC 2015 Table 1006.2.1: Spaces with One Exit or Exit Access Doorway has retained the same number in IBC 2018. Some of the maximum occupant load have changed. In the IBC 2018, Occupancies R-2, R-3, and R-4 now have a maximum occupant load of 20 (in the 2015 IBC the maximum was 10.) Another change to R-4 is that without a sprinkler system and with an occupancy load less than or equal to 30 and for occupancy loads more than 30, one exit is not permitted. (In the 2015 IBC a 75 foot travel distance had been permitted in both instances.)

(Formerly Table 1006.2.1 IBC 2015)

Case Study: Applying the Codes during Schematic Design

Thus far, the occupancy classification, construction type, number of exits, and distance to the exits have been determined. The following four schematic plans are used to show how this might be applied to the spa project. The first phase of the space-planning process was to make sure the design concept was reflected in the plans and that general egress requirements were met.

Space-Planning Refinement Second Iteration: Bathrooms and Accessibility

During the second major iteration of the space-planning process, an additional level of refinement included the integration of accessibility requirements for the public restrooms, at all doors and hallways, and throughout the corridors and rooms.

IBC 2018 TABLE 2902.1 PLUMBING FIXTURE REQUIREMENTS

Table 2902.1 has retained the same number. Assembly has been adjusted to remove the occupancy column that contained A-1, A-2, A-3, A-4, and A-5 from the table. A category for "casino gaming areas" has been added with pertinent plumbing requirements.

As with Assembly, the occupancy column has been removed for Factory (F-1 and F-2) and for Institutional (I-1, I-2, I-3, and I-4). Under Institutional, a new row item has been added for "custodial care facilities," with the pertinent plumbing requirements. Under Institutional a new row item has been added for "Medical care recipients in hospitals and nursing homes," with the pertinent plumbing requirements. (This replaces "Hospitals, ambulatory nursing home care recipient" in the IBC 2015.) "Employees other than residential care" in the IBC 2015 has been replaced by "Employees in hospitals and nursing homes" in the IBC 2018. "Visitors other than residential care" in the IBC 2015 has been replaced with "Visitors in hospitals and nursing homes" in the IBC 2018. Beneath reformatories, "Employees" in the IBC 2015 has been replaced by "Employees in reformatories, detention centers, and correctional centers" in the IBC 2018. The occupancy column has been removed for the Residential classification, eliminating the column with R-1, R-2, R-3, and R-4 in the IBC 2018. The occupancy column has been removed for the Storage classification, eliminating the column with S-1 and S-2 in the IBC 2018.

(Formerly IBC 2015 Table 2902.1)

Table 5.6 IBC 2018 Table 2902.1: Minimum Number of Required Plumbing Fixtures

[P] TABLE 2902.1
MINIMUM NUMBER OF REQUIRED PLUMBING FIXTURES[a]
(See Sections 2902.1.1 and 2902.2)

No.	CLASSIFICATION	DESCRIPTION	WATER CLOSETS (URINALS SEE SECTION 424.2 OF THE *INTERNATIONAL PLUMBING CODE*)		LAVATORIES		BATHTUBS/ SHOWERS	DRINKING FOUNTAINS (SEE SECTION 410 OF THE *INTERNATIONAL PLUMBING CODE*)	OTHER
			Male	Female	Male	Female			
1	Assembly	Theaters and other buildings for the performing arts and motion pictures[d]	1 per 125	1 per 65	1 per 200		—	1 per 500	1 service sink
		Nightclubs, bars, taverns, dance halls and buildings for similar purposes[d]	1 per 40	1 per 40	1 per 75		—	1 per 500	1 service sink
		Restaurants, banquet halls and food courts[d]	1 per 75	1 per 75	1 per 200		—	1 per 500	1 service sink
		Casino gaming areas	1 per 100 for the first 400 and 1 per 250 for the remainder exceeding 400	1 per 50 for the first 400 and 1 per 150 for the remainder exceeding 400	1 per 250 for the first 750 and 1 per 500 for the remainder exceeding 750		—	1 per 1,000	1 service sink

(continued)

Table 5.6　IBC 2018 Table 2902.1: Minimum Number of Required Plumbing Fixtures *(continued)*

PLUMBING SYSTEMS

[P] TABLE 2902.1—(continued)
MINIMUM NUMBER OF REQUIRED PLUMBING FIXTURES[a]
(See Sections 2902.1.1 and 2902.2)

No.	CLASSIFICATION	DESCRIPTION	WATER CLOSETS (URINALS SEE SECTION 424.2 OF THE *INTERNATIONAL PLUMBING CODE*)		LAVATORIES		BATHTUBS/ SHOWERS	DRINKING FOUNTAINS (SEE SECTION 410 OF THE *INTERNATIONAL PLUMBING CODE*)	OTHER
			Male	Female	Male	Female			
1	Assembly	Auditoriums without permanent seating, art galleries, exhibition halls, museums, lecture halls, libraries, arcades and gymnasiums[d]	1 per 125	1 per 65	1 per 200		—	1 per 500	1 service sink
		Passenger terminals and transportation facilities[d]	1 per 500	1 per 500	1 per 750		—	1 per 1,000	1 service sink
		Places of worship and other religious services[d]	1 per 150	1 per 75	1 per 200		—	1 per 1,000	1 service sink
		Coliseums, arenas, skating rinks, pools and tennis courts for indoor sporting events and activities	1 per 75 for the first 1,500 and 1 per 120 for the remainder exceeding 1,500	1 per 40 for the first 1,520 and 1 per 60 for the remainder exceeding 1,520	1 per 200	1 per 150	—	1 per 1,000	1 service sink
		Stadiums, amusement parks, bleachers and grandstands for outdoor sporting events and activities[f]	1 per 75 for the first 1,500 and 1 per 120 for the remainder exceeding 1,500	1 per 40 for the first 1,520 and 1 per 60 for the remainder exceeding 1,520	1 per 200	1 per 150	—	1 per 1,000	1 service sink
2	Business	Buildings for the transaction of business, professional services, other services involving merchandise, office buildings, banks, light industrial, ambulatory care and similar uses	1 per 25 for the first 50 and 1 per 50 for the remainder exceeding 50		1 per 40 for the first 80 and 1 per 80 for the remainder exceeding 80		—	1 per 100	1 service sink[e]
3	Educational	Educational facilities	1 per 50		1 per 50		—	1 per 100	1 service sink
4	Factory and industrial	Structures in which occupants are engaged in work fabricating, assembly or processing of products or materials	1 per 100		1 per 100		—	1 per 400	1 service sink
5	Institutional	Custodial care facilities	1 per 10		1 per 10		1 per 8	1 per 100	1 service sink
		Medical care recipients in hospitals and nursing homes[b]	1 per room[c]		1 per room[c]		1 per 15	1 per 100	1 service sink
		Employees in hospitals and nursing homes[b]	1 per 25		1 per 35		—	1 per 100	—
		Visitors in hospitals and nursing homes	1 per 75		1 per 100		—	1 per 500	—
		Prisons[b]	1 per cell		1 per cell		1 per 15	1 per 100	1 service sink

(continued)

Table 5.6 IBC 2018 Table 2902.1: Minimum Number of Required Plumbing Fixtures *(continued)*

[P] TABLE 2902.1—continued
MINIMUM NUMBER OF REQUIRED PLUMBING FIXTURES[a]
(See Sections 2902.1.1 and 2902.2)

No.	CLASSIFICATION	DESCRIPTION	WATER CLOSETS (URINALS SEE SECTION 424.2 OF THE *INTERNATIONAL PLUMBING CODE*)		LAVATORIES		BATHTUBS OR SHOWERS	DRINKING FOUNTAINS (SEE SECTION 410 OF THE *INTERNATIONAL PLUMBING CODE*)	OTHER
			Male	**Female**	**Male**	**Female**			
5	Institutional	Reformatories, detention centers and correctional centers[b]	1 per 15		1 per 15		1 per 15	1 per 100	1 service sink
		Employees in reformitories, detention centers and correctional centers[b]	1 per 25		1 per 35		—	1 per 100	—
		Adult day care and child day care	1 per 15		1 per 15		1	1 per 100	1 service sink
6	Mercantile	Retail stores, service stations, shops, salesrooms, markets and shopping centers	1 per 500		1 per 750		—	1 per 1,000	1 service sink[e]
7	Residential	Hotels, motels, boarding houses (transient)	1 per sleeping unit		1 per sleeping unit		1 per sleeping unit	—	1 service sink
		Dormitories, fraternities, sororities and boarding houses (not transient)	1 per 10		1 per 10		1 per 8	1 per 100	1 service sink
		Apartment house	1 per dwelling unit		1 per dwelling unit		1 per dwelling unit	—	1 kitchen sink per dwelling unit; 1 automatic clothes washer connection per 20 dwelling units
		One- and two-family dwellings and lodging houses with five or fewer guestrooms	1 per dwelling unit		1 per 10		1 per dwelling unit	—	1 kitchen sink per dwelling unit; 1 automatic clothes washer connection per dwelling unit
		Congregate living facilities with 16 or fewer persons	1 per 10		1 per 10		1 per 8	1 per 100	1 service sink
8	Storage	Structures for the storage of goods, warehouses, storehouses and freight depots, low and moderate hazard	1 per 100		1 per 100		—	1 per 1,000	1 service sink

a. The fixtures shown are based on one fixture being the minimum required for the number of persons indicated or any fraction of the number of persons indicated. The number of occupants shall be determined by this code.

b. Toilet facilities for employees shall be separate from facilities for inmates or care recipients.

c. A single-occupant toilet room with one water closet and one lavatory serving not more than two adjacent patient sleeping units shall be permitted, provided that each patient sleeping unit has direct access to the toilet room and provisions for privacy for the toilet room user are provided.

d. The occupant load for seasonal outdoor seating and entertainment areas shall be included when determining the minimum number of facilities required.

e. For business and mercantile classifications with an occupant load of 15 or fewer, a service sink shall not be required.

f. The required number and type of plumbing fixtures for outdoor swimming pools shall be in accordance with Section 609 of the *International Swimming Pool and Spa Code*.

Plumbing Fixture Requirements

The project prompt includes specific fixture requirements but does not necessarily conform to the building code requirements for plumbing fixtures. This section will discuss how to know the minimum code requirements and then how to design the bathrooms to conform to the project requirements as well.

Code Requirements

Table 2902.1 describes the minimum plumbing fixtures required based on the occupancy group (see Table 5.6).

Based on calculating the fixtures using Table 2902.1, only one lavatory and one water closet are required in each bathroom. The project prompt does not require a drinking fountain, laundry hookups in the residence, or a janitor's sink, which are required by code. The project prompt requires the following:

Women's Room: toilet stall, shower stall, dressing cubicle with bench, two lavatories (one barrier-free), four small lockers

Men's Room: toilet stall, urinal, shower stall, dressing cubicle with bench, two lavatories (one barrier-free), four small lockers

To this, a janitor sink, water fountains, and laundry hookups were added to meet pertinent code requirements.

Accessibility Requirements

In addition to the basic overall egress requirements, general accessibility requirements must also be addressed during schematic design to make sure all spaces provide adequate square footage for accessibility.

Restrooms

For the spa portion of the project, accessible restrooms, dressing rooms, and showers have to be considered (Figures 5.1, 5.2, 5.3).

Reception Desk Design

Based on ADA, a section of the check-in desk must be wheelchair accessible (Figure 5.4).

Water Fountains

For ADA, at least one water fountain must meet accessibility requirements (Figure 5.5).

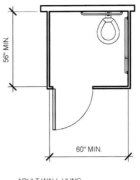
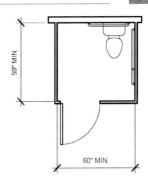

ADULT WALL HUNG WATER CLOSET

ADULT FLOOR MOUNTED WATER CLOSET AND CHILDREN'S WATER CLOSET

Figure 5.1
ADA requirements for stalls

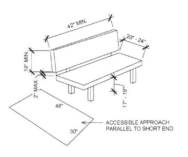

ACCESSIBLE BENCH

ACCESSIBLE BENCH AGAINST A WALL

Figure 5.2
ADA requirements for dressing rooms

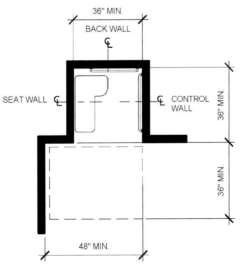

Figure 5.3
ADA requirements for shower stalls

Figure 5.4
ADA reception
desk requirements

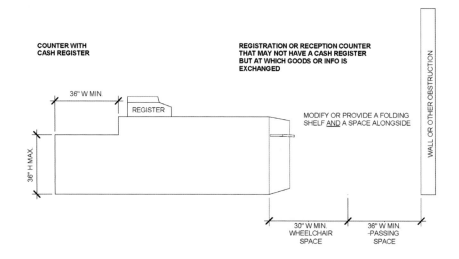

Figure 5.5
ADA water
fountain

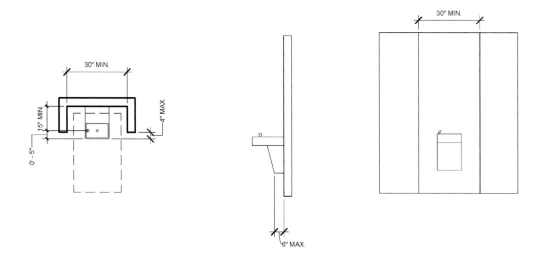

Students' Examples

Case Study 1: "Grandeur"

The movement of plate tectonics near Jackson Wyoming inspires the concept for the "Grandeur" project, where the spa project is to be located. Using this as inspiration, three basic parti diagrams were proposed for the location of the residence within the spa (Figure 5.6).

After selecting one of the schemes, a preliminary floor plan was developed to integrate the design concept into the overall arrangement of the floor plan (Figure 5.7).

A dead-end corridor identified during a preliminary codes review of the design resulted in an opportunity for an additional exit. A second plan review identified some additional code and design issues (Figure 5.8).

The revised plan illustrated corrected problems and posed some new issues, including the water fountains projecting into the path of travel and a problematic turning radius in the residential bathrooms (Figure 5.9).

The final floor plan for schematic design shows the resolution of the many code and ADA issues (Figure 5.10).

GRANDEUR

CONCEPT STATEMENT

BOLD MOVEMENTS & FORMATIONS OF NATURAL FORMS IN THE SURROUNDING LANDSCAPE INSPIRE STRONG ARCHITECTURAL MOVEMENT WITHIN THE INTERIOR.

FURTHER EXPLANATION

MOVEMENT IS PART OF JACKSON, WYOMING AND THE SURROUNDING AREA. MILLIONS OF YEARS AGO REGIONS PLATES SHIFTED TO FORM THE YOUNG FIST RANGE OF THE ROCKY MOUNTAINS. THE GRAND TETONS NEARBY YELLOWSTONE NATIONAL PARK SITS IN ALL HER GLORY FULL OF WONDROUS HOT SPRINGS, BEAUTIFUL FORESTS, BURSTING GEYSERS, AND WILDLIFE.

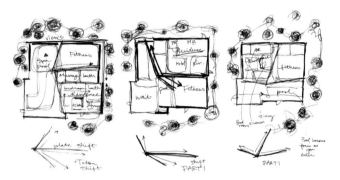

Figure 5.6
Grandeur project
three partis

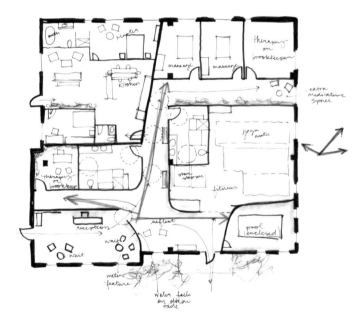

Figure 5.7
Schematic plan
sketch

GRANDEUR

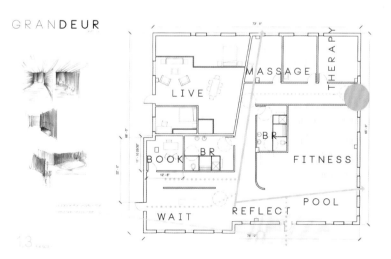

Figure 5.8
Dead-end corridor

Figure 5.9
Space-planning
issues on sketched
plan

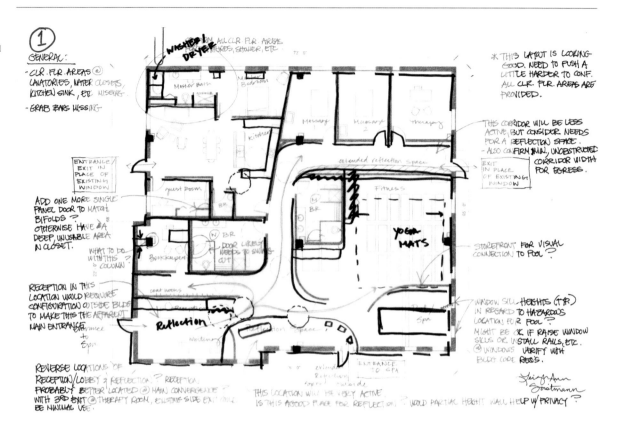

Figure 5.10
Final schematic
plan

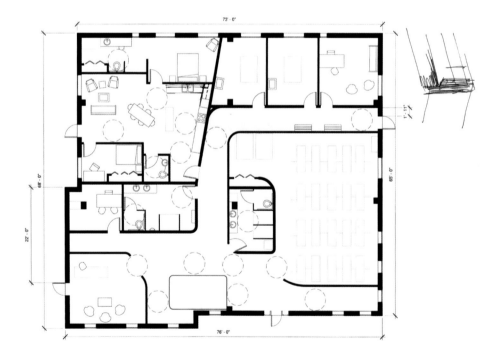

Case Study 2: "Erosion and Uplift"

Inspired by the geological cycles of the Catskill Mountains at the base of which this spa project is located, the Erosion and Uplift project's preliminary plans failed to capture the design concept in the initial space planning. Using the rectilinear plan prototypes developed during the early schematic phase, a parti overlay provided inspiration for a more fluid plan scheme (Figures 5.11, 5.12, 5.13).

Despite their organization, the initial plans for this project failed to incorporate the project concept (Figure 5.14).

Once the parti diagram was revisited, a new sketch plan was produced. This was then used to develop a computerized plan (Figure 5.15).

A marked-up iteration led to a more finalized schematic plan with corrections to code and ADA issues (Figure 5.16).

Figure 5.11
Parti sketch

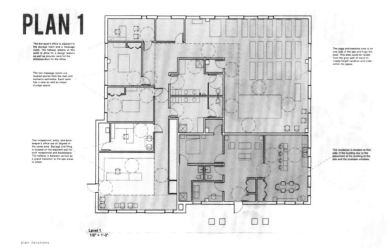

Figures 5.12 and 5.13
Early schemes with rectilinear plan

Figure 5.14
Sketch plan
incorporating parti

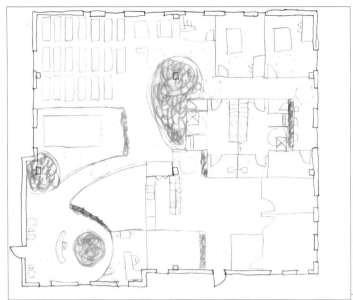

Figure 5.15
Schematic
computer plan

Figure 5.16
Final schematic
plan

Case Study 3: "Lifestream"

The Lifestream spa relies on the healing properties of rain for inspiration. Several aspects of the interior were designed to mimic how various animals respond to rain—for example, seeking cover under an overhang, as found at the reception desk.

The project shows the student working through several of the code and accessibility issues in three dimensions as well as plan. One of the challenges of this project was to integrate universal design into the residence. Although not mandated by code, this meant that all areas of the residence were accessible (Figures 5.17, 5.18, 5.19).

A preliminary computer plan shows a very rectilinear approach to space planning (Figure 5.20).

After several attempts, a final plan integrated the multiple iterations and corrected code and ADA problems, although the door at the bottom of the plan still does not have proper push clearance (Figure 5.21).

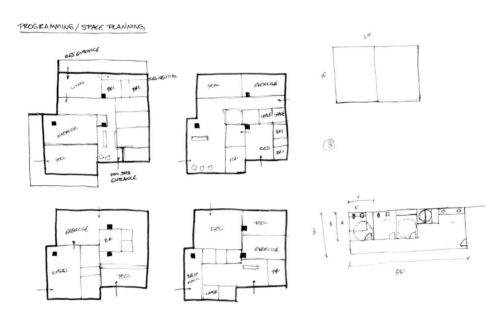

Figure 5.17
Rough plan sketches

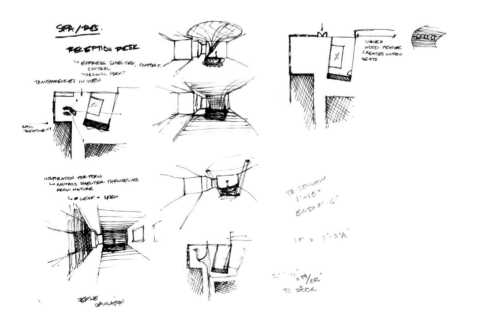

Figure 5.18
Three-dimensional studies

Figure 5.19
Multiple plan
diagrams

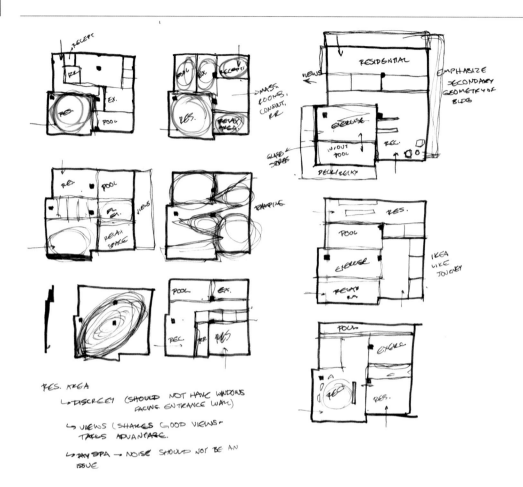

Figure 5.20
Rectilinear
computer plan

Figure 5.21
Final schematic
plan

Power and Data Plan

FINISH PLAN LEGEND

WHITE OAK PLANKS 1,897 SQ. FT		10" X 48" SLATE FLOORING 1,175 SQ. FT	
WHITE TERAZZO 474 SQ. FT		WHITE MARBLE TILE 92 SQ. FT	
24"x24" TEXTURED STONE TILE 630 SQ. FT		HIGH END RESIDENTIAL CARPET 343 SQ. FT	

Finish Floor Plan

NOTE: INADEQUATE CLEARANCE ON PUSH SIDE OF DOOR

Conclusions

The three examples show the students grappling first with how to meet all the program requirements and fulfill on the design concept through schematic design iterations. Once the concept is in place through the use of a parti diagram, the programmatic requirements must again be addressed in order to confirm compliance with all required codes and guidelines.

Diagrams of Building Analysis

The following diagrams provide a summary of the codes and ADA analysis for the building shell provided (Figures 5.22–5.25).

Clarification: Even though half-diagonal is for nonsprinklered buildings, this particular building must be sprinklered because it contains an R occupancy.

Key Terms

dead-end corridor
egress
integrated project delivery
live-work unit
programming
schematic design

Assignment

1. Using each of the code tables provided, look up the required number of exits, travel distance, and plumbing fixture requirements for the building. What would happen if the building was to be used as an ambulatory healthcare facility? As a furniture store? What impact would this have on the number of exits? Number of bathroom fixtures?

Figure 5.22
Overall building
analysis with
percentage for
each use type

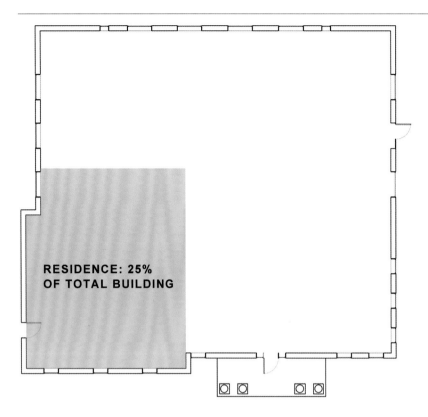

RESIDENCE: 25%
OF TOTAL BUILDING

Figure 5.23
Nonsprinklered—
half-diagonal rule

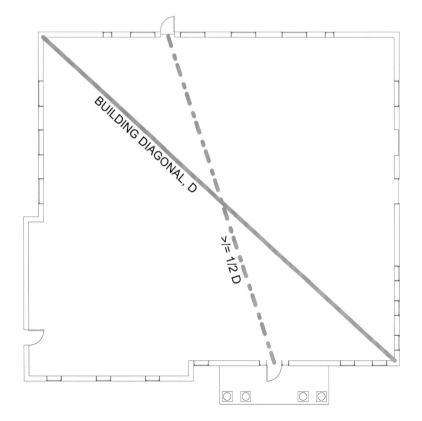

BUILDING DIAGONAL, D

>/= 1/2 D

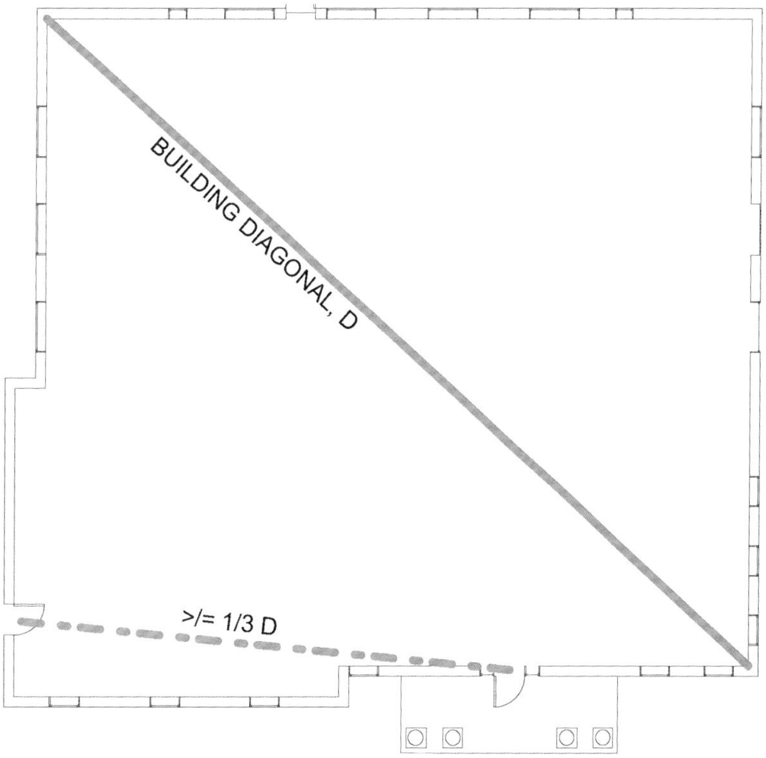

Figure 5.24
Sprinklered—one-third-diagonal rule

Figure 5.25
Corridor widths required with remote exit access placement

Case Study: Hospitality Design—Restaurant

Learning Objectives:

After reading this chapter and doing the exercises, students will be able to

- Go through the basic process of identifying occupancy type and determining construction type, occupancy loads, and required exits
- Evaluate travel distance, number of exits required, and common path of travel
- Determine ADA clearances at all doors and fixtures
- Place grab bars in appropriate locations
- Calculate the number of plumbing fixtures needed for a specific use
- Layout table, chairs, and booths with adequate aisle ways and clearances

Introduction

The chapter presents the design process for a restaurant. Using three different projects, this chapter will illustrate the process of designing the schematic phase of a restaurant using applicable codes and guidelines. This first project consisted of a one-week team project where students were given a generic restaurant building shell and asked to determine the type of restaurant and location. The second restaurant design took place over several weeks and had a more detailed space-planning process. One example was located in Nashville and the other in Wisconsin in a historic building listed on the National Register of Historic Places. All three projects included a sustainability component. This range of projects shows the process three times and layers in additional levels of complexity with each project. For all three projects, a sprinkler system is used. For the two projects connected to a hotel (an R use), a sprinkler system is required. For the other restaurant, located in a four-story historic building, a sprinkler system is also used. A fire separation between occupancies is required.

Project One

As a one-week project, students completed a schematic design for this restaurant in teams of two people. Student teams selected their own location and type of restaurant.

Scope of the Problem

The proposed restaurant connected to a hotel and consisted of approximately 4,900 square feet. The parameters given for the project included a 1,100 to 1,200 square foot kitchen area, a bar and lounge area for twenty to twenty-four people, a variety of seating choices, and men's and women's bathrooms containing two water closets and two lavatories each. Two satellite workstations support waitstaff throughout the restaurant with drink stations and registers. An entertainment area could be added but was not required. The restaurant portion of the building is contained on a single story and is constructed of a steel frame structure encased in concrete with glass storefronts.

Applying the Code

For the restaurant project, students were given the building and that it was of construction Type II. Students then created a code- and ADA-compliant plan and interior space.

Programming Phase

During programming, the students first had to determine the use group for the project. Using Chapter 3 of the IBC, Assembly was the obvious choice, as the project is a building or structure used for food and drink purposes. There are five different levels in the Assembly use category.

Assembly Occupancy

Based on Table 6.1, the A-2 group applies to the restaurant project.

Maximum Floor Area Allowances per Occupant

Using the use group and Table 1004.5 from the IBC, the student teams then calculated the allowable number of occupants for the restaurant.

For maximum floor area allowances per occupant, please refer to Table 4.2 and its accompanying Box 4.1, which summarizes the primary changes to the table.

Of the total square footage of the restaurant's 4,900 square feet, 1,200 square was designated as a commercial kitchen. Using Table 1004.5, the calculations for possible occupants are as follows:

3,700 square feet / 15 net* (unconcentrated tables and chairs) = 247 people

1,200 square feet / 200 gross (kitchens, commercial) = 6 people

These numbers must be reduced as the restaurant number is a net square footage calculation, meaning it will be reduced to the square footage that can be occupied.

*In order to figure out the net square footage, some plan prototypes and a circulation percentage are first needed. A plan prototype for the restrooms (Figure 6.1) can be deducted from the overall square footage, as can the cloakroom, corridors, and service spaces. Until the actual layout is known, this calculation will be approximate. Thus, a conservative circulation factor of 10 percent will be used for this preliminary calculation (370 square feet). Each bathroom is estimated at 160 square feet, based on the plan prototype (320 square feet total).

Table 6.1 Assembly Occupancy

A-1	Motion picture theaters
	Symphony and concert halls
	Television and radio studios
	admitting an audience
	Theaters
A-2	Banquet halls
	Casinos
	Nightclubs
	Restaurants, cafeterias, and
	similar dining facilities (including
	associated commercial kitchens)
A-3	Amusement arcades
	Art galleries
	Bowling alleys
	Community halls
	Courtrooms
	Dance halls
	Exhibition halls
	Funeral parlors
	Gymnasiums
	Indoor swimming pools
	Lecture halls
	Libraries
	Museums
	Places of religious worship
	Pool and billiard halls
	Waiting areas in transportation
	terminals
A-4	Arenas
	Skating rinks
	Swimming pools
	Tennis courts
A-5	Amusement part structures
	Bleachers
	Grandstands
	Stadiums

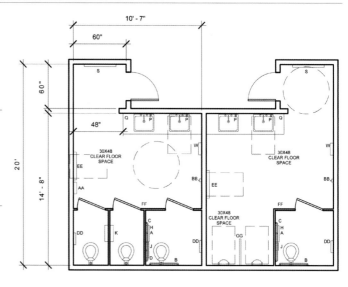

A - VERTICAL GRAB BAR
B - HORIZONTAL GRAB BAR
C = HORIZONTAL GRAB BAR
D - SURFACE-MOUNTED SANITARY
    NAPKIN DISPOSAL
H - SURFACE MOUNTED TOILET SEAT
    COVER DISPENSER
J - SURFACE-MOUNTED MULTI ROLL
    TOILET TISSUE DISPENSER
K - PARTITION-MOUNTED TOILET SEAT
    COVER DISPENSER, SANITARY NAPKIN DISPOSAL,
    TOILET TISSUE DISPENSER WITH THEFT-RESISTANT
    SPINDLE
P - AUTOMATIC, UNIVERSAL COUNTERTOP-MOUNTED
    SOAP DISPENSER
Q - SERIES WALL-TO-WALL MIRROR
S - FULL-LENGTH MIRROR
AA - RECESSED SANITARY NAPKIN/TAMPON VENDOR
BB - DOOR BUMPER
EE - WALL-MOUNTED BABY CHANGING STATION
FF - FLOOR-ANCHORED LAMINATED PLASTIC
    TOILET COMPARTMENTS
GG - WALL-HUNG URINAL SCREEN

Figure 6.1
Restroom plan
prototype

(3,700 square feet − 370 square feet [circulation] − 320 square feet [bathrooms]) = 3010 square feet / 15 net* (unconcentrated tables and chairs) = 200.666 or 201 occupants

1,200 square feet / 200 gross (Kitchens, commercial) = 6 occupants

Total = 207 occupants

Exits Required

Based on the number of occupants, the number and distance of exits can be established. The widths of aisles and access ways within the restaurant must comply with Section 1029. Since the maximum number of occupants with single exit for Assembly is limited to forty-nine

people, at least two exits are required. Based on Table 1006.3.2, two exits are required for 1 to 500 people (see Table 6.2). Table 1017.2 dictates the maximum travel distance to an exit for this project is 200 feet without a sprinkler and 250 feet with a sprinkler. Since this project requires a sprinkler system (as it is attached to a hotel), the maximum travel distance is 250 feet (Table 6.3).

In addition to this exit access travel distance, the common path of travel cannot exceed 30 feet before an occupant has a choice of two exits. The **common path of travel** is the way in which someone would walk through a space (around furniture, for example) from the furthest point in a room in order to get to a point of decision where

Table 6.2 IBC 2018 Table 1006.3.2: Minimum Number of Exits or Access to Exits per Story

TABLE 1006.3.2
MINIMUM NUMBER OF EXITS OR
ACCESS TO EXITS PER STORY

OCCUPANT LOAD PER STORY	MINIMUM NUMBER OF EXITS OR ACCESS TO EXITS FROM STORY
1-500	2
501-1,000	3
More than 1,000	4

> ### IBC 2018 TABLE 1006.3.2: MINIMUM NUMBER OF EXITS OR ACCESS TO EXITS PER STORY
>
> The IBC 2018 table, the Minimum Number of Exits or Access to Exits per Story, is now Table 1006.3.2. The content of the table has not changed.
>
> (Formerly IBC 2015 Table 1006.3.1)

two exit choices are possible. Exits and aisles need to be designed so that the travel distance is not more than 200 feet and the minimum width cannot be less than 0.08 times the number of occupants.

0.08 x 207 occupants = 16.56 inches.

Section 1029.9.1 requires that aisle widths be 48 inches when there is seating on either side, unless there are fewer than fifty seats, in which case a 36 inch aisle is sufficient. Dead-end aisles cannot exceed 20 feet in length. Seating at a counter or table adjacent to an aisle way should allow for a clear width of 19 inches perpendicular to the table or counter (Figures 6.2, 6.3).

Various types of seating arrangements have different spacing requirements. The project prompt requires a variety of seating types, including booths (Figure 6.4).

Preliminary Plumbing Fixture Count

This preliminary occupant count can be used to generally assess the plumbing fixture requirements to see if more are needed than in the project prompt.

Assuming 50 percent female and 50 percent male (103 each), and using Table 2902.1, the required number of water closets is one for every seventy-five people or two each and lavatories is one per two-hundred people or one each. Thus, the prompt exceeds the code requirements. In

Table 6.3 IBC 2018 Table 1017.2: Exit Access Travel Distance

TABLE 1017.2
EXIT ACCESS TRAVEL DISTANCE[a]

OCCUPANCY	WITHOUT SPRINKLER SYSTEM (feet)	WITH SPRINKLER SYSTEM (feet)
A, E, F-1, M, R, S-1	200[e]	250[b]
I-1	Not Permitted	250[b]
B	200	300[c]
F-2, S-2, U	300	400[c]
H-1	Not Permitted	75[d]
H-2	Not Permitted	100[d]
H-3	Not Permitted	150[d]
H-4	Not Permitted	175[d]
H-5	Not Permitted	200[c]
I-2, I-3	Not Permitted	200[c]
I-4	150	200[c]

For SI: 1 foot = 304.8 mm.

a. See the following sections for modifications to exit access travel distance requirements:
  Section 402.8: For the distance limitation in malls.
  Section 404.9: For the distance limitation through an atrium space.
  Section 407.4: For the distance limitation in Group I-2.
  Sections 408.6.1 and 408.8.1: For the distance limitations in Group I-3.
  Section 411.3: For the distance limitation in special amusement buildings.
  Section 412.6: For the distance limitations in aircraft manufacturing facilities.
  Section 1006.2.2.2: For the distance limitation in refrigeration machinery rooms.
  Section 1006.2.2.3: For the distance limitation in refrigerated rooms and spaces.
  Section 1006.3.3: For buildings with one exit.
  Section 1017.2.2: For increased distance limitation in Groups F-1 and S-1.
  Section 1029.7: For increased limitation in assembly seating.
  Section 3103.4: For temporary structures.
  Section 3104.9: For pedestrian walkways.
b. Buildings equipped throughout with an automatic sprinkler system in accordance with Section 903.3.1.1 or 903.3.1.2. See Section 903 for occupancies where automatic sprinkler systems are permitted in accordance with Section 903.3.1.2.
c. Buildings equipped throughout with an automatic sprinkler system in accordance with Section 903.3.1.1.
d. Group H occupancies equipped throughout with an automatic sprinkler system in accordance with Section 903.2.5.1.
e. Group R-3 and R-4 buildings equipped throughout with an automatic sprinkler system in accordance with Section 903.3.1.3. See Section 903.2.8 for occupancies where automatic sprinkler systems are permitted in accordance with Section 903.3.1.3.

> ### IBC 2018 TABLE 1017.2: EXIT ACCESS TRAVEL DISTANCE
>
> Table 1017.2 has retained the same table number. In the IBC 2018, I-4 has been separated from I-2 and I-3 and now permits a maximum travel distance of 150 feet without a sprinkler system. (This was not permitted for I-4 in the IBC 2015.) I-2, I-3, and I-4 still allow a maximum travel distance of 200 feet in a building with a sprinkler system.

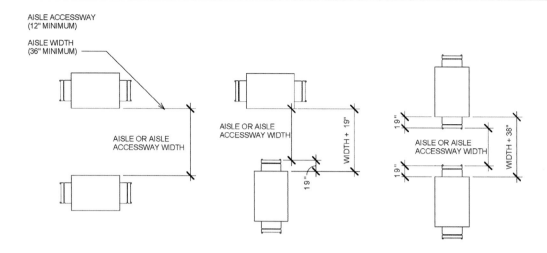

AISLE ACCESSWAY
(12" MINIMUM)

AISLE WIDTH
(36" MINIMUM)

AISLE OR AISLE
ACCESSWAY WIDTH

AISLE OR AISLE
ACCESSWAY WIDTH

WIDTH + 19"

19"

19"

19"

AISLE OR AISLE
ACCESSWAY WIDTH

WIDTH + 38"

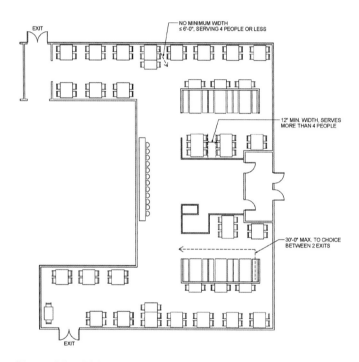

EXIT

NO MINIMUM WIDTH
≤ 6'-0", SERVING 4 PEOPLE OR LESS

12" MIN. WIDTH, SERVES
MORE THAN 4 PEOPLE

30'-0" MAX. TO CHOICE
BETWEEN 2 EXITS

EXIT

Figures 6.2 and 6.3
Egress width
requirements

Figure 6.4
Typical fixed seating

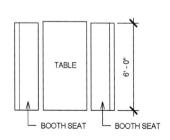

TABLE

6'-0"

BOOTH SEAT   BOOTH SEAT

12'-0"/2'-0" PER OCCUPANT = 6 OCCUPANTS

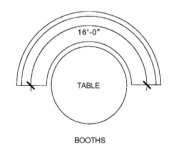

16'-0"

TABLE

BOOTHS

16'-0"/2'-0" PER OCCUPANT = 8 OCCUPANTS

addition, according to Table 2902.1, a drinking fountain and service sink are also required (Table 6.4).

Once the basic information has been gathered during programming, an informed schematic design process can take place. During this iterative process, some adjustments might be made to the initial code calculations as will be seen in the case studies.

Space-Planning Refinement Process—Refinement and Iteration

The first stage of the schematic design is to take the overall code direction and the concept and start to design the restaurant in two and three dimensions. Because the nature of schematic plans on trace is conceptual, several iterations will be needed before a more finalized plan is conceived.

Project Example

The Palisade restaurant team located the design in the Swiss Alps overlooking Lake Gruyere. The restaurant reflected the local traditions in wine, chocolate, and cheese production as inspiration. The team incorporated several sustainability features including a geothermal heating system, a green roof, natural lighting, gray-water reuse, and solar panels to create a Net-Zero project design.

The first image shows the project team beginning to determine the location for the kitchen and circulation (Figures 6.5, 6.6).

A more thorough exploration of the project concept in plan and three dimensions begins to show potential seating areas in the restaurant (Figure 6.7).

Thumbnail sketches throughout this process help ensure that the design concept is expressed in the interior design.

A preliminary section is used to begin to explore some of the sustainability issues for the project in conjunction with the design concept (Figure 6.8).

Table 6.4 Number of Plumbing Fixtures

Calculations

150 occupants
75 female/75 male

	WC	Lavatory
Male	1 per 25 first 50	1 per 50 = 2 each
	1 per 40 first 80	1 per 80 = 1 each
Female	1 per 25 first 50	1 per 50 = 2 each
	1 per 40 first 80	1 per 80 = 1 each

Water Fountain 1 per 100 = 2 required
Service Sink = 1 required

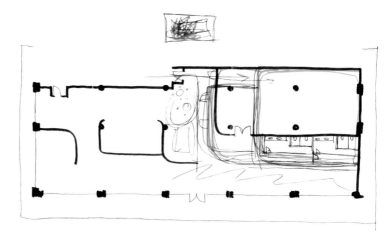

Figure 6.5
Preliminary plan idea showing circulation and two exits with kitchen location

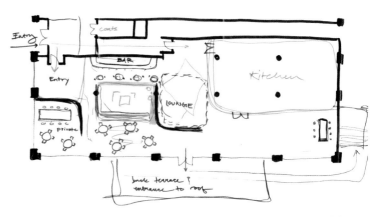

Figure 6.6
More developed plan

Figure 6.7
Three-dimensional
vignettes of
specific parts of
the restaurant

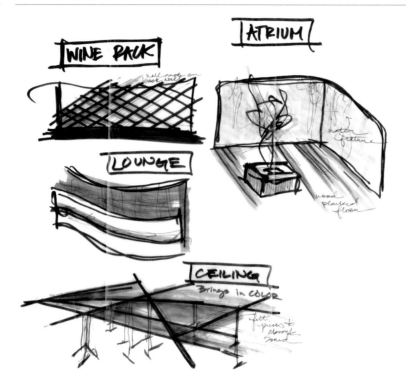

Figure 6.8
Preliminary
section and notes

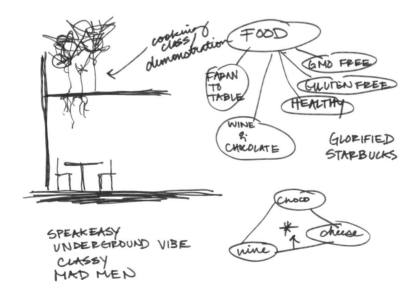

A first draft of the computerized floor plan shows the overall seating arrangement for the restaurant, kitchen location, wait station placement, and restrooms. Some problematic areas include a view into the bathrooms from the lounge and bar areas, as well as some circulation problems into and out of the kitchen (Figure 6.9).

The resulting restaurant schematic design integrates codes, ADA, the conceptual approach, and space-planning refinements. Comments about density and code/ADA are integrated into a second schematic plan (Figure 6.10).

The final schematic submittal integrates sustainability concerns, code requirements, and ADA. The final package also comments on the sustainability features that have been integrated into the project design (Figures 6.11–6.19).

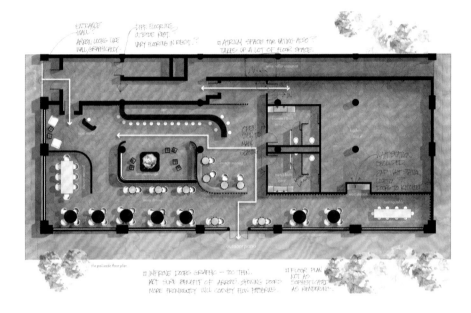

Figure 6.9
Early schematic computerized plan

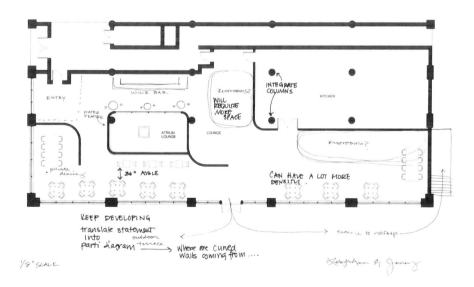

Figure 6.10
Second conceptual plan development

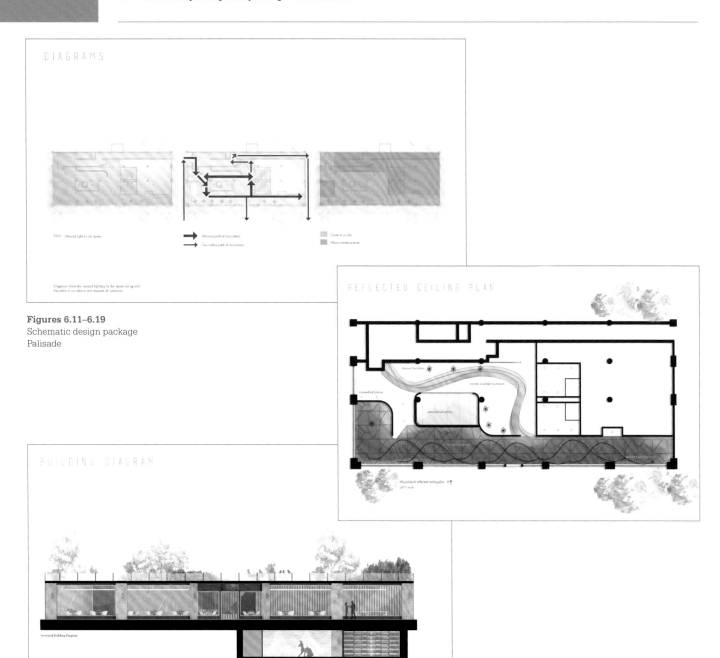

DIAGRAMS

Diagrams show the natural lighting in the space along with the paths of circulation and degrees of openness.

Figures 6.11–6.19
Schematic design package
Palisade

REFLECTED CEILING PLAN

BUILDING DIAGRAM

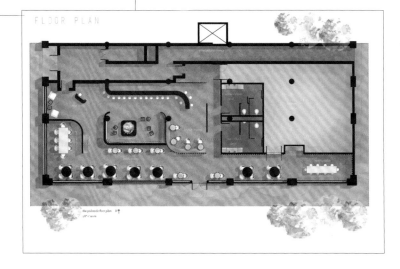

FLOOR PLAN

FURNITURE AND FINISHES

BUILDING AXON

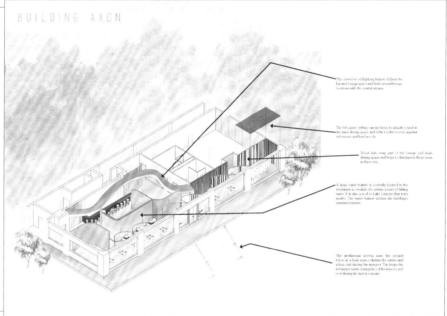

**Figures
6.11–6.19**
(continued)

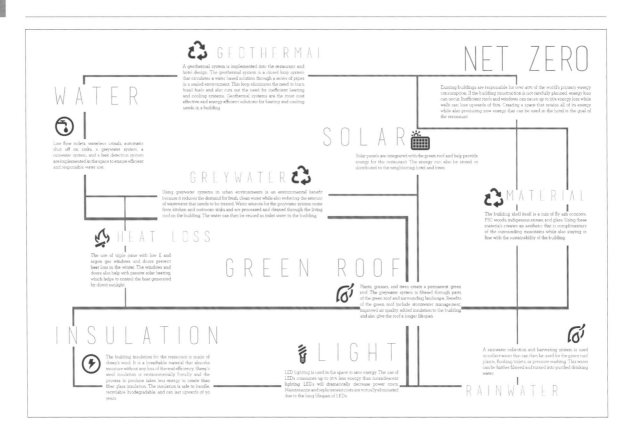

Project Two

The second example was for a restaurant located inside a converted factory building that was to contain both a small hotel and restaurant. Located in Nashville, the restaurant was to be designed as a music venue, serving both the local residents and out-of-town guests. The project was inspired by the way in which music is layered to create a fused whole. Visual representations of sound were used to inspire the parti and ultimately the design. A ceiling feature unifies the space and demonstrates the unification of parts to a whole.

Applying the Code

The brick factory building contains a heavy timber interior structure and is classified as Type IV construction.

Programming Phase

As mentioned in the previous example, Chapter 3 of the IBC was used to determine that Assembly was the appropriate choice for food and drink purposes. Based on Table 6.1, the A-2 group applies to the restaurant project.

Maximum Floor Area Allowance per Occupant

Using the use group and Table 1004.5 from the IBC, the occupancy load for the restaurant was calculated. Of the total square footage of the restaurant 12,064 square feet, 4,826 square feet was designated as a commercial kitchen. An additional 10 percent was dedicated to circulation. Using Table 1004.5, the calculations for possible occupants are as follows:

> 12,064 square feet – (4,826 square feet [kitchen] + 724 square feet [circulation] + 320 square feet [restrooms]) = 6,194 square feet
>
> 6,194 square feet / 15 net* (unconcentrated tables and chairs) = 413 people
>
> 4,826 square feet / 200 gross (kitchens, commercial) = 25 people
>
> Total Occupants = 413 + 25 = 438 total occupants

*As with the previous example, in order to figure out the net square footage, some plan prototypes and a circulation amount are first needed. A plan prototype for the restrooms can be deducted from the overall square footage, as can the cloakroom, corridors, and service spaces. Until the actual layout is known, this calculation will be approximate. Thus, a conservative circulation factor of 10 percent will be used for this preliminary calculation (724 square feet). Each bathroom is estimated at 160 square feet based on the plan prototype (320 square feet total).

Exits Required

Based on the number of occupants, the number and distance of exits can be established. The widths of aisles and access ways within the restaurant must comply with Section 1029. Since the maximum number of occupants with a single exit for Assembly is limited to forty-nine people, at least two exits are required. Based on Table 1006.3.2, two exits are required for 1 to 500 people. Table 1017.2 dictates the maximum travel distance to an exit for this project is 200 feet without a sprinkler and 250 feet with a sprinkler. A sprinkler system is required since the restaurant is attached to a hotel.

In addition to this exit access travel distance, the common path of travel cannot exceed 30 feet before an occupant has a choice of two exits. Exits and aisles need to be designed so that the travel distance is not more than 200 feet and the minimum width cannot be less than 0.08 times the number of occupants.

> 0.08 x 438 occupants = 35.04 inches.

Section 1029.9.1 requires that aisle widths be 48 inches when there is seating on either side, unless there are fewer than fifty seats, in which case a 36 inch aisle is sufficient. Dead-end aisles cannot exceed 20 feet in length. Seating at a counter or table adjacent to an aisle way should allow for a clear width of 19 inches perpendicular to the table or counter.

Various types of seating arrangements have different spacing requirements. In order to reflect the design concept, the designer chose to integrate various types and levels of seating.

Preliminary Plumbing Fixture Count

The preliminary occupancy calculations were used to determine the plumbing fixture requirements.

Assuming 50 percent female and 50 percent male (219 each), and using Table 2902.1, the required number of water closets is one for every seventy-five people or three each and lavatories is one per two-hundred people or two each. As a nightly entertainment venue, the designer chose to add additional fixtures to both restrooms. In addition, according to Table 2902.1, a drinking fountain and service sink are also required.

Once the basic information has been gathered during programming, an informed schematic design process can take place. During this iterative process, some adjustments might be made to the initial code calculations as will be seen in the case studies.

Space-Planning Refinement Process—Refinement and Iteration

The first stage of the schematic design is to take the overall code direction and the concept and start to design the restaurant in two and three dimensions. Because the nature of schematic plans of trace is conceptual, several iterations will be needed before a more finalized plan is conceived.

The first diagrams show the integration of the design concept into a project parti (Figure 6.20).

Blocking diagrams were used to organize the various components of the space (Figures 6.21, 6.22).

Once this was integrated into the computerized plan, additional code work was conducted to determine the number of fixtures and how they met ADA as well as clear paths of travel for egress (Figures 6.23, 6.24).

A refined parti diagram was used to direct the ceiling design feature, connecting the parts of the space (Figure 6.25).

The resulting plan met the various codes and accessibility requirements, as well as the conceptual parameters for the project (Figures 6.26–6.30).

Figure 6.20
Preliminary sketches showing parti and concept work

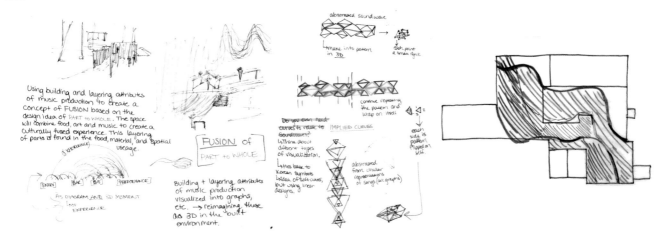

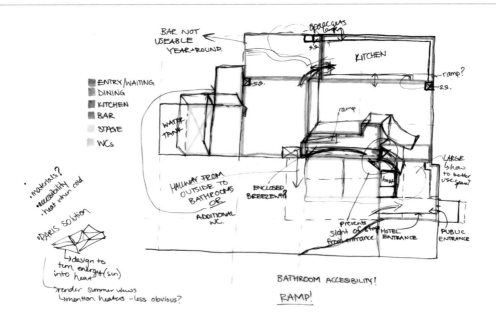

Figures 6.21 and
6.22
Blocking diagrams
showing spaces in
restaurant

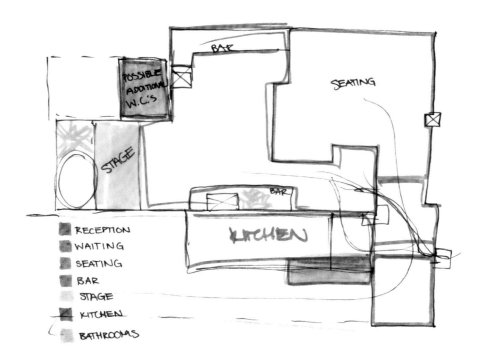

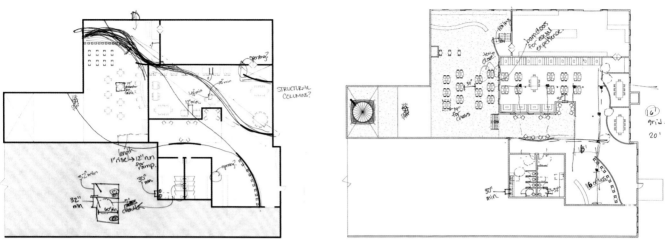

Figures 6.23 and 6.24
Refined plans in the computer showing codes and ADA notations

Figure 6.25
Refined parti

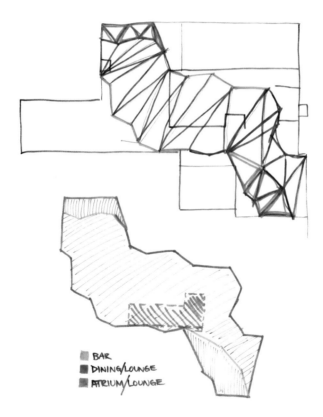

BAR
DINING/LOUNGE
ATRIUM/LOUNGE

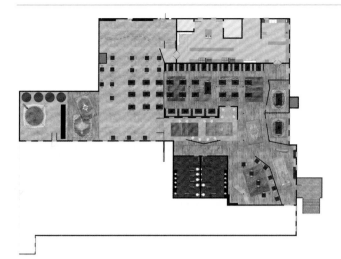

Figures
6.26–6.30
Final schematic
design

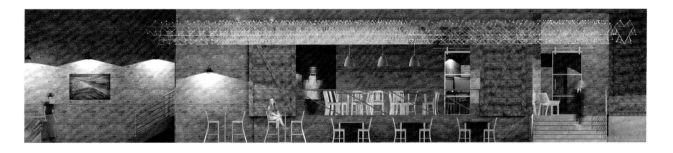

Project Three

The third example is for a brewery that was to be located in an adaptive reuse of a warehouse building constructed circa 1914 and originally designed by Frank Lloyd Wright. In addition to the basic approach used in the first case study, this project also involved working within the confines of a building listed on the National Register of Historic Places.

Applying the Code

For this project, the historic brick building had a concrete column and two-way slab construction on the interior, making it construction Type II.

Programming Phase

As with the previous two examples, the occupancy group was A-2 for the project.

Maximum Floor Area Allowance per Occupant

Using the use group and Table 1004.1.2 from the IBC, the student calculated the number of occupants permitted for the restaurant.

In order to figure out the net square footage, some plan prototypes and a circulation factor are both needed. A plan prototype for the restrooms can be deducted from the overall square footage, as can the entry lobby area, corridors, and service spaces. Until the actual layout is known, this calculation will be approximate. Thus, a conservative circulation factor of 10 percent will be used for this preliminary calculation. Each bathroom is estimated at 160 square feet based on the plan prototype (320 square feet total).

Therefore, of the total square footage of the restaurant 4,500 square feet, 450 square feet is designated toward circulation and 320 square feet for bathrooms, leaving 3,730 square feet. Using a 40 percent factor for the restaurant kitchen, the square footage allotted for that space is 1,492 square feet. Using Table 1004.5, the calculations for possible occupants are as follows:

Preliminary Occupancy Load Calculations

2,238 square feet / 15 net* (unconcentrated tables and chairs) = 150

1,492 square feet / 200 gross (kitchens, commercial) = 8

Total occupants: 150 + 8 = 158 possible occupants

Exits Required

Based on the number of occupants, the number and distance of exits can be established. The widths of aisles and access ways within the restaurant must comply with Section 1029. Since the maximum number of occupants with single exit for Assembly is limited to forty-nine people, at least two exits are required. Based on Table 1006.3.2, two exits are required for 1 to 500 people. Table 1017.2 dictates the maximum travel distance to an exit for this project is 200 feet without a sprinkler and 250 feet with a sprinkler. As a significant historic building, a sprinkler system has been added for protection.

In addition to this exit access travel distance, the common path of travel cannot exceed 30 feet before an occupant has a choice of two exits. Exits and aisles need to be designed so that the travel distance is not more than 200 feet and the minimum width cannot be less than 0.08 times the number of occupants.

$$0.08 \times 158 = 12.64 \text{ inches.}$$

Section 1029.9.1 requires that aisle widths be 48 inches when there is seating on either side unless there are fewer than fifty seats, in which case a 36 inch aisle is sufficient. Dead-end aisles cannot exceed 20 feet in length. Seating at a counter or table adjacent to an aisle way should allow for a clear width of 19 inches perpendicular to the table or counter.

As with the previous two projects, the third example includes a variety of seating types.

Preliminary Plumbing Fixture Count

The occupancy load helps to determine the preliminary plumbing fixture requirements. Assuming 50 percent female and 50 percent male (79 each), and using Table 2902.1, the required number of water closets is one for every seventy-five people or two each and lavatories is one per two-hundred people or one each. A drinking fountain and service sink are also required.

Once the basic information has been gathered during programming, an informed schematic design process can take place. During this iterative process, some adjustments might be made to the initial code calculations, as will be seen in the case studies.

Space-Planning Refinement Process— Refinement and Iteration

The inspiration for the project was beer-making. The restaurant contained a local brewery and specialized in locally available cuisine. The local blue-collar community provided direction the use for this former storage warehouse, which was rehabilitated to include the local restaurant/ brewery and a gallery for local artisans (Figures 6.31–6.34).

The first iteration of the plan shows a series of code issues that had to be resolved. Following this, the kitchen and bathrooms were moved to opposite sides of the plan to better accommodate the use of the space (Figure 6.35).

The second computerized floor plan shows some code problems, including improper door swings and an elevator not separated from the fire stair (Figure 6.36).

The final floor plan (schematic design) accommodates code and ADA concerns, as well as conforms to the design concept (Figure 6.37).

The final floor plan (schematic design) accommodates code and ADA concerns as well as conforms to the design concept (Figures 6.38–6.41).

Historic Preservation Considerations

The building chosen for this project was listed on the National Register and had been designed by world-renowned architect, Frank Lloyd Wright. As such, in addition to the typical code and ADA requirements, the student also had to contend with the Secretary of the Interior's Standards for historic buildings. In this particular case, the student chose to put a very minimal interior invention into the existing building. All historic columns, floor, ceilings, and exteriors were retained.

In order to retain a listing on the National Register of Historic Places, the existing historic building had to be respected. This meant retaining all existing window openings in the size and configuration of the original building. While new egress stairs were appended to the exterior, they were located so that they did not change the view of the building exterior from its major facades. The existing brick exterior and concrete cornice were retained, as were all interior concrete columns, floors, and ceilings. All new work was theoretically reversible, in keeping with the Secretary's Standards.

**Figures
6.31–6.33**
Preliminary
sketches showing
conceptual parti
and basic blocking

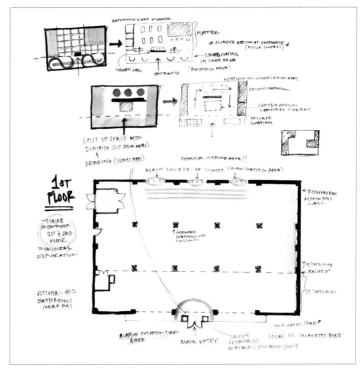

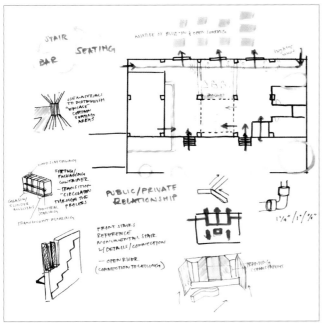

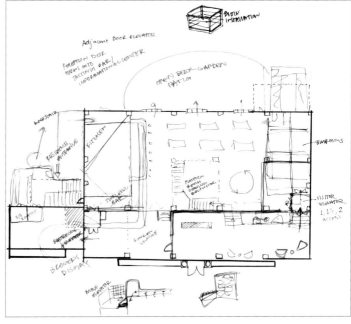

Figure 6.34
Concept notes

Figure 6.35
First floor plan
preliminary

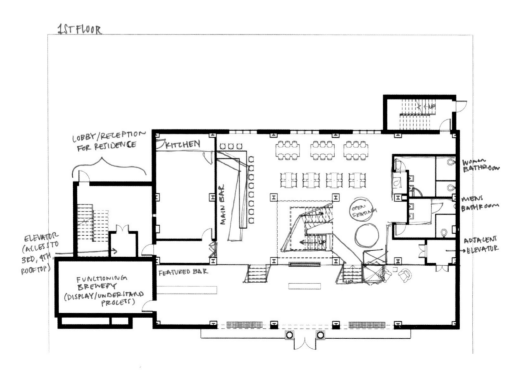

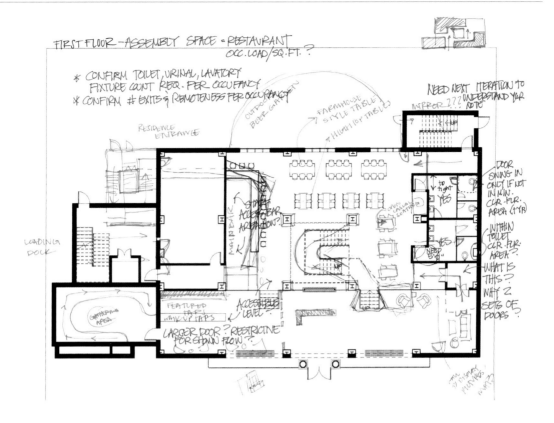

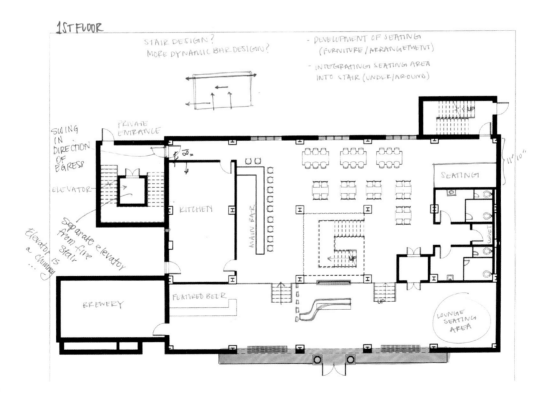

**Figures
6.38–6.41**
Final schematic
design

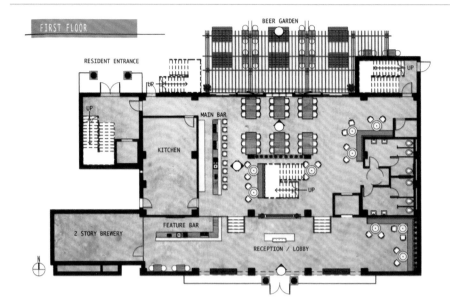

FIRST FLOOR

BEER GARDEN

RESIDENT ENTRANCE

UP

UP

MAIN BAR

KITCHEN

UP

2 STORY BREWERY

FEATURE BAR

RECEPTION / LOBBY

N

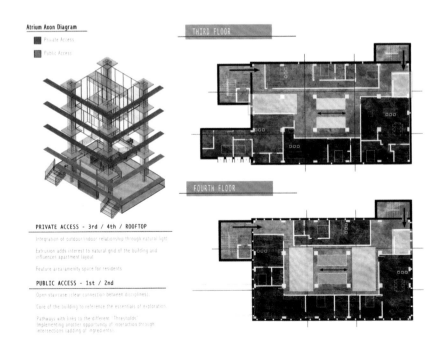

Atrium Axon Diagram

■ Private Access
■ Public Access

THIRD FLOOR

FOURTH FLOOR

PRIVATE ACCESS - 3rd / 4th / ROOFTOP

Integration of outdoor-indoor relationship through natural light.

Extrusion adds interest to natural grid of the building and
influences apartment layout.

Feature area amenity space for residents.

PUBLIC ACCESS - 1st / 2nd

Open staircase (clear connection between disciplines).

Core of the building to reference the essentials of exploration.

Pathways with links to the different Thresholds:
Implementing another opportunity of interaction through
intersections (adding of ingredients).

ROOFTOP TERRACE

The Rooftop Terrace provides an oasis for the building residents as well as a space available for rent for special occasions. Various types of seating are provided to accommodate a wide range of social interactions for individuals and groups. The skylights located central to the rooftop provide a view of the lower levels. An outdoor fireplace provides an intimate area for the residents to unwind. Multiple containers are available for residents to engage in the building's community garden by growing vegetables and herbs.

User Profile Circulation

■ Resident

■ Visitor

□ Local

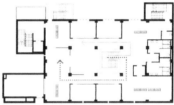

First Floor

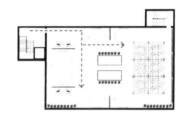

Second Floor

Rooftop

LOCAL

Engages in her community through frequent visits to Forge to grab a bite to eat with friends and keep up with the creations of beutiful artwork by her neighbors. On nice days she enjoys sitting and drinking a pint in the beer garden.

Conclusions

All three examples demonstrate how the design concept and codes work together throughout the design process. Beginning with a basic analysis of the building shell through the final plan for the design, the code shapes the space planning by indicating how many exits will be required, limiting travel distances, and providing other life-safety requirements. The design concept provides creative inspiration for how to accomplish this.

Basic Code Diagrams

Project 1

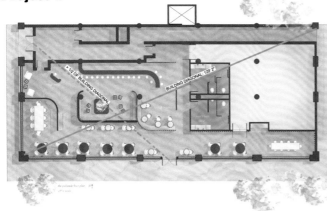

Figure 6.42
Diagram showing diagonal and exit placement

Project 2

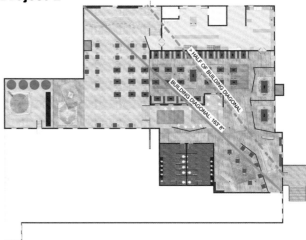

Figure 6.43
Diagram showing diagonal and exit placement

Project 3

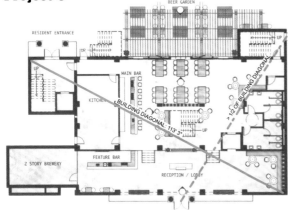

Figure 6.44
Diagram showing diagonal and exit placement

Assignment

1. Visit your favorite restaurant, a local hotel, or other hospitality venue and map code requirements that you can see: number of exits, spacing of aisles and tables, estimates of travel distances, bathroom fixtures counts. What, if anything, could be improved from your perspective? Using the tables included here, do you think the project meets all current requirements?

7

Case Studies: Office Design

Learning Objectives:

After reading this chapter and doing the exercises, students will be able to

- Go through the basic process of identifying occupancy type and determining construction type, occupant loads, and required exits
- Evaluate travel distance, number of exits required, and common path of travel
- Determine ADA clearances at all doors and fixtures
- Place grab bars in appropriate locations
- Calculate the number of plumbing fixtures needed for a specific use
- Identify appropriate strategies for fire separation between use groups

Introduction

This chapter will include three case studies related to new ways of working. The first is a co-working space, the second is a co-working space for retailers, and the third project is for a global design office that integrates the WELL Building Standard.

Co-working Space

This project entailed designing an 11,500 square foot, two-story co-working space in Peachtree, Georgia. Located in an existing office park building, the co-working space occupied the second floor with a small area of the first floor included in the overall square footage for the project. The project includes seven full-time employees with thirty-five to forty-five professionals who shared the co-working environment. The primary spaces included private offices, open office space, private enclaves, a work café, an ideation zone, a video conference room, forum space, project rooms, a studio work space, a reception area, resource center, and in-between spaces.

NEXT PROJECT: CO-WORKING

Building Location & Description

Location

1545 Peachtree Street
Suite 280
One Peachtree Point
Atlanta, GA 30309

Scope

1st and 2nd Floors (approximately 11,500 ft²)

Program Requirements

Next Spaces

Private Offices/Enclaves

Quantity: Minimum of 5

Space Allocation: 100–125 ft² (9.29 m²–11.61 m²) each

Consider making these spaces multipurpose. An enclave can support one to two people in private conversation or work and is not individually owned.

Function: An environment that allows for heads-down, focused work in either an owned or shared setting. Provide work surfaces, outfitted with technology, such that in-person and virtual meetings may occur seamlessly.

Lighting: Direct/indirect lighting; Make fixture recommendations, reflected ceiling plan not required

Furniture: Choose the most appropriate Steelcase Inc. product(s) for this space based on the client's vision and needs.

Construction: Minimal use of drywall to divide space. Consider the use of Steelcase Inc. movable or demountable wall products. One wall must have glass incorporated for visibility in and from the space. Acoustics should be taken into consideration.

Open Office / Individual Work Areas

Quantity: 35–40

Space Allocation: Up to 48 ft² (4.46 m²) each

Function: Work settings that allow people to be immersed into the brand of the organization, promote flexibility and choice (spaces do not have to be owned), and provide access the latest technology. The space must provide options that allow employees to shift seamlessly through the four modes of work (socializing, collaborating, focusing, and learning). Diversity of individual workspaces (types and sizes) is encouraged.

Lighting: Direct/indirect lighting, supplemented by individual task lighting; make fixture recommendations; reflected ceiling plan not required.

Furniture: Choose the most appropriate Steelcase Inc. product(s) for this space based on the client's vision and needs. If panels are used, consider LEED requirements for daylighting and views from the seated position.

Construction: Walls may be used to delineate this work zone, but no millwork materials should be used to divide individual work spaces. Consider Steelcase Inc. wall solutions vs. traditional construction wherever possible.

Private Enclaves

Quantity: Minimum of 4

Space Allocation: 25–40 ft² (2.32–3.7 m²) each

Consider making the space multipurpose.

Function: An environment that allows for rejuvenation/respite or heads-down focused work in a relaxed setting that minimizes visual and auditory distractions.

Lighting: Direct/indirect lighting; make fixture recommendations; reflected ceiling plan not required.

Furniture: Choose the most appropriate Steelcase Inc. product(s) for this space based on the client's vision and needs.

Construction: Minimal use of drywall to divide space. Consider the use of Steelcase Inc. movable or demountable wall products. A minimum of one wall should incorporate glass for visibility in and from the space. Acoustics must be taken into consideration for this space.

WorkCafe

Quantity: 1

Space Allocation: 750–1,000 ft² (69.77 m²–92.93 m²)

Function: A space where employees can decompress and enjoy a meal together at any time during the day. As part of the NEXT culture, workers are encouraged to eat with others vs. alone at one's desk. During nonpeak meal times, the space should serve as an alternative meeting space. Consider making this environment multifaceted and multipurpose. Incorporate a range of settings to support individual focus work and peer to peer collaboration. Maximizing real estate, this area works hard during peak social hours as well as supporting individual and group work. Collaboration area should include one to two project studio spaces where teams can work together on long-term projects using analog and digital tools. *Food preparation spaces are not needed for this project.*

Lighting: A combination of lighting sources is recommended. All selections should be energy efficient. Fixture selections and reflected ceiling plan required.

Furniture: Choose the most appropriate Steelcase Inc. product(s) for this space based on the client's vision and needs.

Construction: Consider Steelcase Inc. wall solutions in conjunction with traditional construction.

Ideation Zone

Quantity: 1

Space Allocation: Approximately 200 ft^2 (18.58 m^2)

Function: NEXT members will use this space to share products or services they want to introduce to the market. These projects may be displayed physically, virtually, or both. The ideation zone can be incorporated into another larger space but does need to be branded and within an environment that would be "customer friendly."

Lighting: Retail lighting solutions should be considered to supplement general lighting for appropriate product display. All should be energy efficient selections. Make fixture recommendations; reflected ceiling plan not required.

Furniture: As needed, choose the most appropriate Steelcase Inc. product(s) for this space based on the client's vision and needs.

Construction: Consider Steelcase Inc. wall solutions in conjunction with traditional construction.

Videoconference

Quantity: 1

Space Allocation: Seats 8 people

Function: A space that accommodates telepresence technology for a minimum of eight people.

NEXT members often collaborate with partners all over the world and will need technology that better supports these distributed teams for both scheduled and impromptu discussions.

Lighting: Students should research the best lighting solutions for telepresence environments and make energy efficient fixture recommendations, but no reflected ceiling plan is required.

Furniture: As needed, choose the most appropriate Steelcase Inc. product(s) for this space based on the client's vision and needs.

Construction: Consider Steelcase Inc. wall solutions.

Forum Space—Active/Distance Learning Classroom

Quantity: 1

Space Allocation: Supports 18 to 24 people

Must be able to break into individual teams of equal size within classrooms.

Function: Create an active/distance learning environment that drives member engagement and supports blended learning. Active learning design principles should be used.

Active Distance Learning Classroom with HDVC camera that acts as the main classroom for satellite locations to connect into the live class. These spaces are also available to be rented by the community.

Provide diverse offerings of analog and digital tools, mobility, palette of posture, and choice and control.

Lighting: Direct/indirect lighting; make fixture recommendations; reflected ceiling plan not required. All lighting choices should be energy efficient selections.

Furniture: Choose the most appropriate Steelcase Inc. product(s) for this space based on the client's vision and needs.

Construction: Consider Steelcase Inc. wall solutions vs. traditional construction wherever possible. Acoustics must be taken into consideration for this space.

Project Rooms

Quantity: 3

Space Allocation: Seats 6 to 8 people

Function: A space that accommodates six to eight people and allows for quick reconfiguration based on project team needs.

Lighting: Energy efficient direct/indirect lighting. Make fixture recommendations but reflected ceiling plan not required.

Furniture: As needed, choose the most appropriate Steelcase Inc. product(s) for this space based on the client's vision and needs.

Construction: Consider Steelcase Inc. wall solutions.

Studio/Workspace

Quantity: 1

Space Allocation: Approximately 300 ft^2 (27.87 m^2)

Function: A raw space that houses equipment to be used during prototype development.

Equipment includes 3D printer, belt sander, laser cutter, table saw, etc.

Lighting: Energy efficient direct lighting recommended. Make fixture recommendations, reflected ceiling plan not required.

Furniture: Minimal furniture is required for this space. As needed, choose the most appropriate Steelcase Inc. product(s) for this space based on the client's vision and needs.

Construction: Traditional construction and millwork is encouraged in this space.

In-between Spaces

Quantity: Varies

Space Allocation: 25–100 ft^2 (7.6–30.5 m^2)

Function: Must support individuals and small groups who extend learning before, during and after meetings. Can consider a range of open, shielded, and closed spaces. A palette of posture should be available for short- and long-term stays. Areas to include are spaces outside of classrooms for feedback and mentoring, touchdown spaces for individuals, and places for one-on-one conversations, including a variety of setting types for one to four members.

Lighting: Direct/indirect lighting. Make fixture recommendations; reflected ceiling plan not required. All lighting choices should be energy efficient selections.

Furniture: Choose the most appropriate Steelcase Inc. product(s) for this space based on the client's vision and needs.

Construction: Consider Steelcase Inc. wall solutions in conjunction with traditional construction.

Reception/First Impression

Quantity: 1

Space Allocation: Approximately 350 ft² (32.51 m²)

Function: A full-time receptionist/office manager will reside in this space.

As people enter the space, provide a space that is welcoming, technology-savvy and seats four to six guests. The receptionist needs a work desk with a modesty panel, a place for his/her personal printer, CPU, and dual monitors.

Lighting: Energy efficient direct/indirect lighting recommended. Make fixture recommendations; reflected ceiling plan not required.

Furniture: As needed, choose the most appropriate Steelcase Inc. product(s) for this space based on the client's vision and needs.

Construction: Consider Steelcase Inc. wall solutions in conjunction with traditional construction.

Resource Center

Quantity: 1

Space Allocation: Approximately 250 ft² (23.22 m²)

Function: A space for the entire office that houses the main printers, copiers, mail sorting area, and counter space for sorting documents and a table for layout space.

Lighting: Energy efficient direct/indirect lighting recommended.

Make fixture recommendations; reflected ceiling plan not required.

Furniture: Minimal furniture is required but as needed, choose the most appropriate Steelcase Inc. product(s) for this space based on the client's vision and needs.

Construction: Traditional construction/millwork is suitable for this space but feel free to also consider Steelcase products used in conjunction with traditional construction.

Applying the Code

Programming Phase

During the programming phase for this project, the designer first determined the occupancy use group. Based on this and the preliminary occupancy calculations, some basic assumptions about egress could be made.

Student Project One

The design concept for the first project relates the way this Peachtree, Georgia, based co-working office brings people together to the way the local fruit, the peach, is connected. Layers of fruit and an external skin surround a central pit. This arrangement was abstracted to the space to show the growth and development that takes place in a co-working office (Figures 7.1, 7.2).

Developed through multiple iterations, the plan has a centralized work café (pit) surrounded by the workers (the fruit) and an external skin (enclosed offices and enclaves) (Figures 7.3, 7.4).

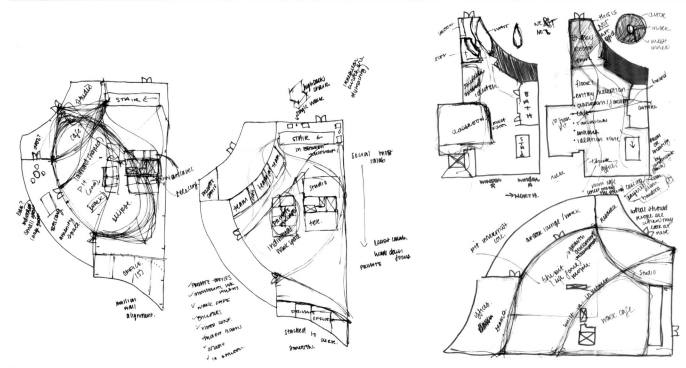

Figures 7.1 and 7.2
Conceptual design sketches

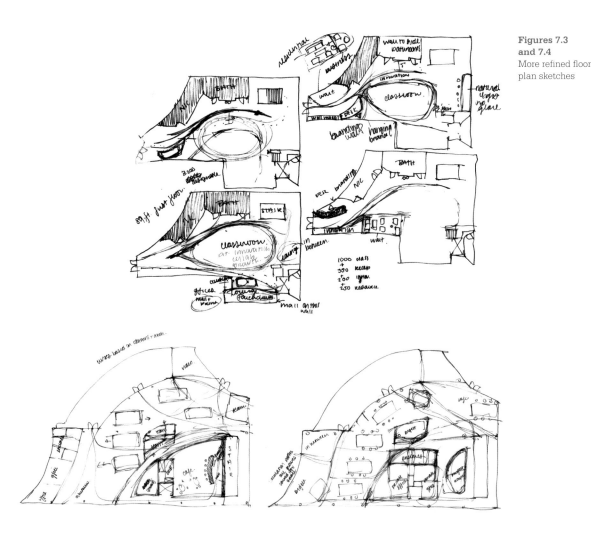

Figures 7.3 and 7.4
More refined floor plan sketches

Occupancy Classification

The primary function for the space is Business (B). The project indicated that the client had spaces located on two floors. The first floor consisted of 4,185 square feet and the second floor 7,316 square feet, for a total of 11,500 square feet. The use group for the offices was B with an occupancy load factor of 150 gross.

For maximum floor area allowances per occupant, please refer to Table 4.2 and its accompanying Box 4.1, which summarizes the primary changes to the table.

Accessibility Requirements

In order to accommodate all possible users, the entire facility is accessible (Figures 7.5, 7.6).

Design Development

Once the preliminary planning was done to accommodate codes and accessibility, students selected finishes appropriate to the use that also met code requirements.

Codes for Interior Finishes

For this facility type (sprinklered), the finishes requirements are found in Table 803.13 (see Table 7.1 and Figures 7.7–7.9).

Student Project Two

A second example of this same project used a nest as inspiration. In addition to meeting all of the above requirements, this project also included several sustainable materials and furniture selections to meet LEED Guidelines (Figures 7.10–7.12).

The final design combines the next concept with a sustainable interior that also meets code and ADA requirements (Figures 7.13–7.15).

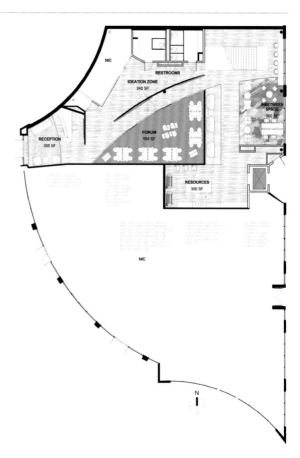

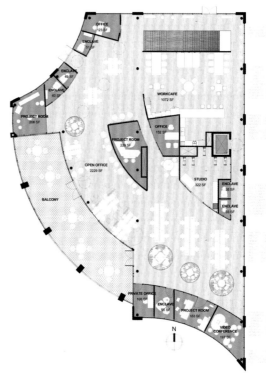

Figures 7.5 and 7.6
Final plans

Table 7.1 IBC 2018 Table 803.13: Interior Wall and Ceiling Finish Requirements by Occupancy

TABLE 803.13
INTERIOR WALL AND CEILING FINISH REQUIREMENTS BY OCCUPANCY[k]

GROUP	SPRINKLERED[l]			NONSPRINKLERED		
	Interior exit stairways and ramps and exit passageways[a, b]	Corridors and enclosure for exit access stairways and ramps	Rooms and enclosed spaces[c]	Interior exit stairways and ramps and exit passageways[a, b]	Corridors and enclosure for exit access stairways and ramps	Rooms and enclosed spaces[c]
A-1 & A-2	B	B	C	A	A[d]	B[e]
A-3[f], A-4, A-5	B	B	C	A	A[d]	C
B, E, M, R-1	B	C[m]	C	A	B	C
R-4	B	C	C	A	B	B
F	C	C	C	B	C	C
H	B	B	C[g]	A	A	B
I-1	B	C	C	A	B	B
I-2	B	B	B[h, i]	A	A	B
I-3	A	A[j]	C	A	A	B
I-4	B	B	B[h, i]	A	A	B
R-2	C	C	C	B	B	C
R-3	C	C	C	C	C	C
S	C	C	C	B	B	C
U	No restrictions			No restrictions		

For SI: 1 inch = 25.4 mm, 1 square foot = 0.0929 m².

a. Class C interior finish materials shall be permitted for wainscotting or paneling of not more than 1,000 square feet of applied surface area in the grade lobby where applied directly to a noncombustible base or over furring strips applied to a noncombustible base and fireblocked as required by Section 803.15.1.

b. In other than Group I-3 occupancies in buildings less than three stories above grade plane, Class B interior finish for nonsprinklered buildings and Class C interior finish for sprinklered buildings shall be permitted in interior exit stairways and ramps.

c. Requirements for rooms and enclosed spaces shall be based on spaces enclosed by partitions. Where a fire-resistance rating is required for structural elements, the enclosing partitions shall extend from the floor to the ceiling. Partitions that do not comply with this shall be considered to be enclosing spaces and the rooms or spaces on both sides shall be considered to be one room or space. In determining the applicable requirements for rooms and enclosed spaces, the specific occupancy thereof shall be the governing factor regardless of the group classification of the building or structure.

d. Lobby areas in Group A-1, A-2 and A-3 occupancies shall be not less than Class B materials.

e. Class C interior finish materials shall be permitted in places of assembly with an occupant load of 300 persons or less.

f. For places of religious worship, wood used for ornamental purposes, trusses, paneling or chancel furnishing shall be permitted.

g. Class B material is required where the building exceeds two stories.

h. Class C interior finish materials shall be permitted in administrative spaces.

i. Class C interior finish materials shall be permitted in rooms with a capacity of four persons or less.

j. Class B materials shall be permitted as wainscotting extending not more than 48 inches above the finished floor in corridors and exit access stairways and ramps.

k. Finish materials as provided for in other sections of this code.

l. Applies when protected by an automatic sprinkler system installed in accordance with Section 903.3.1.1 or 903.3.1.2.

m. Corridors in ambulatory care facilities shall be provided with Class A or B materials.

IBC 2018 TABLE 803.13 INTERIOR WALL AND CEILING FINISH REQUIREMENTS BY OCCUPANCY

Table 803.11 in the IBC 2015 has been replaced by Table 803.13 in the IBC 2018. Note "m" has been added in the 2018 IBC, stating that corridors in ambulatory care facilities shall be provide with Class A or B materials.

(Formerly Interior Wall and Ceiling Finish Requirements IBC 2015 Table 803.11)

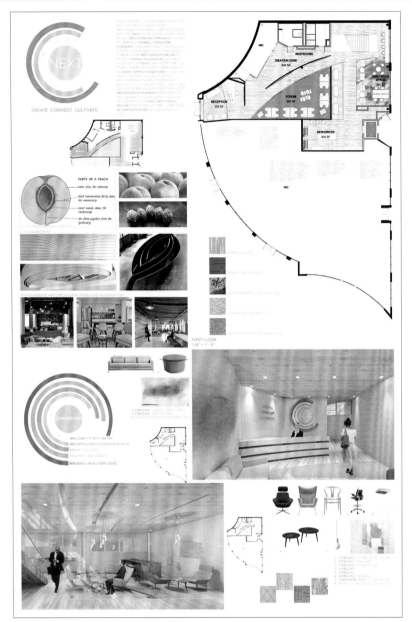

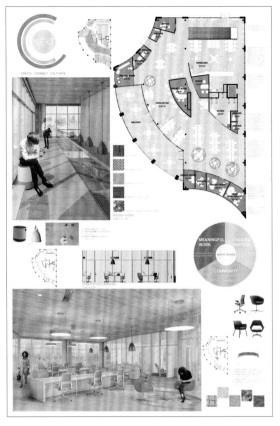

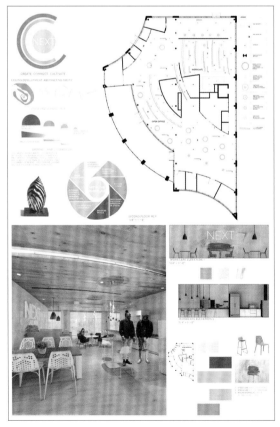

Figures 7.7–7.9
Final project
boards

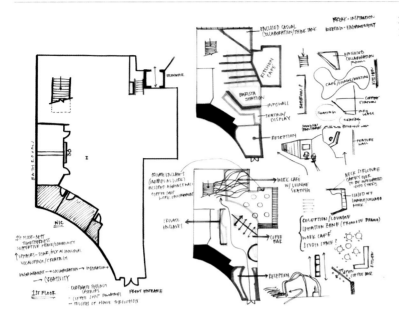

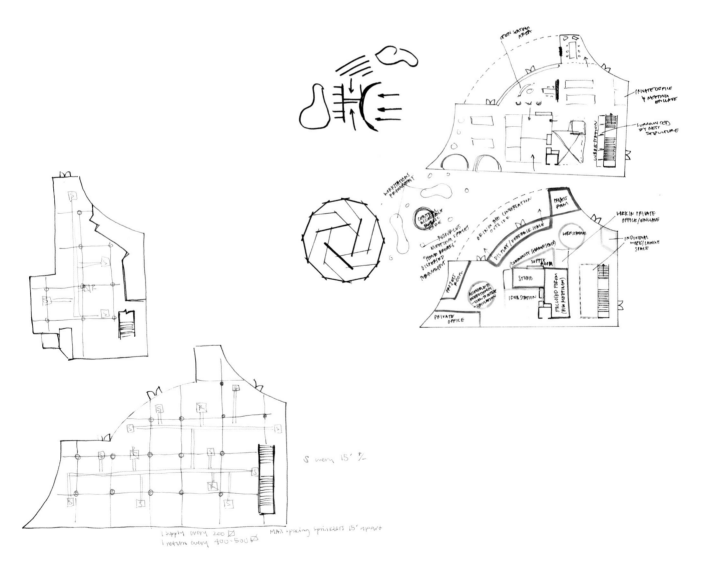

**Figures
7.13–7.15**
Final boards

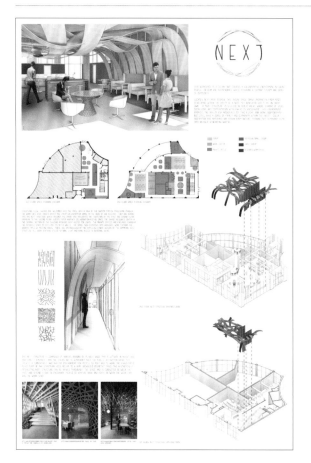

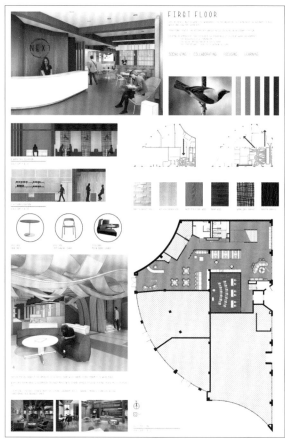

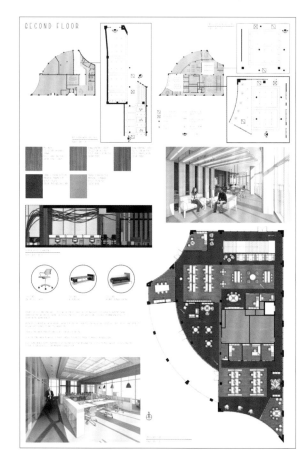

Co-working Retail Space

Based on the 2016 IIDA "Social Station" Student Competition, this project tackled a new office project type: co-working for retailers. With the rise of the internet and the closing of many physical retail establishments, many startup retailers have resorted to online shops that still require a physical presence for photographing merchandise, shipping and handling orders, and handling other business operations. This 18,000 square foot site located on the seventh floor of a historic building in Dallas, Texas, included co-working space for up to sixty tenants and an evening retail/event environment.

In addition to the basic program requirements, students were required to follow the LEED CI version 4.0 guidelines.

PROJECT DESCRIPTION IIDA SOCIAL STATION

Building Location & Description

The 2016 IIDA SDC invites you to create Social Station—a first-of-its-kind co-working space specialized for today's social retailers. Your program should be the integration of both social retail and a high-functioning co-working space. Encouraging adaptability, health, and well-being, and an emphasis on an active, engaging space should be priorities in your final design. It should also address new models and approaches to the co-working space.

The reference site of where your design will be located is 603 Munger Avenue, an iconic property known for its three roof-top cylindrical water tanks and red brick façade visible from Woodall Rodgers Freeway in Dallas, Texas. Specifically, the seventh floor will be the location of Social Station, with floorplans and other dimensions provided. The design solution must take into account working space, meeting space, lounge space, retail space, and a variety of other touchdown areas for personal and hands-on work.

Program Requirements

Co-working Office Space Program Requirements

1. Flexible workspace for up to sixty co-working tenants
   a. Average occupancy will range from 40 to 85 percent at any given time, with an average of 60 percent capacity.
   b. Workspace should be able to accommodate single-employee companies up to companies of four employees.
2. Minimum of three collaborative workspaces/meeting spaces for up to four people
3. Communal lounge space
4. Secure storage space for tenant's personal belongings, including, but not limited to, coats, bags, laptops, small tools, and limited inventory.
   a. This space may be centralized, multiple smaller spaces, or a hybrid.
5. Small prep-kitchen that includes a shared refrigerator, microwave, counter/storage space, coffee maker, and recycling/composting/refuse area
6. Minimum of three private touchdown spaces for private phone calls, private one-on-one meetings, etc.
7. Minimum of three heads-down workspaces that allow concentration and individual work.
8. Light duty maker workshop for 3D printing, product development/testing, and hands-on product customization.

Evening Retail/Event Program Requirements

The space will need to transform into an event/retail space in the evenings, taking no more than two hours to complete.

1. Flexible display options for between one and four tenant brands per event
   a. Items to be sold can range from clothing, home décor, essential oils, custom products, and more
   b. Consider modular workstations
2. Event space to accommodate up to seventy-five guests
3. Ability to serve food and beverages buffet style or passed hors d'oeuvres

Applying the Code

Programming Phase

During the programming phase for this project, the designer first determined the occupancy use group. Based on this and the preliminary occupancy calculations, some basic assumptions about egress could be made. Two existing fire stairs provide access from the seventh floor, where the project is located, to the first floor exit from the building. Three elevators also provide access to the seventh floor. While the northern-most stair can accommodate an area of refuge within the fire-rated stair enclosure, the one near the elevators cannot. This meant that students were required to create a fire-rated enclosed lobby area, including the elevators and second fire stair.

The total square footage for this project was approximately 15,000 square feet. The occupancy type was Business (B) with an occupant load factor of 150 gross (see Table 4.2).

15,000 / 150 = 100 occupants

Using this load, the plumbing fixture requirements could be verified using Table 7.2 (see also Table 7.3).

Table 7.2 IBC 2018 Table 2902.1: Minimum Number of Required Plumbing Fixtures

[P] TABLE 2902.1
MINIMUM NUMBER OF REQUIRED PLUMBING FIXTURES[a]
(See Sections 2902.1.1 and 2902.2)

No.	CLASSIFICATION	DESCRIPTION	WATER CLOSETS (URINALS SEE SECTION 424.2 OF THE *INTERNATIONAL PLUMBING CODE*)		LAVATORIES		BATHTUBS/ SHOWERS	DRINKING FOUNTAINS (SEE SECTION 410 OF THE *INTERNATIONAL PLUMBING CODE*)	OTHER
			Male	Female	Male	Female			
1	Assembly	Theaters and other buildings for the performing arts and motion pictures[d]	1 per 125	1 per 65	1 per 200		—	1 per 500	1 service sink
		Nightclubs, bars, taverns, dance halls and buildings for similar purposes[d]	1 per 40	1 per 40	1 per 75		—	1 per 500	1 service sink
		Restaurants, banquet halls and food courts[d]	1 per 75	1 per 75	1 per 200		—	1 per 500	1 service sink
		Casino gaming areas	1 per 100 for the first 400 and 1 per 250 for the remainder exceeding 400	1 per 50 for the first 400 and 1 per 150 for the remainder exceeding 400	1 per 250 for the first 750 and 1 per 500 for the remainder exceeding 750		—	1 per 1,000	1 service sink

(continued)

Table 7.2 IBC 2018 Table 2902.1: Minimum Number of Required Plumbing Fixtures *(continued)*

PLUMBING SYSTEMS

[P] TABLE 2902.1—(continued)
MINIMUM NUMBER OF REQUIRED PLUMBING FIXTURES[a]
(See Sections 2902.1.1 and 2902.2)

No.	CLASSIFICATION	DESCRIPTION	WATER CLOSETS (URINALS SEE SECTION 424.2 OF THE *INTERNATIONAL PLUMBING CODE*)		LAVATORIES		BATHTUBS/ SHOWERS	DRINKING FOUNTAINS (SEE SECTION 410 OF THE *INTERNATIONAL PLUMBING CODE*)	OTHER
			Male	Female	Male	Female			
1	Assembly	Auditoriums without permanent seating, art galleries, exhibition halls, museums, lecture halls, libraries, arcades and gymnasiums[d]	1 per 125	1 per 65	1 per 200		—	1 per 500	1 service sink
		Passenger terminals and transportation facilities[d]	1 per 500	1 per 500	1 per 750		—	1 per 1,000	1 service sink
		Places of worship and other religious services[d]	1 per 150	1 per 75	1 per 200		—	1 per 1,000	1 service sink
		Coliseums, arenas, skating rinks, pools and tennis courts for indoor sporting events and activities	1 per 75 for the first 1,500 and 1 per 120 for the remainder exceeding 1,500	1 per 40 for the first 1,520 and 1 per 60 for the remainder exceeding 1,520	1 per 200	1 per 150	—	1 per 1,000	1 service sink
		Stadiums, amusement parks, bleachers and grandstands for outdoor sporting events and activities[f]	1 per 75 for the first 1,500 and 1 per 120 for the remainder exceeding 1,500	1 per 40 for the first 1,520 and 1 per 60 for the remainder exceeding 1,520	1 per 200	1 per 150	—	1 per 1,000	1 service sink
2	Business	Buildings for the transaction of business, professional services, other services involving merchandise, office buildings, banks, light industrial, ambulatory care and similar uses	1 per 25 for the first 50 and 1 per 50 for the remainder exceeding 50		1 per 40 for the first 80 and 1 per 80 for the remainder exceeding 80		—	1 per 100	1 service sink[e]
3	Educational	Educational facilities	1 per 50		1 per 50		—	1 per 100	1 service sink
4	Factory and industrial	Structures in which occupants are engaged in work fabricating, assembly or processing of products or materials	1 per 100		1 per 100		—	1 per 400	1 service sink
5	Institutional	Custodial care facilities	1 per 10		1 per 10		1 per 8	1 per 100	1 service sink
		Medical care recipients in hospitals and nursing homes[b]	1 per room[c]		1 per room[c]		1 per 15	1 per 100	1 service sink
		Employees in hospitals and nursing homes[b]	1 per 25		1 per 35		—	1 per 100	—
		Visitors in hospitals and nursing homes	1 per 75		1 per 100		—	1 per 500	—
		Prisons[b]	1 per cell		1 per cell		1 per 15	1 per 100	1 service sink

(continued)

Table 7.2 IBC 2018 Table 2902.1: Minimum Number of Required Plumbing Fixtures *(continued)*

[P] TABLE 2902.1—continued
MINIMUM NUMBER OF REQUIRED PLUMBING FIXTURES[a]
(See Sections 2902.1.1 and 2902.2)

No.	CLASSIFICATION	DESCRIPTION	WATER CLOSETS (URINALS SEE SECTION 424.2 OF THE INTERNATIONAL PLUMBING CODE)		LAVATORIES		BATHTUBS OR SHOWERS	DRINKING FOUNTAINS (SEE SECTION 410 OF THE INTERNATIONAL PLUMBING CODE)	OTHER
			Male	Female	Male	Female			
5	Institutional	Reformatories, detention centers and correctional centers[b]	1 per 15		1 per 15		1 per 15	1 per 100	1 service sink
		Employees in reformitories, detention centers and correctional centers[b]	1 per 25		1 per 35		—	1 per 100	—
		Adult day care and child day care	1 per 15		1 per 15		1	1 per 100	1 service sink
6	Mercantile	Retail stores, service stations, shops, salesrooms, markets and shopping centers	1 per 500		1 per 750		—	1 per 1,000	1 service sink[e]
7	Residential	Hotels, motels, boarding houses (transient)	1 per sleeping unit		1 per sleeping unit		1 per sleeping unit	—	1 service sink
		Dormitories, fraternities, sororities and boarding houses (not transient)	1 per 10		1 per 10		1 per 8	1 per 100	1 service sink
		Apartment house	1 per dwelling unit		1 per dwelling unit		1 per dwelling unit	—	1 kitchen sink per dwelling unit; 1 automatic clothes washer connection per 20 dwelling units
		One- and two-family dwellings and lodging houses with five or fewer guestrooms	1 per dwelling unit		1 per 10		1 per dwelling unit	—	1 kitchen sink per dwelling unit; 1 automatic clothes washer connection per dwelling unit
		Congregate living facilities with 16 or fewer persons	1 per 10		1 per 10		1 per 8	1 per 100	1 service sink
8	Storage	Structures for the storage of goods, warehouses, storehouses and freight depots, low and moderate hazard	1 per 100		1 per 100		—	1 per 1,000	1 service sink

a. The fixtures shown are based on one fixture being the minimum required for the number of persons indicated or any fraction of the number of persons indicated. The number of occupants shall be determined by this code.

b. Toilet facilities for employees shall be separate from facilities for inmates or care recipients.

c. A single-occupant toilet room with one water closet and one lavatory serving not more than two adjacent patient sleeping units shall be permitted, provided that each patient sleeping unit has direct access to the toilet room and provisions for privacy for the toilet room user are provided.

d. The occupant load for seasonal outdoor seating and entertainment areas shall be included when determining the minimum number of facilities required.

e. For business and mercantile classifications with an occupant load of 15 or fewer, a service sink shall not be required.

f. The required number and type of plumbing fixtures for outdoor swimming pools shall be in accordance with Section 609 of the *International Swimming Pool and Spa Code.*

IBC 2018 TABLE 2902.1: MINIMUM NUMBER OF REQUIRED PLUMBING FIXTURES

IBC 2015, Table 2902.1 has retained the same number. Assembly has been adjusted to remove the occupancy column that contained A-1, A-2, A-3, A-4, and A-5 from the table. A category for "casino gaming areas" has been added with pertinent plumbing requirements.

As with Assembly, the occupancy column has been removed for Factory (F-1 and F-2) and for Institutional (I-1, I-2, I-3, and I-4). Under Institutional, a new row item has been added for "custodial care facilities," with the pertinent plumbing requirements. Under Institutional a new row item has been added for "Medical care recipients in hospitals and nursing homes," with the pertinent plumbing requirements. (This replaces "Hospitals, ambulatory nursing home care recipient" in the IBC 2015.) "Employees other than residential care" in the IBC 2015 has been replaced by "Employees in hospitals and nursing homes" in the IBC 2018. "Visitors other than residential care" in the IBC 2015 has been replaced with "Visitors in hospitals and nursing homes" in the IBC 2018. Beneath reformatories, "Employees" in the IBC 2015 has been replaced by "Employees in reformatories, detention centers, and correctional centers" in the IBC 2018. The occupancy column has been removed for the Residential classification, eliminating the column with R-1, R-2, R-3, and R-4 in the IBC 2018. The occupancy column has been removed for the Storage classification eliminating the column with S-1 and S-2 in the IBC 2018.

(Formerly IBC 2015 Table 2902.1)

Table 7.3 Required Plumbing Fixtures for Co-working Retail Space

100 occupants
50 female/50 male

	WC	Lavatory
Male	1 per 25 first 50 = 2	1 per 40 first 80 = 2
		1 per 80 after = 1
		Total = 3
Female	1 per 25 first 50 = 2	1 per 40 first 80 = 2
		1 per 80 after = 1
		Total = 3

Water Fountain 1 per 100 = 2 required
Service Sink = 1 required

In addition to meeting building code requirements for the project, students were also asked to comply with the LEED CI v.4 Green Building Rating System. Certain assumptions were inherent in the project approach. For example, it was assumed all prerequisites were met, leaving students to identify other areas they were pursuing with the design.

Project One

The first student example used the chameleon as inspiration for the space that changed throughout the day. During the day, the seventh floor served as a co-working space for retailers. This was transformed into a display and social space after hours at night. All of the product vendors who use the Social Station create products that appeal to the local demographic and are sustainable.

Beginning with the way in which scales overlap on a chameleon, a series of overlapping organic forms were used to inspire the space planning.

Movable panels, organic shaped voids, and raised rooms were used to create areas for privacy and establish a hierarchy of spaces (Figure 7.16).

The parti diagram was a reflection of these early design explorations (Figure 7.17).

As the plan was developed, the rounded shapes gave way to more hexagonal ones closer to the structure of the scale. The interlocking "scales" established a circulation path that was highlighted using the ceiling and materials throughout the space. The preliminary plan did not include a fire-rated lobby entry area that was required for an area of refuge (Figure 7.18).

Refinements to the Plan

The plan was refined to integrate the required lobby. As can be seen in the diagram, the initial plan had one of the doors swinging the wrong way (not in the direction of egress) (Figures 7.19, 7.20).

As the plan was being developed, dimensional sketches explored some of the concepts as well (Figure 7.21).

Materials reinforcing the concept were also being selected (Figure 7.22).

A series of four refined diagrams directed the project and ensured adherence to the design concept (Figure 7.23).

A more finalized schematic plan adds some finishes but fails to show the corrected door swing (Figure 7.24).

The axonometric details the integration of key design ideas in three dimensions (Figure 7.25).

The final project illustrated the integration of all code and ADA concerns, as well as the inclusion of LEED criteria (Figures 7.26–7.35).

Figure 7.16
Conceptual
diagrams

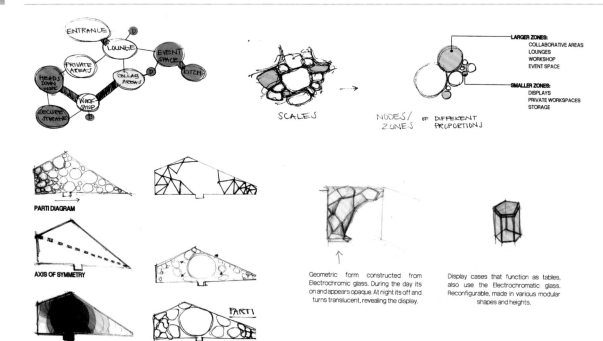

SCALES

NODES/ ZONES   OF DIFFERENT PROPORTIONS

LARGER ZONES:
COLLABORATIVE AREAS
LOUNGES
WORKSHOP
EVENT SPACE

SMALLER ZONES:
DISPLAYS
PRIVATE WORKSPACES
STORAGE

PARTI DIAGRAM

AXIS OF SYMMETRY

POINTS OF ENTRY

PARTI

Geometric form constructed from Electrochromic glass. During the day its on and appears opaque. At night its off and turns translucent, revealing the display.

Display cases that function as tables, also use the Electrochromatic glass. Reconfigurable, made in various modular shapes and heights.

Figure 7.17
Parti diagram

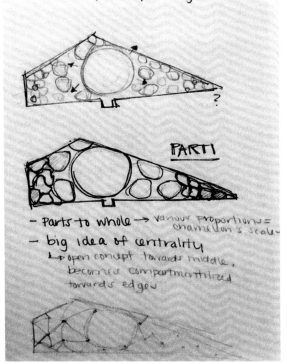

Adaptation

Drawing inspiration from the chameleon; its extreme ability to adapt, and its scales proportion influences spatial planning.

PARTI

- Parts to whole → various proportions = chameleon's scales
- big idea of centrality
  ↳ open concept towards middle, becomes compartmentalized towards edges

organic → center
geometric → edges
P
P
P
P
P?
W
HD
②
MANNEQ. DISPLAY
EVENT/ DISPLAYS
③
KITCHEN
CONF.
①
C?
ALCOVE
PRIVATE NOOK
LOUNGE NOOK
RECEP. + LOCKERS
DISPLAY WALL
GYM.
COMPOST GARDEN
shaped indoor gardens
1,2,3 = white, pops of color from merchandise
enclosed spaces = buckets of color

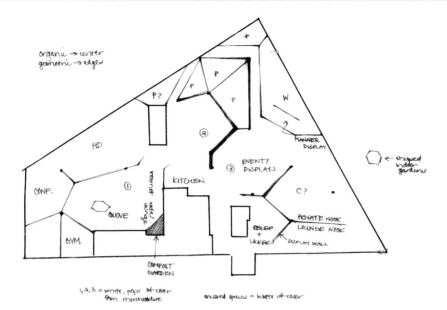

Figure 7.18
Preliminary plan

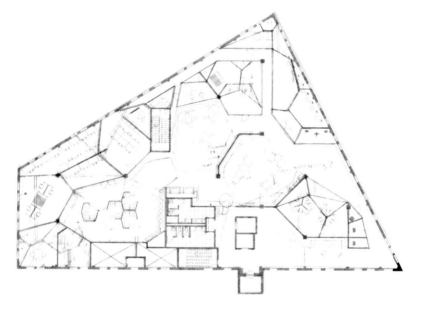

Figure 7.19
Refined plan with code problems

A. RECEPTION
B. LOBBY
C. PRIVATE TOUCH DOWN SPACES
D. COLLAB. WORKSPACES
E. LOUNGE / EVENT SPACE
F. WORKSHOP, with pinup space, mannequins, sewing stations, and a space for fittings.
G. INFORMAL MEETING SPACE
H. FORMAL MEETING SPACE, with videoconferencing.
I. SITTING AREA
J. LOCKERS / COAT CLOSET
K. HEADS DOWN WORKROOM
L. CONFERENCE ROOM
M. YOGA / MULTIPURPOSE SPACE
N. COLLAB. LOUNGE
O. CHARGING STATIONS
P. BOOTH SEATING
Q. KITCHENETTE
R. COLLAB / PRESENTATION SPACE, with bluescape wall.
Need to close off for fire
overall good!

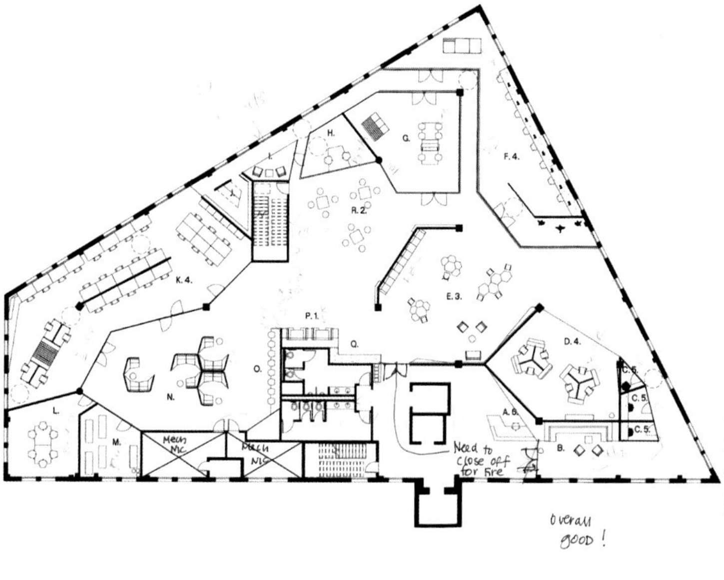

Figure 7.20
Refined plan with code problems

Figure 7.21
Four interior
thumbnail
sketches

PRIVATE SPACES,

With frosted glass.

INTERNET LOUNGE

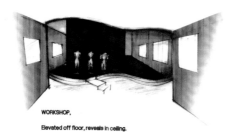

WORKSHOP,

Elevated off floor, reveals in ceiling.

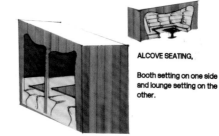

ALCOVE SEATING,

Booth setting on one side
and lounge setting on the
other.

Figure 7.22
Preliminary
material selections

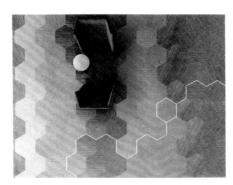

Figure 7.23
Four refined
diagrams

Concept of **adaptation**, drawing inspiration from the **chameleon**. Its scale s becomes a motif that influences
spatial planning which is demonstrated through **proportion** and **color**.

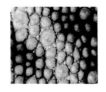
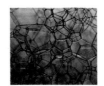

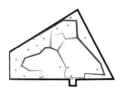

CIRCULATION.

The space features an open concept towards the center, and becomes more compartmentalized towards the edges.

CONCEPT. PARTS TO WHOLE.

The biggest piece is for the lounge, then the collaboration spaces, and the smaller areas are dedicated for more private, quiet activities.

HIERARCHY. PROPORTIONS.

In the evenings, retail events are centralized within the space. With the larger displays in the center, and smaller displays scattered outwards.

WORKSPACES.

Many different workspaces to cater to each different personality type. From light to dark, collaboration, heads down, and private spaces are represented.

S.O.C.I.A.L.

↑ COOL!

I know you are concerned about colors — but I think they work.

↓ Direction of egress

WORK ON this layout

A. RECEPTION

B. LOBBY

C. PRIVATE TOUCH DOWN SPACES

D. HEADS DOWN WORKSPACES

E. LOUNGE / EVENT SPACE

F. WORKSHOP, with pinup space, mannequins, sewing stations, and a space for fittings.

G. INFORMAL MEETING SPACE

H. FORMAL MEETING SPACE, with videoconferencing.

I. SITTING AREA

J. LOCKERS / COAT CLOSET

K. CONFERENCE ROOM

L. YOGA / MULTIPURPOSE SPACE

M. COLLAB. LOUNGE

N. CHARGING STATIONS

O. COMPOST GARDEN

P. KITCHENETTE

Q. COLLAB / PRESENTATION SPACE, with bluescape wall.

Figure 7.24
Refined schematic plan with finishes

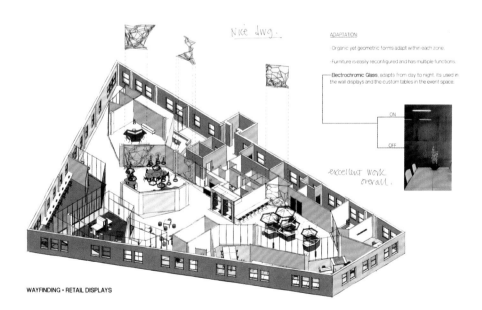

Nice dwg.

ADAPTATION:

· Organic yet geometric forms adapt within each zone.

· Furniture is easily reconfigured and has multiple functions.

— Electrochromic Glass, adapts from day to night. Its used in the wall displays and the custom tables in the event space.

ON

OFF

excellent work overall.

WAYFINDING · RETAIL DISPLAYS

Figure 7.25
Axonometric

Concept of **adaptation**, drawing inspiration from the **chameleon**. Its scales becomes a motif that influences spatial planning which is demonstrated through **proportion** and **color**.

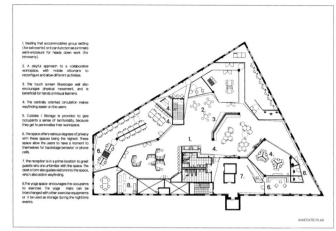

1. Seating that accommodates group setting (for extroverts) or it can function as a intimate semi-enclosure for heads down work (for introverts).

2. A playful approach to a collaborative workspace, with mobile ottomans to reconfigure and allow different activities.

3. The touch screen Bluescape wall also encourages physical movement, and is beneficial for hands on/visual learners.

4. The centrally oriented circulation makes wayfinding easier on the users.

5. Cubbies / Storage is provided to give occupants a sense of territoriality, because they get to personalize their workspace.

6. The space offers various degrees of privacy with these spaces being the highest. These space allow the users to have a moment to themselves for backstage behavior or phone calls.

7. The reception is in a prime location to greet guests who are unfamiliar with the space. The desk is form also guides visitors into the space, which also aids in wayfinding.

8. The yoga space encourages the occupants to exercise. The yoga mats can be interchanged with other exercise equipments or it be used as storage during the nighttime events.

ANNOTATED PLAN

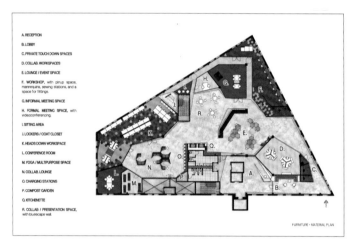

A. RECEPTION

B. LOBBY

C. PRIVATE TOUCH DOWN SPACES

D. COLLAB. WORKSPACES

E. LOUNGE / EVENT SPACE

F. WORKSHOP, with pinup space, mannequins, sewing stations, and a space for fittings.

G. INFORMAL MEETING SPACE

H. FORMAL MEETING SPACE, with videoconferencing.

I. SITTING AREA

J. LOCKERS / COAT CLOSET

K. HEADS DOWN WORKSPACE

L. CONFERENCE ROOM

M. YOGA / MULTIPURPOSE SPACE

N. COLLAB. LOUNGE

O. CHARGING STATIONS

P. COMPOST GARDEN

Q. KITCHENETTE

R. COLLAB / PRESENTATION SPACE, with bluescape wall.

FURNITURE + MATERIAL PLAN

In the logo, emphasis is placed on the C, to symbolize how the Social Station is a place that encourages creativity, collaboration, and celebrating innovative ideas and products.

WW-Graphic system is applied to columns and hanging signage. This allows signage to be easily changed for events or different companies start using the space. It can be reflected onto the signs. Its also extremely sustainable because the product can be recycled at the end of its life cycle.

LOGO + FIRST FLOOR SIGNAGE

RECEPTION // LOBBY

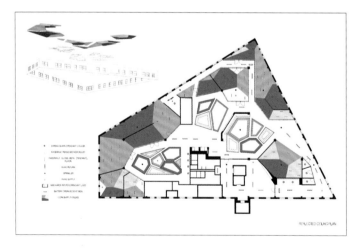

REFLECTED CEILING PLAN

INTERNET LOUNGE // COLLAB. SPACE

Figures 7.26–7.35
Final schematic drawings

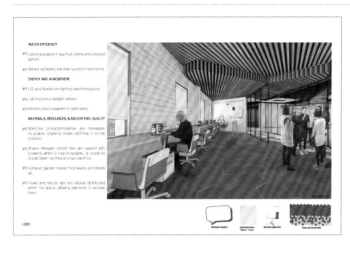

WATER EFFICIENCY

[✓] Use of gray water in dual flush toilets and compost garden.

[✓] Sensor activated, low flow faucets in restrooms.

ENERGY AND ATMOSPHERE

[✓] LED and fluorescent lighting used throughout.

[✓] Lighting is on a daylight sensor.

[✓] Kitchen placed adjacent to restrooms.

MATERIALS, RESOURCES, & INDOOR ENV. QUALITY

[✓] Specified products/materials are renewable, recyclable, Cradle to Cradle certified, or locally sourced.

[✓] Shaw's Hexagon carpet tiles are backed with Ecoworx, which is fully recyclable, is Cradle to Cradle Silver Certified and has low VOCs.

[✓] Compost garden reuses food waste and cleans air.

[✓] Views and natural light are equally distributed within the space, allowing everyone to access them.

LEED

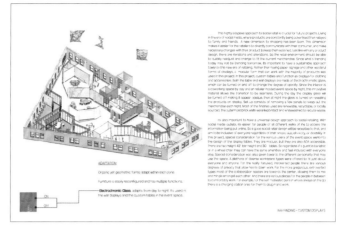

This highly adaptive approach to social retail is crucial for future projects. Living in the era of social media, where products are constantly being advertised than relayed to family and friends. A new dimension to shopping has been born. This dimension makes it easier for the retailers to directly communicate with their consumer, and make necessary changes with their product to keep them relevant. Just like with any product design, there are iterations and alterations. So the retail environment should be able to subtly readjust and change to fit the current merchandise. Since what is trending today may not be trending tomorrow, its important to have a sustainable approach toward this new era of retailing. Rather than having paper signage and other wasteful forms of displays, a modular form that can work with the majority of products was used in this project. In this project, custom tables also function as displays for clothing and accessories. Both the table and wall displays are made of Electrochromic glass, which can be turned on and off to change the degree of opacity. Since the interior is a coworking space by day and a retailer-hosted event space by night, this innovative material allows the transition to be seamless. During the day the display glass will be turned off making it appear opaque, then at night the glass is turned on revealing the products on display. Set up consists of removing a few panels to swap out the merchandise each night. Most of the finishes used are renewable, recyclable, or locally sourced. The outermost brick walls were kept intact and whitewashed to reduce waste.

Its also important to have a universal design approach to social retailing. With social media outlets, its easier for people of all different walks of life to access the information being put online. So a good social retail design will be receptive to that, and aim to be inclusive of everyone regardless of their shape, size, ethnicity, or disability. In this project, special consideration for the various users of the event space went into the design of the display tables. They are modular, but they are also ADA accessible. There are two height (42" bar height and 36" tables. So regardless of a guest is bariatric or in a wheel chair they can have the same amenities and feel included with everyone else. Special consideration was also given toward the different personality that may use the space. A plethora of diverse workspace types were offered to 'it just about everyone and anyone. For the reality focused, introverted people there are various degrees of privacy that allow hearts down work. For the more gregarious, extroverted types most of the collaboration spaces are towards the center, allowing them to mix and mingle amongst each other. And there are various places for the people in-between to comfortably work. For example, for the self-motivated person whos always on the go there is a charging station area for them to plug in and work.

ADAPTATION

Organic yet geometric forms adapt within each zone.

Furniture is easily reconfigured and has multiple functions.

ON / OFF — **Electrochromic Glass**, adapts from day to night. Its used in the wall displays and the custom tables in the event space.

WAY FINDING · CUSTOM DISPLAYS

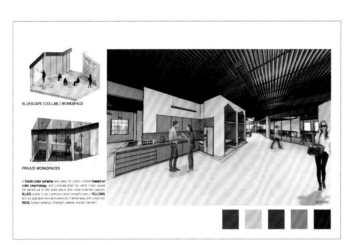

BLUESCAPE (COLLAB.) WORKSPACE

PRIVATE WORKSPACES

A **triadic color scheme** was used. All colors chosen **based on color psychology**, and consideration to what trait would be beneficial in the work place and retail-oriented spaces. **BLUES**, guide trust, communication and efficiency. **YELLOWS**, encourage optimism, extraversion, friendliness, and creativity. **REDS**, fosters energy, strength, desire, and excitement.

KITCHEN

BAR HEIGHT

TABLE HEIGHT, FOR ADA USERS

Custom display tables provide **universal design** by accommodating guests of all types. These tables can also stack for retail displays. The merchandise can be secured inside the E-Glass or laid atop the surface.

EVENT SPACE

Tiffany Stool · Pelcraft LVT Deepete · Marsh · Epixon Upholstery, Venture · Naws · Penelope Chair · Epixon Upholstery, Wizard · Vapor · 3Form, Ecoresin Spider

Project Two

Inspired by the dry soil of Texas, this project used a series of level changes in all directions to reflect the heaving and settling that happens within the structure of the soil layers.

A series of schematic design sketches explore this idea as applied to the potential design of the space (Figures 7.36, 7.37).

The resulting parti diagram included two axes along which the spaces would shift (Figure 7.38).

This was used to organize the spaces into specific types of functions within the space, as demonstrated in the bubble diagram (Figure 7.39).

A preliminary computerized plan shows the application of the conceptual approach and some resulting code issues, including the need for a fire-rated lobby with area of refuge and the necessity of some clear paths of egress. Other space-planning issues were also identified (Figure 7.40).

A second more refined plan also failed to include the fire-rated lobby (Figure 7.41).

A third iteration of the floor plan includes the lobby, but it has doors swinging the wrong way, a ramp that needs to accommodate ADA concerns, and some egress paths that are insufficient (Figure 7.42).

Figure 7.36
Conceptual exploration sketches

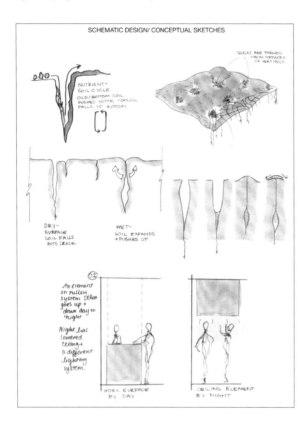

Figure 7.37
Conceptual exploration sketches

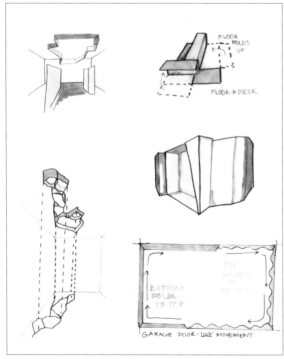

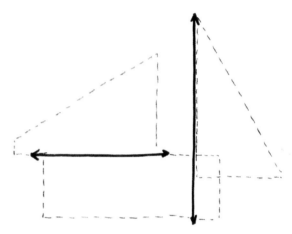

Figure 7.38
Parti diagram

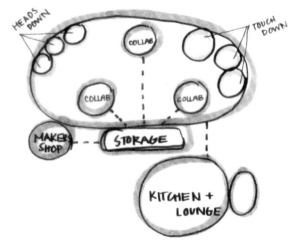

Figure 7.39
Bubble diagram

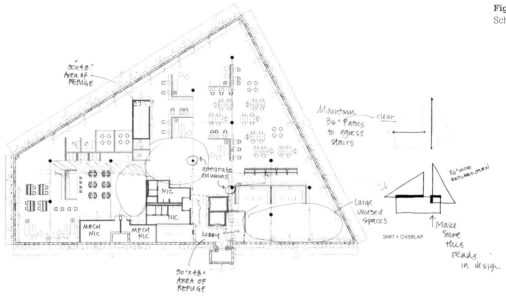

Figure 7.40
Schematic plan 1

Figure 7.41
Schematic plan 2

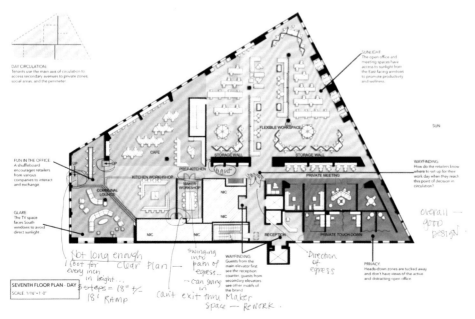

Figure 7.42
Schematic plan 3

Schematic Design Phase

The final proposal includes all corrected code and ADA information, as well as information on how the project met LEED requirements.

Accessibility Requirements

The final design includes an accessible ramp and restrooms (Figures 7.43–7.54).

**Figures
7.43–7.54**
Schematic design proposal

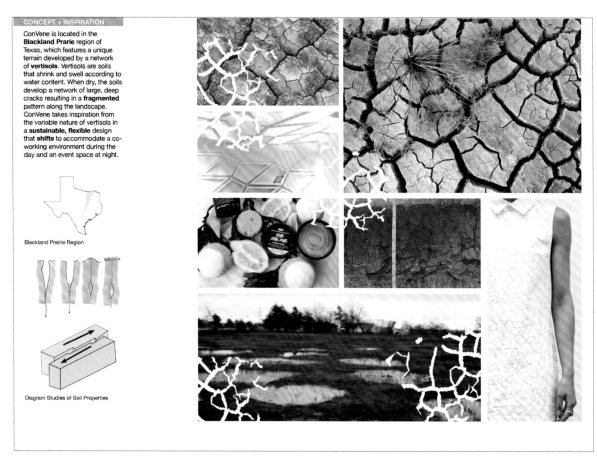

CONCEPT + INSPIRATION

ConVene is located in the **Blackland Prarie** region of Texas, which features a unique terrain developed by a network of **vertisols**. Vertisols are soils that shrink and swell according to water content. When dry, the soils develop a network of large, deep cracks resulting in a **fragmented** pattern along the landscape. ConVene takes inspiration from the variable nature of vertisols in a **sustainable, flexible** design that **shifts** to accommodate a co-working environment during the day and an event space at night.

Blackland Prairie Region

Diagram Studies of Soil Properties

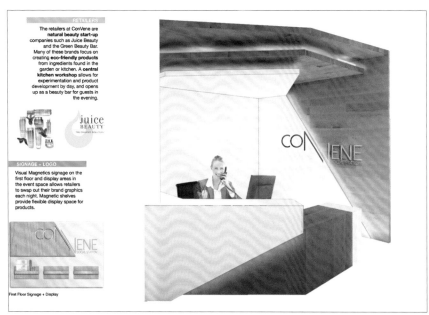

RETAILERS

The retailers at ConVene are **natural beauty start-up** companies such as Juice Beauty and the Green Beauty Bar. Many of these brands focus on creating **eco-friendly products** from ingredients found in the garden or kitchen. A **central kitchen workshop** allows for experimentation and product development by day, and opens up as a beauty bar for guests in the evening.

juice
BEAUTY

SIGNAGE + LOGO

Visual Magnetics signage on the first floor and display areas in the event space allows retailers to swap out their brand graphics each night. Magnetic shelves provide flexible display space for products.

First Floor Signage + Display

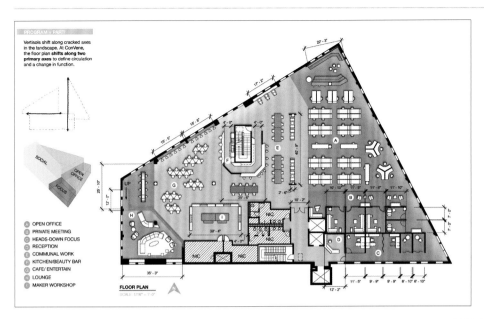

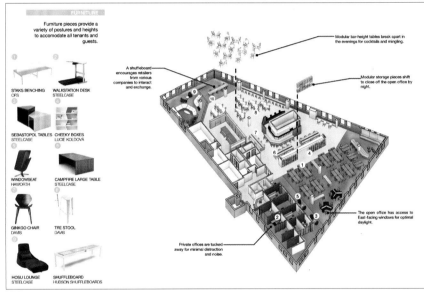

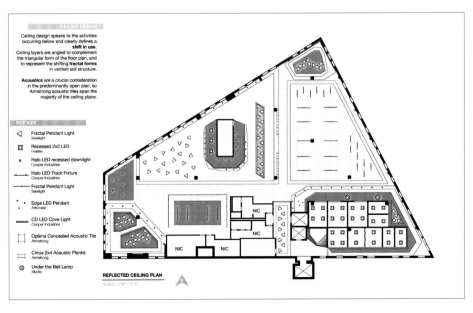

LIFE SAFETY + HVAC KEY

LIFE SAFETY + HVAC KEY

Ceiling Mounted Sprinkler ⊛

Plumbing supply Line —

Supply ⊠

Return ⊡

Ceiling Mounted Exit Sign ⊕

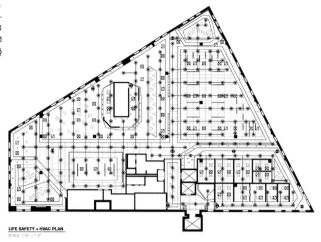

LIFE SAFETY + HVAC PLAN
SCALE: 1/16" = 1'-0"

LEED v4 for Interior Design and Construction
Checklist + Application

LOCATION + TRANSPORTATION

Access to Quality Transit:
• Lamar @ Munger - S - NS bus stop one block away.

• West End Train Station a five minute walk away.

Bicycle Facilities:
• Bike storage is provided near reception.

WATER EFFICIENCY

Indoor Water Use Reduction:
• Kohler Numi Duel-Flush Toilet.

• Moen STo Low Flow MotionSense™ Faucets.

Optimize Energy Performance:

• Occupancy sensors in offices and meeting rooms.

• All specified lighting fixtures use LEDs.

• Fisher and Paykel ActiveSmart™ Refrigerator with Energy Star award.

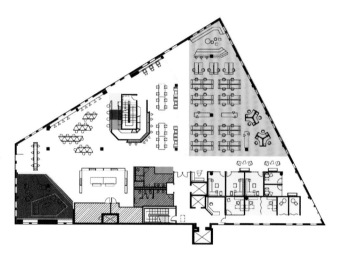

MATERIALS + RESOURCES

Storage and Collection of Recyclables:
• Steelcase Victor AWRF254836 4-opening recycling center in kitchen.

Building Product Disclosure and Optimization:
• Sourcing of Raw Materials- Terrazzo aggregate material sourced 200 miles away at Bilbrough Marble Co in Burnet, TX.

Material Ingredients and Environmental Product Declarations:
• Maharam Upholstery Greenguard Gold Certified and Rapidly Renewable Content Mr Credit 6.

• Staybull Hard Maple Recycled Wood Flooring

• Shaw Vantage Tile Carpet Cradle-to-Cradle® v2 Silver with EcoWorx® Backing.

INTERIOR ENVIRONMENTAL QUALITY

Low-Emitting Materials:
• Sherwin Williams ProMar® 200 Zero VOC Interior Latex Paint

Thermal Comfort:
•Steelcase Intelligent Divisio™ Screen displays time, date and temperature information.

Daylight:
• The open office has access to North-East-facing windows for optimal daylight. All enclosed offices are pulled away from the windowline and have glass curtain walls.

Acoustic Performance:
• EcoSorpt Acoustic Baffles in open office.

Ⓐ HARD MAPLE FLOORING
STAYBULL FLOORING

Ⓑ TERRAZZO FLOORING
BILBROUGH MARBLE, TEXAS

Ⓒ 2"x4" CLAY WALL TILE
FIRECLAY TILE

Ⓓ PROMAR 200 ZERO VOC
INTERIOR LATEX PAINT
SHERWIN WILLIAMS

Ⓔ FLOCK UPHOLSTERY
HIGHSEA
MAHARAM

Ⓕ DIVINA MILANGE UPHOLSTERY
920
MAHARAM

Ⓖ POSTIANO UPHOLSTERY
GREEN APPLE
ARCHITEX

Ⓗ COINCIDE UPHOLSTERY
CARIBBEAN
MAHARAM

Ⓘ MODE UPHOLSTERY
ODYSSEY
MAHARAM

Ⓙ DIVINA MILANGE UPHOLSTERY
154
MAHARAM

Ⓚ VANTAGE CARPET TILE
AZURE HEATHER
SHAW

THE CYCLE OF WORK

Work styles are represented by the different layers of vertisol soil which cycle from bottom to top. Ceiling planes are layered at varying heights according to the type of activity occurring below. Heads-down work has a low ceiling height while social, high-traffic areas are higher.

SOCIAL

OPEN WORK

HEADS-DOWN

COLLABORATE

Workspace shifts to become more active and social when traveling through the plan. Stadium seating in the North-East corner of the floor allows for casual collaboration at a variety of heights.

FitzFelt Draperies provide thermal comfort and acoustic control in the collaborative corner.

BuzziBalance and BuzziCubes create a playful environment and encourage movement.

FOCUS

The ceiling layers downward in the focus work zone of the office. Private meeting rooms allow for teams of 2-4 to collaborate without distraction.

The Muuto Under the Bell Lamp absorbs noise and defines informal meeting spots.

Nooks provide a quiet place to retreat to.

Visual Magnetics walls in closed collaboration rooms provide a writable surface for brainstorming.

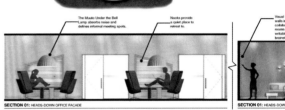

SECTION 01: HEADS-DOWN OFFICE FACADE
SCALE 1/4" = 1'-0"

SECTION 01: HEADS-DOWN OFFICE INTERIOR
SCALE 1/4" = 1'-0"

DISPLAY

In the evenings, the kitchen workshop becomes a beauty bar for retailers to display and share their new products.

PALETTE + FEEL

Pops of blue and green are consistent throughout the space and contrast warm golden hues in Maple finishes to create a split-complementary color scheme. Blue was originally derived from the blue hues found in vertisol soil where basalt rock minerals are leached from the soil. Green is culturally associated with "natural" products, and is found in the packaging for many of ConVene's retailers.

ENTERTAIN + LOUNGE

Both floor and ceiling **layer upward** to define the lounge space. Hosu lounge chairs and BuzziCubes are low to the ground and playful to encourage flexible seating arrangements. Window seats are carved into the walls to create intimate seating within the open area.

Design Development

Codes for Interior Finishes

As a part of the design process, students completed series of worksheets designed to keep both building code and design concept concerns in the forefront. The first worksheet (Table 7.4) generally considered the design concept and material selections for sustainability. See Table 7.1 for code requirements for interior finishes.

Another worksheet addressed the reflected ceiling plan and the need for sprinklers, exit signs, and lighting (including emergency lighting) (Table 7.5).

Table 7.4 Worksheet Material Palette and F, F & E Justifications

How do your materials and F, F & E selections meet sustainability guidelines? Why did you select what you selected? Include everything that shows up on your renderings and final project documents

Item	Location	Description	Manufacturer	Sustainability information	Rating? Possible LEED points?	Other Comments about finishes/ F, F & E (Justify the selections)
Ex. Flooring	Restroom	Rubber	Nora	PVC-free Halogen-free	Greenguard gold low VOC	Use with low-VOC adhesive

Table 7.5 Worksheet for Reflected Ceiling Plans and Life Safety

Sprinklers
- Ceiling mounted—spread 16 feet distribution in diameter
- Must be aligned—plumbing supply (water)

Exit Signs
- Visible from all occupied spaces
- At every change in direction
- Above each exit door

HVAC
- All spaces must have a supply and a return
- In large spaces, one supply every 200 square feet or so and one return for every 400 to 500 square feet
- If using exposed ceiling, you will see duct work connecting supplies and returns

Exposed Ceilings
- If you are using an exposed ceiling, you will see the underside of the structure above

Legends
- You must have a legend, and it needs to include information on the fixture and lamps you use in your space (use only LED or fluorescent); HID Metal halide (color corrected) is also a possible lamp type to use
- You should include exit signs, smoke detectors, supply and return, and ceiling finishes on your legend *and* all light fixtures

Dimensions
- RCPs should include ceiling heights of all ceilings, dropped soffits, and other design details
- Special features need to be dimensioned

Materials
- Materials should be indicated and differentiated

Other Life-Safety Items
- Smoke alarm in all corridors and open office spaces
- Fire alarm with visible strobe and sound in each enclosed space with multiple occupants

Design Office

The last project to be discussed in this chapter is a design office located in Los Angeles. In addition to meeting all codes and accessibility requirements, this project also used the WELL Building Standard.

PROJECT DESCRIPTION NEXT DESIGN OFFICE

Building Location & Description

Location

1150 S Olive Street
32nd floor
Los Angeles, CA 90015

Scope

Plan and design NEXT's new, top floor office space, measuring approximately 11,300 square feet. Do not include building core elements, such as restrooms, elevators, stairs, and utility rooms labeled NIC (Not in Contract) and shaded on the floorplan.

Program Requirements

Currently, there are thirty-five total NEXT employees. These employees are divided into three studios focused on Corporate, Education, and Healthcare Design.

Management

- Managing Director (1) – mobile worker – Uses laptop and docking station with dual monitors
- Studio Director (3) – mobile workers – One per studio; all use laptop and docking station with dual monitors
- Design Director (3) – mobile worker – One per studio; all use laptops and docking stations with dual monitors
- Marketing Director (1) – mobile worker – Uses laptop and docking station with dual monitors

Design Staff

- Designers (8) – All use CPU with dual monitors; one is a mobile worker with a laptop and docking station
- Project Managers (7) – All use laptop and docking station with dual monitors; one PM is a mobile worker
- Job Captains (6) – All use laptops and docking stations with dual monitors; two captains are mobile workers
- Intern (1) – Functions as the librarian and vendor contact; uses CPU with dual monitors

Administrative Staff

- Office Manager (1) – Uses CPU with dual monitors
- Project Coordinators (3) – One coordinator per studio; all use CPUs with dual monitors
- Receptionist (1) – Uses CPU with dual monitors

Extended Team

- CEO, COO, CFO, Finance team, Human Resources, and Information Technology – These individuals work from New York headquarters but occasionally visit branch offices and need touchdown workspace. Typical visits last one to two days.

Include five additional workspaces for NEXT's remote/mobile workers and interns. The NEXT Los Angeles team is projected to grow to forty-five total people by the end of this year. Your workplace design concept should have the flexibility to accommodate full capacity distributed through the range of settings.

Next Spaces/Program Requirements

Though not a formal part of the required settings in the program provided below, consideration should be made regarding places where colleagues cross paths throughout the day that naturally become hotspots for impromptu collaboration. Maximize real estate by supporting these informal interactions along circulation routes.

Reception

Quantity: 1

Space Allocation: Approximately 200–250 ft^2 (18.6–23.2 m^2)

Function: Provide an inspiring and welcoming space that communicates NEXT's culture and incorporates branding. Provide seating for two to four guests who typically wait for short periods of time. Occasionally, several groups of guests may arrive at the same time to meet with different design teams. A full-time receptionist will reside in this space to greet guests, offer drinks, answer phones, sign for packages, and complete light administrative work.

The receptionist has requested furniture that allows him/her the flexibility to sit or stand in the future space. The desk should have a modesty panel, a place for CPU, dual monitors, phone, printer, and storage for personal items. Ideally, the desk will hide most of the equipment from the visitor's view.

Lighting: Energy efficient, direct/indirect lighting recommended. Make fixture recommendations; reflected ceiling plan not required.

Furniture: Choose the most appropriate Steelcase Inc. product(s) for this space based on the client's vision and needs.

Construction: Consider Steelcase Inc. wall solutions in conjunction with traditional construction.

Design Library

Quantity: 1

Space Allocation: Approximately 300 ft^2 (27.9 m^2)

Function: NEXT has recently downsized their library and would like to maximize real estate in the new space. They will only keep items in the library that clients need to touch and feel—like carpet books, fabrics, laminates, wood, stone, etc. The library should include appropriate storage to hold loose samples, as well as current finish palettes for at least twenty projects at one time. NEXT has decided to eliminate code reference books, lighting catalogs, and furniture binders, as most of the updated information can be found online.

The library is typically managed by an intern or junior designer, so that these employees get exposure to the latest and greatest products while developing relationships with manufacturer representatives. Small, informal vendor presentations (up to four people) take place in the library, while larger, formal presentations take place in other areas of the office. Product representatives will also bring refreshments, so there should be a hospitality surface. Vendors like a space to display new products and typically leave presentation materials, brochures, physical samples, and even larger products like chairs and small tables. Designers may bring their clients to the library to select finishes, requiring large layout work surface and seating.

Lighting: Provide natural, fluorescent, and LED lighting so that designers can view samples under a variety of lighting conditions. Retail lighting solutions may also be considered for supplementing general lighting at product display. All fixtures should be energy efficient.

Make fixture recommendations; reflected ceiling plan not required.

Furniture: Choose the most appropriate Steelcase Inc. product(s) for this space based on the client's vision and needs.

Construction: Consider Steelcase Inc. wall solutions in conjunction with traditional construction.

Large Conference

Quantity: 1

Space Allocation: Seats 14+ people (Square footage not given to provide design flexibility)

Function: This space is used for large client presentations, formal vendor presentations, staff meetings, and project team meetings. The room should be flexible and large enough to add additional seating for up to ten or more people. Provide whiteboards, pin-up space, layout surface for finish presentations, and a hospitality counter. NEXT employees often collaborate with partners all over the world and need HDVC telepresence technology.

Lighting: Students should research the best lighting solutions for telepresence environments and make energy efficient fixture recommendations; reflected ceiling plan not required.

Furniture: Choose the most appropriate Steelcase Inc. product(s) for this space based on the client's vision and needs.

Construction: Consider Steelcase Inc. wall solutions. Acoustics must be taken into consideration.

BIM/VR/Training Room

Quantity: 1

Space Allocation: Seats 14+ people (Square footage not given to provide design flexibility)

Function: NEXT would like to design a new multipurpose room satisfying a variety of needs. In this room, they will collaborate with engineers, contractors, landscape architects, and other consultants—all using BIM (Building Information Modeling) programs to create buildings and interiors in three dimensions. The space should include technology for viewing digital content on a large scale, with multiple views. Technology must enable spontaneous and simultaneous sharing and content creation. NEXT has been using virtual reality headsets to present design ideas to their clients. This room should have capabilities to augment the virtual reality experience. Last, the space will also function as an educational/training environment and should contain whiteboards, pin-up space, and telepresence technology.

Lighting: Students should research the best lighting solutions for telepresence environments and make energy efficient fixture recommendations; reflected ceiling plan is not required.

Furniture: Choose the most appropriate Steelcase Inc. product(s) for this space based on the client's vision and needs.

Construction: Consider Steelcase Inc. wall solutions. Acoustics must be taken into consideration as well as flexibility for incorporating future technology.

Medium Conference

Quantity: 1

Space Allocation: Seats 6–8 people (Square footage not given to provide design flexibility)

Function: This space is used for smaller client presentations, informal vendor meetings, and project team meetings. Include whiteboards, pin-up space, layout surface for finish presentations, and telepresence technology.

Lighting: Students should research the best lighting solutions for telepresence environments and make energy efficient fixture recommendations; reflected ceiling plan is not required.

Furniture: Choose the most appropriate Steelcase Inc. product(s) for this space based on the client's vision and needs.

Construction: Consider Steelcase Inc. wall solutions. Acoustics must be taken into consideration.

Small Conference

Quantity: 2

Space Allocation: 100–150 ft^2 (9.3–13.9 m^2) each

Function: This space should seat two to four people. It will primarily be used for planned and impromptu project meetings and will occasionally function as a dedicated project room for a couple of days. The space should accommodate technology, whiteboards, pin-up space, and storage for finishes and tools. Include HDVC telepresence technology such that employees can connect with teammates and clients via WebEx conference calls.

Lighting: Energy efficient, direct/indirect lighting recommended. Make fixture recommendations; reflected ceiling plan not required.

Furniture: Choose the most appropriate Steelcase Inc. product(s) for this space based on the client's vision and needs.

Construction: Consider Steelcase Inc. wall solutions. Acoustics must be taken into consideration.

Phone/Quiet Rooms

Quantity: Minimum of 2

Space Allocation: 36–48 ft^2 (3.3–4.5 m^2) each

Function: NEXT wants to provide employees with spaces for private phone calls. The footprint is purposefully small to help ensure availability for short-duration use. Consider audio and visual privacy when designing this space—employees will prefer shielded privacy during stressful phone calls.

Lighting: Energy efficient, direct/indirect lighting recommended. Make fixture recommendations; reflected ceiling plan not required.

Furniture: Choose the most appropriate Steelcase Inc. product(s) for this space based on the client's vision and needs.

Construction: Consider Steelcase Inc. wall solutions. Acoustics must be taken into consideration.

Mother's Room/Relaxation Room
Quantity: 1

Space Allocation: 36–64 ft^2 (3.3–5.9 m^2)

Function: Consider making the space multipurpose for either a nursing mother or an employee who needs time to relax or rejuvenate. The room should minimize auditory distractions and must have visual privacy.

Lighting: Energy efficient, direct/indirect lighting recommended. Make fixture recommendations; reflected ceiling plan not required.

Furniture: Choose the most appropriate Steelcase Inc. product(s) for this space based on the client's vision and needs.

Construction: Consider Steelcase Inc. wall solutions. Acoustics must be taken into consideration.

Private Offices
Quantity: Minimum of 3

Space Allocation: 100–150 ft^2 (9.3–13.9 m^2) each

Function: NEXT would like to eliminate all owned/assigned private offices, making private space available to the entire staff. Consider making these spaces multipurpose and varying the design layout and furniture selection between rooms to maximize employee choice.

The managing director, studio directors, and design directors will use these rooms when additional privacy is required for working with HR and other leaders. Designers will use these spaces to focus by themselves or collaborate with one to two other teammates without disturbing others in the open office.

Lighting: Energy efficient direct/indirect lighting recommended. Make fixture recommendations; reflected ceiling plan not required.

Furniture: Choose the most appropriate Steelcase Inc. product(s) for this space based on the client's vision and needs.

Construction: Consider Steelcase Inc. wall solutions. Acoustics must be taken into consideration.

Open Office/Individual Work Areas
Quantity: 45

Space Allocation: Up to 48 ft^2 (4.5 m^2) each

Function: NEXT wants their future workspaces to be open, collaborative, and functional. They want to move to a free address system for their mobile workers, where spaces are not owned by these individuals, and they can select from the variety of workspaces provided in the program based on the work being performed at that time. Their former office had only one style of workstation that didn't suit everyone's preferences. Because employees have varying needs that constantly change, the new office must allow employees to shift seamlessly through the four modes of work (socializing, collaborating, focusing, learning).

A diversity of individual workspaces that vary in type and size is encouraged.

NEXT management has decided to provide height-adjustable work surfaces for all employees with fixed technology and to provide mobile workers with choices for alternative postures.

Designers have requested height-adjustable work surfaces. These should accommodate dual monitors and either a laptop or keyboard/CPU. A second work surface (either adjacent to or contiguous with the first) should accommodate a 30 inch by 42 inch drawing for reference when drafting by computer or by hand. Designers need access to storage for both large-size drawing sets (30" x 42") and half-size sets, bins to hold two to three finish palettes, and a place for personal storage (purse, bag, pens, notebook, etc.).

Designers collaborate often and invite their teammates to view their screen. They have requested additional shared layout spaces where they can flip through a large set of drawings as a team. Project managers primarily work on the phone and on laptops. They mostly use half-size drawing sets and don't often need access to finish palettes. Job captains alternate between the field, during project construction, and the office, where they are primarily drawings-focused. They use both full- and half-size drawings sets and keep bins of submittals at their desk.

Project coordinators perform administrative functions for the project team and don't keep drawings or finishes at their desk. They may have stacks of paper and folders but hope to become paperless in the future.

Managers (managing director, studio director, design director, and marketing director) don't need as much storage as their staff. They use laptops and split time between leading teams in the office and business development outside the office.

Lighting: Energy efficient direct/indirect lighting recommended. Supplement with individual task lighting. Fixture selections and a reflected ceiling plan is required (only one if broken into different areas on the floor plan).

Furniture: Choose the most appropriate Steelcase Inc. product(s) for this space based on the client's vision and needs. If panels are used, consider LEED requirements for day lighting and views from the seated position.

Construction: Walls may be used to delineate this work zone but no millwork materials should be used to divide individual work spaces. Consider Steelcase Inc. wall solutions vs. traditional construction wherever possible.

Pin-Up & Ideation Zone

Quantity: Minimum of 2 locations

Function: Pin-up and display spaces should be located throughout the office, with a minimum of two locations. These spaces not only show off work to potential clients but also expose the entire staff to projects that designers might be working on with other NEXT offices.

Employees are encouraged to share ideas, engage others to comment, and provide mentoring to each other. Display may be analog or digital—or both. The ideation zone can be incorporated into a larger space but does need to be branded and "customer friendly."

Lighting: Retail lighting solutions should be considered to supplement general lighting for appropriate product display. All should be energy efficient selections. Make fixture recommendations; reflected ceiling plan not required.

Furniture: Choose the most appropriate Steelcase Inc. product(s) for this space based on the client's vision and needs.

Construction: Consider Steelcase Inc. wall solutions in conjunction with traditional construction.

WorkCafe

Quantity: 1

Space Allocation: 750–1000 ft^2 (69.7–93 m^2)

Function: The WorkCafe allows employees to decompress and socialize at any time of day. As part of the NEXT culture, workers are encouraged to eat with others versus alone at one's desk. During nonpeak meal times, the café provides a place to host all-staff meetings, team building activities, large vendor presentations, parties, and events. Employees will also use the space for casual client meetings and as an alternative work place when they desire a change of scenery. Incorporate a wide range of settings to support individual focus work, socialization, collaboration, and rejuvenation. Provide a sink, refrigerator, microwave, coffee machine, storage, and adequate counter space for hospitality. Food preparation spaces are not needed for this project. Most events and meetings are catered from an outside vendor and brought up to the WorkCafe.

Lighting: A combination of lighting sources is recommended. All selections should be energy efficient. Fixture selections and reflected ceiling plan required.

Furniture: Choose the most appropriate Steelcase Inc. product(s) for this space based on the client's vision and needs.

Construction: Consider Steelcase Inc. wall solutions in conjunction with traditional construction.

Resource Center

Quantity: 1

Space Allocation: Approximately 200–250 ft^2 (18.6–23.2 m^2)

Function: The resource center serves as a copy/print, mail, and storage room. It contains (1) large scale plotter, (1) copier/printer, (1) desk top printer, mail boxes or trays, and adequate counter space. Work surface should be large enough to hold 30 inch by 42 inch drawings for collating into sets for clients, engineers, consultants, and to the city for permit. Storage is required for plotter paper, general office supplies, and marketing brochures. This is also the place where received packages are temporarily stored.

Lighting: Energy efficient, direct/indirect lighting recommended. Make fixture recommendations; reflected ceiling plan not required.

Furniture: Minimal furniture is required. Choose the most appropriate Steelcase Inc. product(s) for this space based on the client's vision and needs.

Construction: Traditional construction/millwork is suitable for this space but feel free to also consider Steelcase products used in conjunction with traditional construction.

Maker Space/Model Shop

Quantity: 1

Space Allocation: Approximately 200–250 ft^2 (18.6–23.2 m^2)

Function: NEXT would like to incorporate a creative studio space for designers to tinker and build physical objects and models to inform their design process. It promotes experimentation and prototyping. The space holds a 3D printer, belt sander, laser cutter, table saw, and various hand tools. Provide storage for raw materials and tools as well as display space for models and artifacts. Provide durable, flexible, mobile work surfaces.

Lighting: Energy efficient, direct/indirect lighting recommended. Make fixture recommendations; reflected ceiling plan not required.

Furniture: Minimal furniture is required. Choose the most appropriate Steelcase Inc. product(s) for this space based on the client's vision and needs. Consider Steelcase Education.

Construction: Traditional construction/millwork is suitable for this space but feel free to also consider Steelcase products used in conjunction with traditional construction.

Applying the Code

Programming

During the preliminary phase of the project, the maximum number of occupants was first calculated. As an 11,300 square foot space with a Business (B) use, the space for the design firm used an occupant load factor of 150 gross.

11,300 / 150 = 76 occupants maximum

Project One

The project example included here used the local concrete textile block houses designed by architect Frank Lloyd Wright as inspiration for this architecture and design firm's offices in Los Angeles. Using Froebel blocks as a source for how to layer and interconnect the various spaces in the office, the designer followed a process of design inspired by Wright. Modular furniture and abstracted geometric forms were used to organize the space along a strong central axis.

Once the preliminary occupant load had been calculated, the next set of concerns related to accessibility and egress. The designer first did preliminary plumbing calculations to make sure the existing restrooms satisfied the numbers required for this use. Assuming a 50/50 split of men and women, the plumbing fixture requirements were as follows: thirty-eight men and thirty-eight women (Table 7.6).

Based on occupancy classification Business (B), three water closets and two lavatories are required for men and women, respectively. The existing bathrooms provided in the building exceed this and are therefore adequate.

Using Section 1006 of the IBC, the number of exits required falls between occupant load of 1 to 500, and two exits are required (Table 1006.3.2). As a sprinklered space, the maximum travel distance is 300 feet according to Table 1017.2. (If it was not a sprinklered building, this maximum travel distance would be 200 feet.) (See Figures 7.55–7.62.)

Table 7.6 Plumbing Calculations

76 occupants
38 female/38 male

	WC	Lavatory
Male	1 per 25 first 50 (2 required)	1 per 40 first 80
	1 per 50 = 1 additional required (3 total)	2 required
Female	1 per 25 first 50 (2 required)	1 per 40 first 80
	1 per 50 = 1 additional required (3 total)	2 required

Water Fountain 1 per 100 = 1 required
Service Sink = 1 required

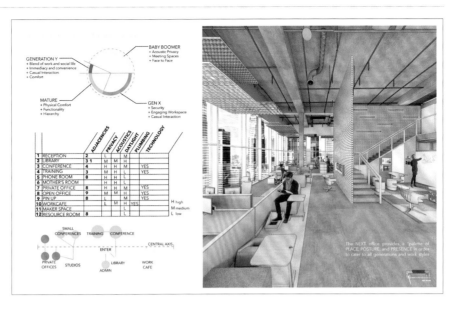

Figures 7.55–7.62
Schematic design
proposal

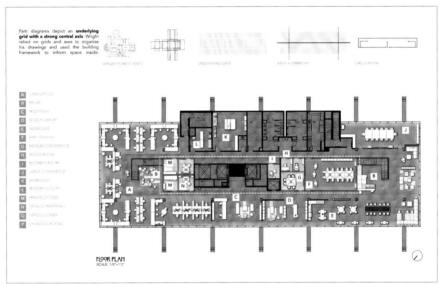

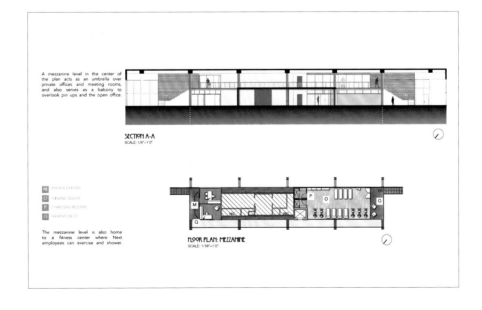

Figures 7.55–7.62
Schematic
design proposal
(continued)

PALETTES OF POSTURE AND OF PATTERN

Classic forms take on a new life in bold colors and contemporary finishes.

Ergonomics and comfort are key in a resilient workplace. The Gesture office chair provides ample back support, and lounge settings throughout the office give designers relief.

Pops of yellow in upholstery and the Holy Day table tie in Next's brand. The Campfire Big Table is perfect for designers to spread out large drawings.

Frank Lloyd Wright often looked to nature for inspiration in his design process. **Analogous colors, green and yellow**, brighten up the predominantly concrete interior. **Abstracted nature** is represented through patterns in finish materials.

Layered lighting in the design library allows designers to play with color temperature and intensity; and nearby windows provide ample daylight.

EXISTING CONCRETE FLOORING

LIGHT MAPLE WOOD AND LAMINATE

DESIGNTEX UPHOLSTERY

FLOR CARPET TILES

A RESILIENT WORKSPACE: THE WELL BUILDING STANDARD

AIR: Optimize and achieve indoor air quality. Strategies include removal of airborne contaminants, prevention and purification.
+ Close off copy and resource room
+ VOC reduction in paint, flooring, furniture and finishing
+ Entryway walk-off system

WATER: Optimize water quality while promoting accessibility.
+ Access to drinking fountains from all spaces

NOURISHMENT: Encourage healthy eating habits.
+ Availability and promotion of fruits and vegetables
+ Proper hand washing facilities with paper towels and liquid soap
+ Nutrition information and signage in the cafe

LIGHT: Minimize disruption to the body's circadian rhythm; improve energy, mood and productivity.
+ Circadian lighting fixtures in private offices and conference
+ Glare reduction and shade controls
+ Window access for at least 75% of occupants

FITNESS: Utilize building design technologies and knowledge-based strategies to encourage physical activity.
+ Wide stair tread for ease of use
+ Artwork and asthetic appeal in stair design
+ Fitness programs
+ Shower and changing facility

COMFORT: Create an indoor environment that is distraction-free, productive, and soothing.
+ Comply with ADA standards for accessible design
+ An acoustic plan that separates loud and quiet zones
+ Sound barriers and acoustic materials
+ Separate work areas from cafe food smells

MIND: Support mental and emotional health.
+ Consider the unique needs of the user
+ Celebration of place and culture
+ Access to privacy
+ Ceiling height proportional to room dimensions
+ Wayfinding elements to provide spatial familiarity

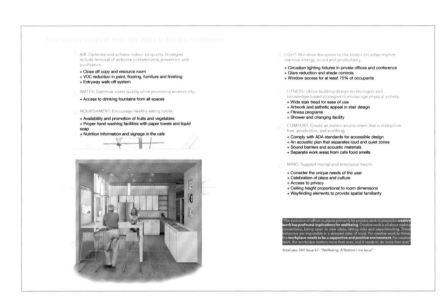

"The evolution of offices as places primarily for process work to places for **creative work has profound implications for wellbeing.** Creative work is all about making connections, being open to new ideas, taking risks and experimenting. These behaviors are impossible in a stressed state of mind. For creative work to thrive, the **workplace needs to be a supportive and positive environment.** For creative work, the workplace matters more than ever, and it needs to do more than ever."

Steelcase 360 Issue 67: "Wellbeing: A Bottom Line Issue"

FLEXIBILITY + MODULARITY

Just as Froebel Blocks allow students to tinker and stack, modular furniture in the Next office encourages designers to play with space and rearrange. Turnstone Campfire Lounge chairs become pieces of a puzzle when stacked on top of a platform.

White boards, cork, and magnetic slats give unlimited opportunities for collaboration and presentations.

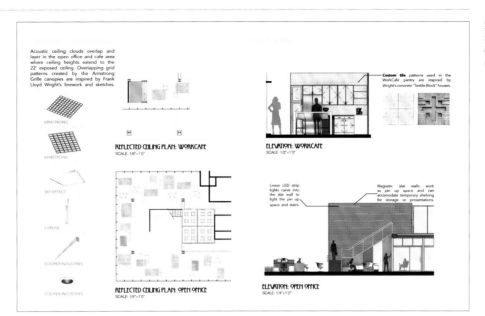

Acoustic ceiling clouds overlap and layer in the open office and cafe area where ceiling heights extend to the 22' exposed ceiling. Overlapping grid patterns created by the Armstrong Grille canopies are inspired by Frank Lloyd Wright's linework and sketches.

ARMSTRONG

ARMSTRONG

SKY EFFECT

EUREKA

COOPER INDUSTRIES

COOPER INDUSTRIES

REFLECTED CEILING PLAN: WORKCAFE
SCALE: 1/8"=1'0"

REFLECTED CEILING PLAN: OPEN OFFICE
SCALE: 1/8"=1'0"

Custom tile patterns used in the WorkCafe pantry are inspired by Wright's concrete "Textile Block" houses.

ELEVATION: WORKCAFE
SCALE: 1/2"=1'0"

Linear LED strip lights carve into the slat wall to light the pin up space and stairs.

Magnetic slat walls work as pin up space and can accomodate temporary shelving for storage or presentations.

ELEVATION: OPEN OFFICE
SCALE: 1/4"=1'0"

Figures 7.55–7.62
Schematic
design proposal
(continued)

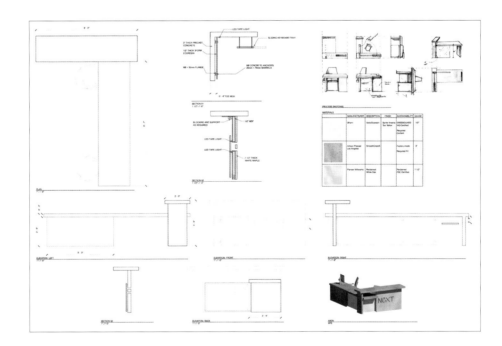

WELL Building Standard

Having satisfied the basic code and accessibility requirements during schematic design, the project also sought to meet WELL Building Standard requirements. In this particular project, that was accomplished in several ways.

Air

The Air Concept was fulfilled by closing off the copy and resource rooms to reduce indoor air toxins; low- and no-VOC paints, flooring, and furniture selections were made; and an entry walk-off system was incorporated into the project in the lobby.

Water

Drinking fountains provided access to water from all spaces. Further, water testing confirmed compliance with all required contaminant levels.

Nourishment

Fresh fruits and vegetables served in the café provided healthy choices to building occupants. Proper handwashing facilities and paper towels with liquid soap provided additional compliance features with WELL. Nutritional information posted in the café allowed users to make good food choices.

Light

At least 75 percent of occupants had access to windows that were also equipped with glare reduction and shade controls. Circadian rhythm lighting provided in private office and conference areas provided occupants with a lighting solution that promotes better sleep and improved productivity.

Fitness

Building users had access to a wide stair that incorporated artwork as well as access to a fitness program, showers, and changing areas.

Comfort

The entire space meets ADA standards. An acoustical plan established loud and quiet zones in the office with sound barriers and acoustical materials. Work areas are separated from the smells of the café.

Mind

The space design celebrates the local place and culture. Wayfinding elements help to make the space easy to navigate and users have access to privacy. A mother room allows nursing mothers to have privacy.

Conclusions

This chapter demonstrates how to integrate the WELL Building Standard into an office space, while also meeting code requirements and following the design concept. The WELL Standard was originally developed for office spaces and fits well with that function, but it can also be applied to all other commercial project types.

Assignments

1. Review the WELL Building Standard. How might this inform a design project?

2. What are the overlaps between code requirements for interior finishes and rating systems such as LEED, Green Globes, or WELL?

> **Key Terms**
>
> WELL Concepts: Air, Water, Nourishment, Comfort, Mind, Light, Fitness

8

Case Studies:
Designs for Living

Learning Objectives:

After reading this chapter and doing the exercises, students will be able to

- Go through the basic process of identifying occupancy type and determining construction type, occupant loads, and required exits
- Evaluate travel distance, number of exits required, and common path of travel and other egress requirements
- Apply universal design principles to the interior
- Place grab bars in appropriate locations (or provide blocking for their future installation)
- Apply sustainability criteria

Introduction

This chapter will provide a series of case studies for living facilities, including a high-end residential application and a small, universally designed apartment. Residential design is covered under both the International Building Code (IBC) and the **International Residential Code (IRC)**. Typically detached, single-family homes fall under the IRC, while most other types of living quarters are covered under the IBC.

The R group in the IBC refers to all portions of buildings dedicate to sleeping purposes, which are not defined under Group I: Institutional or the IRC (Table 8.1).

The type of sleeping conditions covered under Group I: Institutional are found in Table 4.2.

Under all conditions, the occupancy factor for R is 200 gross. For Institutional (I), with overnight occupancy, the factor is 120 gross.

Table 8.1 Section 310.1 Residential R, IBC 2018

Residential Group R includes, among others, the use of a building or structure, or a portion thereof, for sleeping purposes when not classified as an Institutional Group I or when not regulated by the *International Residential Code*.

International Residential Code

The IRC applies to all one- and two-family detached dwellings and townhouses that are not more than three stories. Exceptions include live-work units and owner-occupied lodging houses with five or fewer guestrooms—both of which can fall under the IRC if equipped with a fire sprinkler system in accordance with Section P2904, IRC 2018.

According to the IRC, all residences must have a means of egress and continuous unobstructed path opening directly into a public way or yard or court that opens to a public way. The door must have a clear width of at least 32 inches, when open 90 degrees, and a height of 78 inches (IRC 2018 Chapter 3).

Every sleeping room must have an operable emergency escape opening with a net clear opening of not less than 5.7 square feet. The net clear height cannot be less than 24 inches and the net clear width must be at least 20 inches. (IRC 2018 Chapter 3).

Smoke alarms must be located in all sleeping rooms and outside of each separate sleeping area. These devices must be interconnected such that when one alarm is activated, all other alarms are activated as well (IRC 2018 Chapter 3). An automatic fire sprinkler system is required in all residential buildings, but some states have amended the IRC to not require fire sprinklers for single-family and duplex homes.

If the dwelling unit is more than one story, the stairway must be 36 inches wide and designed so that there is not less than 27 inches clear between handrails if they are installed on both sides. The clear headroom required is 6 feet, 8 inches, and the riser and tread relationships are maximum riser height 7 and 3/4 inches, with a minimum tread width of 10 inches. This information should always be reviewed with the local code enforcement authority, as it may be different in various locations. Open risers are permitted as long as a 4-inch-diameter sphere cannot pass through the opening. The handrail height required is between 34 and 38 inches. (Some states have amended the stair riser and tread requirements.)

Scope of the Problem— Project 1: High-End Residential

Located in the multistory Astor building overlooking Central Park in New York City, this project involved the design of a high-end residence for an art collector that entertained extensively. The art played an important role in the design of the apartment that included servants' quarters and an art gallery. Graceful living was inspired by the paintings of Degas for this collector's residence.

As a multistory building over three stories, this project fell under the IBC. The construction type for this brick bearing-wall building with a slate roof was Type II.

Programming and Schematic Design

The use group for this project was **Residential (R)**. Using Table 8.1, the specific classification was R-2. Chapter 12 of the IBC dictated certain minimum requirements for interior space planning, including that all interior rooms have to be at least 7 feet wide (except for kitchens), with ceiling heights of at least 7 feet, 6 inches (except kitchens, bathrooms, storage areas, and laundry rooms). In addition, every dwelling unit had to have at least one room that was more than 120 square feet, and all other rooms had to have a net area of not less than 70 square feet (except kitchens). A 3-foot clear path is required for kitchens.

The square footage of the apartment was 4,224. Dividing this number by 200, the possible number of occupants was twenty-two. This covered the owner's family, as well as the household helpers.

The preliminary phase of the project involved the creation of an adjacency matrix (Figure 8.1) and zoning, block, and bubble diagrams (Figures 8.2–8.4).

Additional diagramming separated loud and quiet areas as well as public and private zones (Figure 8.5).

A computerized plan was reviewed for clearance, elevator access, and circulation (Figure 8.6).

Alterations were made to integrate changes (Figure 8.7).

Revisions were reflected in a partially rendered floor plan (Figure 8.8).

The final design integrated all required codes as well as the Degas artwork (Figures 8.9–8.11).

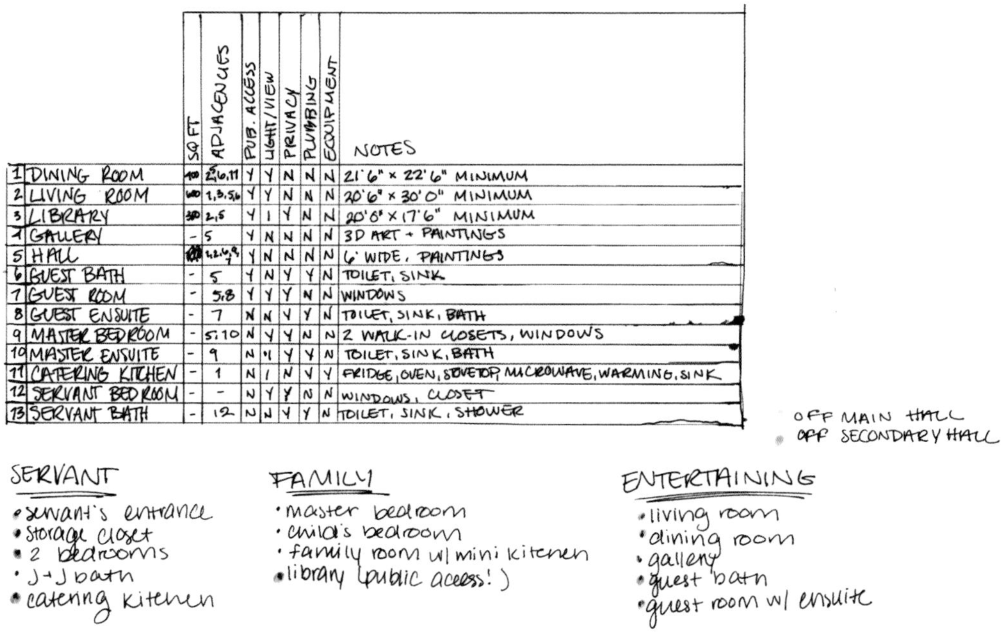

Figure 8.1
Adjacency matrix

Figure 8.2
Zoning diagram

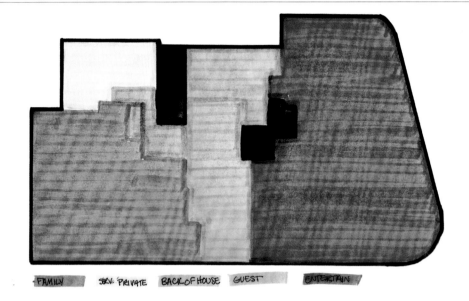

FAMILY   SERV. PRIVATE   BACK OF HOUSE   GUEST   ENTERTAIN

Figure 8.3
Block diagram

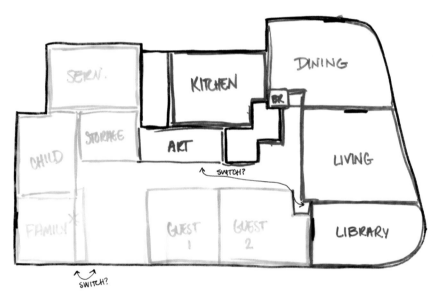

Figure 8.4
Bubble diagram

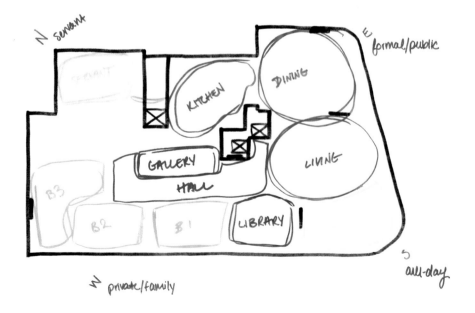

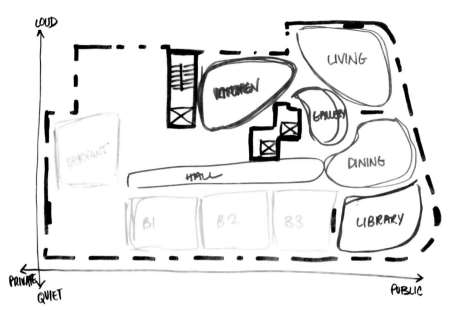

Figure 8.5
Diagram showing loud to quiet areas and public versus private

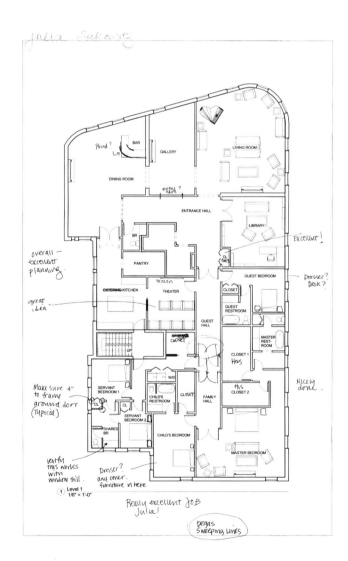

Figure 8.6
Computer plan 1

Figure 8.7
Rendered floor plan

Guests enter the spacious **entrance hall**, where they can view some of the client's collection of Degas paintings as they walk to the dining room, living room, or library.

The L-shaping **dining room** includes a long, dramatic dining table on the long end and a large bar on the short end, where guests can walk through into the gallery space.

The **gallery** features seven Degas paintings as well as two sculptures, all featuring ballerinas. The colors in this room were kept minimal in order to draw attention to the art on display.

The expansive **living room** allows for multiple seating arrangements that are symmetrical within themselves, mimicking the furniture of Degas' time.

The **library** features a large executive desk as well as a seating area and, of course, walls filled with books. This is a more "private" public space, with double doors that allow the room to be separated from the other public areas.

The **guest room** features its own closet and private restroom for guests to use during overnight visits.

The **theater**, placed off of the guest hall, allows for a more intimate, informal gathering with quick access to the kitchen for popcorn and snacks.

The **master bedroom** features a dramatic king size bed and a seating area in front of a gracious fireplace. An en-suite master bathroom and two oversized closets are available beyond the main bedroom space.

The **child's bedroom** is a more expansive version of the guest bedroom.

The **servant and back-of-house areas** are divided by the servant's entrance. On one side are the bedrooms with a shared bathroom, as well as the family's storage space and laundry closet, easily accessible to the family. On the opposite side is the catering kitchen, allowing hourly employees to quickly enter the space they will most likely be working in. The catering kitchen features a counter with barstools for quick meals, an large storage pantry, and quick access to the dining room through double-action doors.

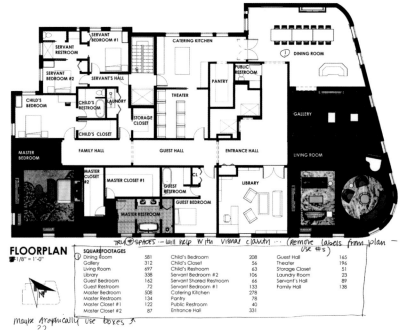

FLOORPLAN
1/8" = 1'-0"

TRU(#)SPACES - will help with visual clarity ... (remove labels from plan -- use #'s)

SQUARE FOOTAGES

Dining Room	581	Child's Bedroom	208	Guest Hall	165
Gallery	312	Child's Closet	56	Theater	196
Living Room	697	Child's Restroom	63	Storage Closet	51
Library	338	Servant Bedroom #2	106	Laundry Room	23
Guest Bedroom	162	Servant Shared Restroom	66	Servant's Hall	89
Guest Restroom	72	Servant Bedroom #1	133	Family Hall	138
Master Bedroom	508	Catering Kitchen	278		
Master Restroom	134	Pantry	78		
Master Closet #1	122	Public Restroom	40		
Master Closet #2	87	Entrance Hall	331		

(This page a bit dense)

Maybe graphically use boxes ??

Figure 8.8
Final floor plan

Guests enter the spacious **entrance hall**, where they can view some of the client's collection of Degas paintings.

The L-shaping **dining room** includes a long, dramatic dining table and a large bar. Guests can walk through into the gallery space.

The **gallery** features seven Degas paintings and two sculptures, all featuring ballerinas. The colors in this room were kept minimal in order to draw attention to the art on display.

The expansive **living room** allows for multiple seating arrangements that are symmetrical within themselves, mimicking the furniture of Degas' time.

The **library** features a large executive desk as well as a seating area and, of course, walls filled with books. This is a more "private" public space, with double doors that allow the room to be separated from the other public areas.

The **theater**, placed off of the guest hall, allows for a more intimate, informal gathering with quick access to the kitchen for popcorn and snacks.

The **master bedroom** features a dramatic king size bed and a seating area in front of a gracious fireplace. An en-suite master bathroom and two oversized closets are available beyond the main bedroom space.

The **servant and back-of-house areas** are divided by the servant's entrance. On one side are the bedrooms with a shared bathroom, the family's storage space and laundry closet, easily accessible to the family. On the opposite side is the catering kitchen, allowing hourly employees to quickly enter the space they will most likely be working in. The catering kitchen features a counter with barstools for quick meals, a large storage pantry, and quick access to the dining room.

FLOOR PLAN
1/8" = 1'-0"

SQUARE FOOTAGES

1. Dining Room	581	11. Child's Bedroom	208	21. Guest Hall	165
2. Gallery	312	12. Child's Closet	56	22. Theater	196
3. Living Room	697	13. Child's Restroom	63	23. Storage Closet	51
4. Library	338	14. Servant Bedroom #2	106	24. Laundry Room	23
5. Guest Bedroom	162	15. Servant Shared Restroom	66	25. Servant's Hall	89
6. Guest Restroom	72	16. Servant Bedroom #1	133	26. Family Hall	138
7. Master Bedroom	508	17. Catering Kitchen	278		
8. Master Restroom	134	18. Pantry	78		
9. Master Closet #1	122	19. Public Restroom	40		
10. Master Closet #2	87	20. Entrance Hall	331		

LIVING ROOM (CIRCULAR)

LIVING ROOM

DEGAS GALLERY

Figures 8.9–8.11
Interior rendered
views showing
living room views
and gallery

Scope of the Problem— Project 2: Live-Work Space with Universal Design Apartment

This project was a design for a small apartment located in Jackson Hole, Wyoming, in a live-work building. As such, it fell under the R-2 use group. A universal design approach ensured equal experiences for people of all sizes and abilities. The building construction type for this project is Type II. The walls are steel with brick cladding, and the roof is also steel framed.

As a residential project in a commercial building, a one-hour fire separation was required between the commercial business use and the residential apartment (Table 8.2).

In accordance with Chapter 12 of the IBC, all interior rooms have to be at least 7 feet wide (except for kitchens) with ceiling heights of at least 7 feet, 6 inches (except kitchens, bathrooms, storage areas, and laundry rooms). In addition, every dwelling unit had to have at least one room that was more than 120 square feet, and all other rooms have to have a net area of not less than 70 square feet (except kitchens).

The square footage of the apartment was 990 square feet. Dividing by 200 gross (the occupancy factor) resulted in a total possible occupant load of five people (Figure 8.12).

The plan shows that the apartment is accessible and meets all minimum code room sizes and square footages. Two exits are provided for the main living spaces. All sleeping rooms contain windows large enough for egress.

> **IBC 2018 TABLE 508.4: REQUIRED SEPARATION OF OCCUPANCIES**
>
> Table 508.4 has retained the same number in the IBC 2018 and no changes have been made to the table except the addition of footnote f.
>
> (Formerly IBC 2015 Table 508.4)

Table 8.2 IBC 2018 Table 508.4: Required Separation of Occupancies

GENERAL BUILDING HEIGHTS AND AREAS

TABLE 508.4
REQUIRED SEPARATION OF OCCUPANCIES (HOURS)[f]

OCCUPANCY	A, E		I-1[a], I-3, I-4		I-2		R[a]		F-2, S-2[b], U		B[e], F-1, M, S-1		H-1		H-2		H-3, H-4		H-5	
	S	NS	S	NS	S	NS	S	NS	S	NS	S	NS	S	NS	S	NS	S	NS	S	NS
A, E	N	N	1	2	2	NP	1	2	N	1	1	2	NP	NP	3	4	2	3	2	NP
I-1[a], I-3, I-4	—	—	N	N	2	NP	1	NP	1	2	1	2	NP	NP	3	NP	2	NP	2	NP
I-2	—	—	—	—	N	N	2	NP	2	NP	2	NP	NP	NP	3	NP	2	NP	2	NP
R[a]	—	—	—	—	—	—	N	N	1[c]	2[c]	1	2	NP	NP	3	NP	2	NP	2	NP
F-2, S-2[b], U	—	—	—	—	—	—	—	—	N	N	1	2	NP	NP	3	4	2	3	2	NP
B[e], F-1, M, S-1	—	—	—	—	—	—	—	—	—	—	N	N	NP	NP	2	3	1	2	1	NP
H-1	—	—	—	—	—	—	—	—	—	—	—	—	N	NP	NP	NP	NP	NP	NP	NP
H-2	—	—	—	—	—	—	—	—	—	—	—	—	—	—	N	NP	1	NP	1	NP
H-3, H-4	—	—	—	—	—	—	—	—	—	—	—	—	—	—	—	—	1[d]	NP	1	NP
H-5	—	—	—	—	—	—	—	—	—	—	—	—	—	—	—	—	—	—	N	NP

S = Buildings equipped throughout with an automatic sprinkler system installed in accordance with Section 903.3.1.1.

NS = Buildings not equipped throughout with an automatic sprinkler system installed in accordance with Section 903.3.1.1.

N = No separation requirement.

NP = Not Permitted.

a. See Section 420.

b. The required separation from areas used only for private or pleasure vehicles shall be reduced by 1 hour but not to less than 1 hour.

c. See Section 406.3.2.

d. Separation is not required between occupancies of the same classification.

e. See Section 422.2 for ambulatory care facilities.

f. Occupancy separations that serve to define fire area limits established in Chapter 9 for requiring fire protection systems shall also comply with Section 707.3.10 and Table 707.3.10 in accordance with Section 901.7.

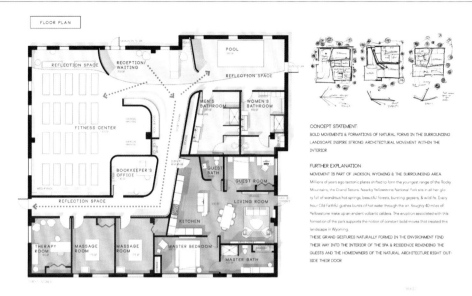

Figure 8.12
Floor plan of apartment

The Principles of Universal Design

Universal design asks designers to consider all people, regardless of size, age, or ability, in designing space. Since everyone is different, this really means designing for all people who could potentially use a space. Universal design considerations are important because they make spaces easy to use and occupy for all people to the greatest extent possible. Although universal design is most often discussed with regard to residential environments, the principles can (and should) apply to all interiors.

PRINCIPLE ONE: Equitable Use

The design is useful and marketable to people with diverse abilities.

PRINCIPLE TWO: Flexibility in Use

The design accommodates a wide range of individual preferences and abilities.

PRINCIPLE THREE: Simple and Intuitive Use

Use of the design is easy to understand, regardless of the user's experience, knowledge, language skills, or current concentration level.

PRINCIPLE FOUR: Perceptible Information

The design communicates necessary information effectively to the user, regardless of ambient conditions or the user's sensory abilities.

PRINCIPLE FIVE: Tolerance for Error

The design minimizes hazards and the adverse consequences of accidental or unintended actions.

PRINCIPLE SIX: Low Physical Effort

The design can be used efficiently and comfortably and with a minimum of fatigue.

PRINCIPLE SEVEN: Size and Space for Approach and Use

Appropriate size and space is provided for approach, reach, manipulation, and use regardless of user's body size, posture, or mobility.

Source: Copyright 1997, NC State University, The Center for Universal Design

Interior views show other universal design attributes of the space, including varying counter top heights, clear space below the sink and cooktop (when cabinet doors are retracted), and level-operated faucets (Figure 8.13).

The apartment design included sustainability features, including locally sourced FSC wood and stone, no-VOC paints, high efficiency Energy Star rated appliances, and automatic sensor faucets (Figures 8.14, 8.15).

Figure 8.13
Kitchen
perspective view

A LIVE EDGE WOOD SLAB
BUILT INTO THE KITCHEN
ISLAND ALLOWS FOOD
PREP ACCESSIBILITY AT A
LOWER HEIGHT

POLISHED BRASS PENDANT
LIGHTS ADD CONTRAST
TO THE WOOD SLATED
CEILINGS AND WHITE ASH
WOOD CABINETRY

THE CABINETRY OPENS
WITH A PUSH AND RE-
LEASE SYSTEM

KITCHEN

Figure 8.14
Details for kitchen
selections

KITCHEN

1 WOOD SLATED CEILING ELEMENT

2 LIGHT WHITE ASH WOOD

3 MONTCLAIR DANBY VEIN CUT STONE

4 GAGGENAU REFRIGERATION

5 GAGGENAU WALL MOUNTED OVEN

6 GAGGENAU GAS STOVE TOP

7 LIVE EDGE BUILT IN COUNTER TOP

Figure 8.15
Details for
bathroom
selections

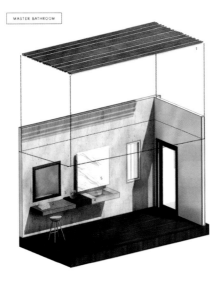

MASTER BATHROOM

1 WOOD SLATED CEILING ELEMENT
   THE WOOD SLATES DROP THE
   CEILING DOWN TO CREATE
   A WARM, SERENE BATHROOM
   EXPERIENCE

2 WARM WOOD
   VANITY COUNTER SURFACE
   SPACE

3 DARK WOOD SLAB
   CREATES CONTRAST AGAINST
   THE WARM WOOD AND SERVES
   AS A RESTING PLACE FOR
   SOAPS AND LOTIONS

4 POURED CONCRETE SINK
   THE POURED CONCRETE
   CREATES A ROUGH, RUSTIC
   TEXTURE AGAINST THE SOFT
   WOOD COUNTER SURFACES

5 WALL MOUNTED STONE SLAB
   SENSORS INDICATE MOVEMENT
   BELOW THE STONE ALLOWING A
   FREE FLOW OF WATER

Scope of the Problem— Project 3: Art Gallery with Universal Design Apartment

The third project example combines an art gallery on the first two floors with a gallery owner's apartment on the upper level. Dale Chihuly's glass work was used as the inspiration for the design. In addition to meeting accessibility standards and universal design, the designer integrated multiple sustainability features. The building construction for this project is Type II (brick bearing walls with an asphalt roof).

Accessibility and Universal Design

Both an elevator and a stair provide access to the third floor apartment. All paths of travel and bathrooms are barrier-free and include blocking in the walls for the installation of grab bars should they be needed by the occupants. All bathrooms include proper clearances for universal access. The kitchen design included multiple counter heights, as well as knee space below the cooktop and sink locations.

Sustainability

The materials selected for the apartment are locally sourced and sustainable, including SFC hardwood flooring, Crossville tile (with 20 percent recyclable material content), and nontoxic paints by Earthpaint. A wireless shading system (Lutron) allows lighting and temperature control, as well as maximum access to daylight and views (Figure 8.16).

A second example of this project was inspired by nature photography and sought to bring nature into the space. One way in which this was accomplished was through the use of skylights and abundant natural lighting. A porch garden provided an additional connection to the outdoors.

As with the previous project, the entire apartment was designed to meet universal design components (Figure 8.17).

The kitchen integrated multiple countertop and work-surface levels, a side-by-side refrigerator, and microwave and oven accessible to a person in a wheelchair (Figure 8.18).

In support of sustainability objectives for the project, all-natural materials and reclaimed lumber were used throughout (Figures 8.19, 8.20).

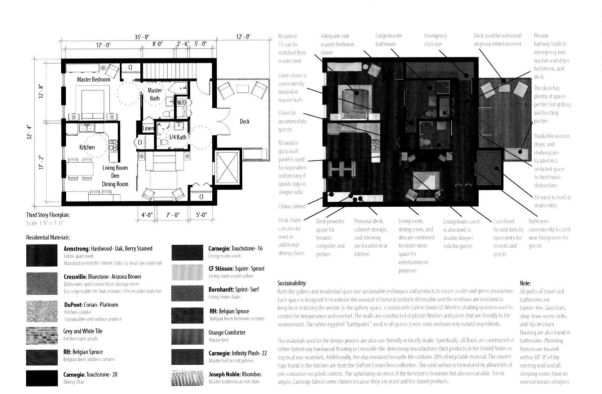

Figure 8.16
Plan showing universal design and sustainable materials

Figure 8.17
Plan showing
porch and
universal design

RESIDENTAL SPACE
LEVEL 3

1   main entrance
2   living room
3   dining room
4   kitchen
5   den & guest bedroom
6   master bedroom
7   master bathroom
8   3/4 bathroom
9   laundry & coat closet
10   porch garden
11   elevator entry

PORCH GARDEN

scale: 1/8" = 1'-0"

LEVEL 3: UNIVERSAL DESIGN FLOOR PLAN

scale: 1/8" = 1'-0"

LEVEL 3: RENDERED FLOOR PLAN

Bienenstock

Figure 8.18
Interior view

RESIDENTIAL SPACE LEVEL 3

Bienenstock

Figure 8.19
Interior view

LEEWARD SOFA

RECYCLED GLASS TILE   REFURBISHED WALNUT   WHITE QUARTZ

KITCHEN & DINING ROOM

Bienenstock

Figure 8.20
Interior view

REFURBISHED OAK   100% PURE COTTON   REFURBISHED MAPLE

HAVANA SLEEPER SOFA

DEN & GUEST ROOM

Bienenstock

Conclusions

The use of a universal design approach to design surpasses the minimum requirements for residential design in accordance with the building code. It helps to create larger spaces that can be used by all people of all sizes and abilities. Residential living areas can be found in three different areas of the code—IRC and the IBC either under R or I use groups—depending on the actual occupant and use of the space.

Key Terms

International Residential Code (IRC)
Residential (R) use group
Type II construction

Assignments

1. Compare the chapters contained within the IRC and the IBC. What are the primary differences in approach?

2. Make a listing of what types of residential projects fall under the IRC versus the IBC.

9

Case Study: Healthcare Design

Learning Objectives:

After reading this chapter and doing the exercises, students will be able to

- Go through the basic process of identifying occupancy type and determining construction type, occupant loads, and required exits
- Evaluate travel distance, number of exits required, and common path of travel
- Determine ADA clearances at all doors and fixtures
- Place grab bars in appropriate locations
- Calculate the number of plumbing fixtures needed for a specific use
- Identify appropriate strategies for fire separation between use groups

Introduction

The chapter includes three designs for healthcare facilities, including the broad issues related to codes and accessibility for healthcare. Healthcare projects fall into one of two categories under the International Building Code—either Business or Institutional. When the project is run as a business—for example an outpatient or ambulatory clinic—it falls under **Business (B)**. If the project is a part of a healthcare facility, such as a hospital, it is an **Institutional (I)** use (see Tables 9.1 and 9.2 and Figure 9.1).

Table 9.1 Section 308: Institutional Occupancy

Institutional	
I-1	Alcohol and drug centers
	Assisted-living facilities
	Congregate care facilities
	Group homes
	Halfway houses
	Residential board and care facilities
I-2	Foster care facilities
	Detoxification facilities
	Hospitals
	Nursing homes
	Psychiatric hospitals
I-3	Correctional centers
	Detention centers
	Jails
	Prerelease centers
	Prisons
	Reformatories

Table 9.2 Section 304: Business Occupancy

Business
Animal hospitals, kennels, and ponds
Banks
Barber and beauty shops
Car wash
Civil administration
Clinic—outpatient
Educational occupancies above twelfth grade
Laboratories—testing and research
Motor vehicle showrooms
Post offices
Print shops
Professional services
Radio and television stations
Training and skill development

Scope of the Problem—Project 1

The first project consisted of a 16,000 square foot clinic for AIDS patients located in Durban, South Africa. The building construction is Type I with noncombustible construction for the exterior walls and roof. Construction techniques in this part of South Africa consist primarily of concrete block wall construction and steel with poured concrete roof construction. The premise of the project was to create a community and educational environment where locals would feel welcome and not stigmatized because of their illness. A café and gym on the first floor invited people to the facility, with more private treatment rooms located on the second floor. The symbolism found in native beadwork provided the inspiration for the conceptual approach. South Africa does not use the ICC codes, so this was a project funded by a US entity, which required the IBC be used.

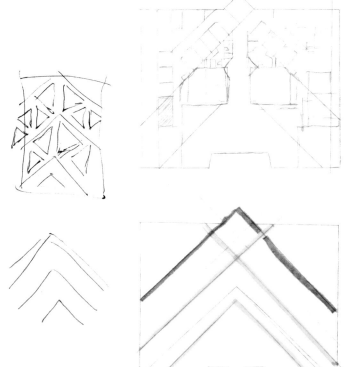

Figure 9.1
Concept and parti diagram

Applying the Code

Programming Phase

During programming, the student gathered overall information about the occupancy group and healthcare guidelines for the project. As an ambulatory clinic, the applicable use group was Business (B). The first floor contained 9,717 square feet resulting in approximately ninety-eight possible occupants (Figure 9.2).

9,717 / 150 gross occupant factor = 64.78 occupants or 65 people.

For maximum floor area allowances per occupant, please refer to Table 4.2 and its accompanying Box 4.1, which summarizes the primary changes to the table.

Schematic Design Phase

During schematic design, actual space-by-space calculations were completed, and plumbing fixture totals were assessed. During the early schematic process, the designer decided to allot much of the first floor to a café space and gymnasium area, with classrooms and a yoga studio to support the design concept of well-being for the patients and as a way to draw people into the facility. These changes resulted in the use group change to Assembly and a subsequent increase in allowable occupants (Figures 9.3–9.5).

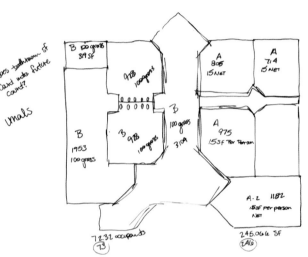

Figure 9.2
Programming occupancy calculations

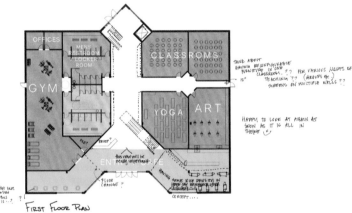

Figure 9.3
Schematic floor plans

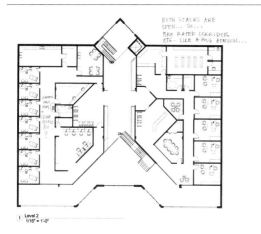

Figure 9.4
Schematic floor plans with code calculations

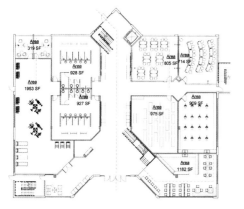

Figure 9.5
Schematic floor plans with code corrections

Scope of the Problem—Project 2

A cardiac health clinic provided the second example. Connected to an existing hospital complex in Melbourne, the heart wellness clinic served the four phases of heart healthcare. The construction type for this project was a concrete frame and wall as well as concrete roof and floor, which is Type I. Although Melbourne, Australia, uses its own buildings codes, a US entity funded this project and required use of the IBC.

Programming

Conceptually, the three floors of the project were dedicated to heart, health, and wellness and the three phases of healthcare delivery: education, rehabilitation, and assisted rehabilitation. The concept was to make a facility that felt welcoming and comfortable so that cardiac patients would not feel intimidated or afraid following a life-altering cardiac event (Figures 9.6–9.9).

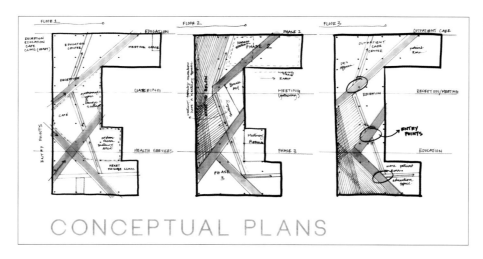

Figures 9.6–9.9
Schematic diagrams for design approach

CONCEPTUAL PLANS

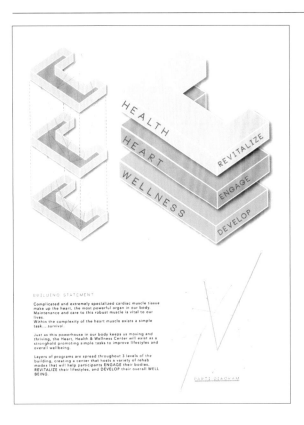

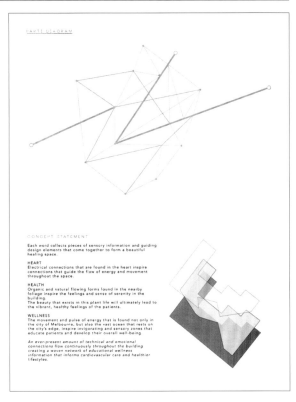

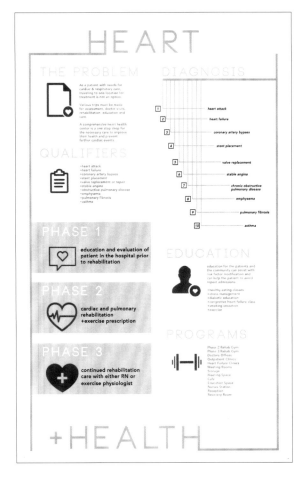

Schematic Design

An integral part of the project was how to connect the three levels while allowing for visual connections and differing functions. A series of three-dimensional explorations resulted in connecting bridges that would encourage walking between the floors, although elevators were also provided (Figures 9.10–9.12).

The floor plans that resulted needed considerable study for building code compliance (Figure 9.13).

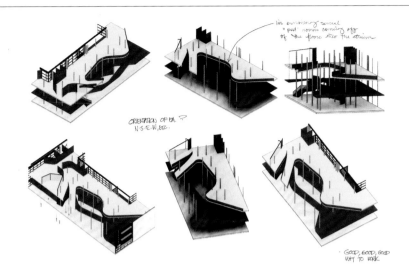

Figures 9.10 and 9.11
Three-dimensional exploration of connections between floors

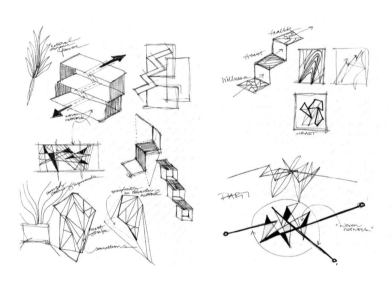

Figure 9.12
Exploration of connections between floors

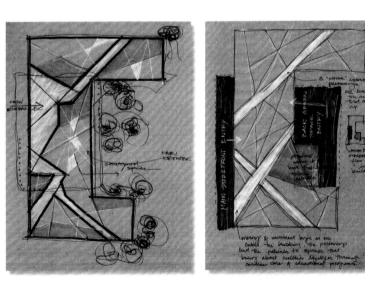

PROCESS SKETCHES

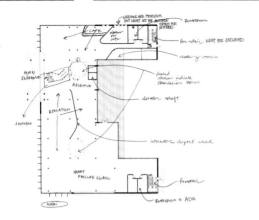

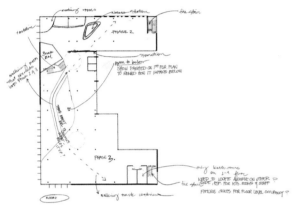

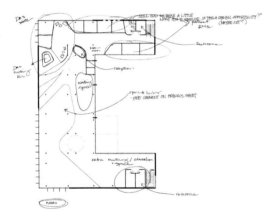

Figure 9.13
Preliminary floor
plans with code
markups

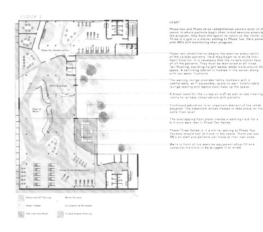

Figure 9.14
Design
development
revised plans

Design Development

The design development plan integrated corrections of the potential code problems of the schematic plan (Figure 9.14).

The resulting interiors show a clean and welcoming space with easy wayfinding for reduced stress and cleanable, hygienic surfaces (Figures 9.15–9.22).

Figures 9.15–9.22
Interior perspectives

Figures 9.15–9.22
Interior perspectives *(continued)*

Construction Documents

A limited set of construction documents was completed for this project. Included in this was a set of egress plans with travel distances and exits for each floor (Figures 9.23–9.25).

Interior Finishes

As an ambulatory clinic, the project was classified as a Business (B) use. As such the interior finishes for the project were in accordance with Table 803.13 on interior walls and ceiling finishes required by occupancy (Table 9.3).

As a sprinklered building in Group B, all interior exit stairways and ramps and exit passageways had to be Class B, while enclosed spaces could be Class C. The actual finishes selected were inspired by the landscape surrounding location in Melbourne. Sustainability was a key factor in the final selections that includes a white IceStone recycled glass, a blue sea glass tile, and white ceramic subway tiles. Sustainable fabrics were treated with Crypton for a healthcare installation. Since the three floors are open to one another, the space has to be treated as an atrium. As such, the travel distance through the atrium cannot exceed 200 feet, and it must be sprinklered.

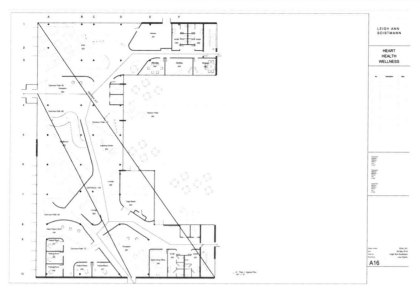

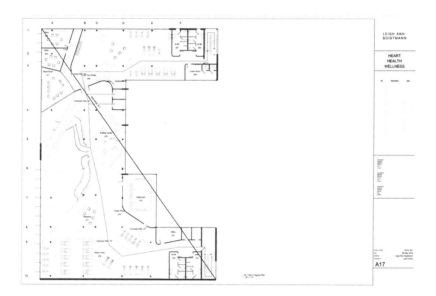

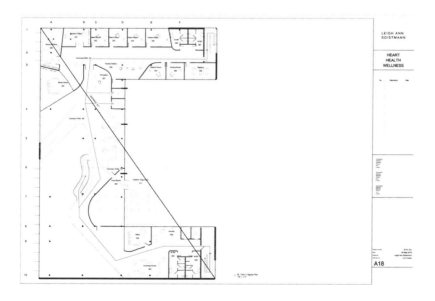

Figures 9.23–9.25
Egress plans all three floors

Table 9.3 IBC 2018 Table 803.13: Interior Finishes

TABLE 803.13
INTERIOR WALL AND CEILING FINISH REQUIREMENTS BY OCCUPANCY[k]

GROUP	SPRINKLERED[l]			NONSPRINKLERED		
	Interior exit stairways and ramps and exit passageways[a, b]	Corridors and enclosure for exit access stairways and ramps	Rooms and enclosed spaces[c]	Interior exit stairways and ramps and exit passageways[a, b]	Corridors and enclosure for exit access stairways and ramps	Rooms and enclosed spaces[c]
A-1 & A-2	B	B	C	A	A[d]	B[e]
A-3[f], A-4, A-5	B	B	C	A	A[d]	C
B, E, M, R-1	B	C[m]	C	A	B	C
R-4	B	C	C	A	B	B
F	C	C	C	B	C	C
H	B	B	C[g]	A	A	B
I-1	B	C	C	A	B	B
I-2	B	B	B[h, i]	A	A	B
I-3	A	A[j]	C	A	A	B
I-4	B	B	B[h, i]	A	A	B
R-2	C	C	C	B	B	C
R-3	C	C	C	C	C	C
S	C	C	C	B	B	C
U	No restrictions			No restrictions		

For SI: 1 inch = 25.4 mm, 1 square foot = 0.0929 m².
a. Class C interior finish materials shall be permitted for wainscotting or paneling of not more than 1,000 square feet of applied surface area in the grade lobby where applied directly to a noncombustible base or over furring strips applied to a noncombustible base and fireblocked as required by Section 803.15.1.
b. In other than Group I-3 occupancies in buildings less than three stories above grade plane, Class B interior finish for nonsprinklered buildings and Class C interior finish for sprinklered buildings shall be permitted in interior exit stairways and ramps.
c. Requirements for rooms and enclosed spaces shall be based on spaces enclosed by partitions. Where a fire-resistance rating is required for structural elements, the enclosing partitions shall extend from the floor to the ceiling. Partitions that do not comply with this shall be considered to be enclosing spaces and the rooms or spaces on both sides shall be considered to be one room or space. In determining the applicable requirements for rooms and enclosed spaces, the specific occupancy thereof shall be the governing factor regardless of the group classification of the building or structure.
d. Lobby areas in Group A-1, A-2 and A-3 occupancies shall be not less than Class B materials.
e. Class C interior finish materials shall be permitted in places of assembly with an occupant load of 300 persons or less.
f. For places of religious worship, wood used for ornamental purposes, trusses, paneling or chancel furnishing shall be permitted.
g. Class B material is required where the building exceeds two stories.
h. Class C interior finish materials shall be permitted in administrative spaces.
i. Class C interior finish materials shall be permitted in rooms with a capacity of four persons or less.
j. Class B materials shall be permitted as wainscotting extending not more than 48 inches above the finished floor in corridors and exit access stairways and ramps.
k. Finish materials as provided for in other sections of this code.
l. Applies when protected by an automatic sprinkler system installed in accordance with Section 903.3.1.1 or 903.3.1.2.
m. Corridors in ambulatory care facilities shall be provided with Class A or B materials.

IBC 2018 TABLE 803.13: INTERIOR FINISHES

Table 803.11 in the IBC 2015 had been replaced by Table 803.13 in the IBC 2018. Note that "m" has been added in the 2018 IBC, stating that corridors in ambulatory care facilities shall be provided with Class A or B materials.

(Formerly Interior Finishes from IBC 2015 Table 803.11)

Scope of the Problem—Project 3

The third project example was for a pediatric wing of a hospital. The pink dike flower found in Australia inspired the central concept. Using biophilic design principles, the student integrated nature into the project, providing indoor and outdoor connections. The construction type for this project was also Type I (Figure 9.26).

Programming

During the initial project programming phase, the use group was identified as Institutional (I). As a primarily outpatient facility, overnight patients were located on the second floor of the hospital, with the first floor dedicated to exam rooms and doctor offices.

Schematic Design

As a part of the schematic design process, exit routes and fire separations were established, as well as restrooms (Figures 9.27, 9.28).

Additional work was done to determine how the interior spaces would be developed and articulated consistent with the original concept. A significant component impacting the space planning was the required hallway width. In accordance with Table 1020.2 of the IBC, the required corridor width for facilities serving stretcher traffic is 72 inches, and for those with bed movement, I-2, the required width is 96 inches (see Table 9.4). This far exceeds the typical width of 44 inches, and therefore it required additional square footage allotted to circulation. Dead-end corridors are limited to 20 feet in length, with some exceptions noted in Section 1020.4 (Figure 9.29).

The triangulated shape was then integrated into the three-dimensional spatial concepts (Figure 9.30).

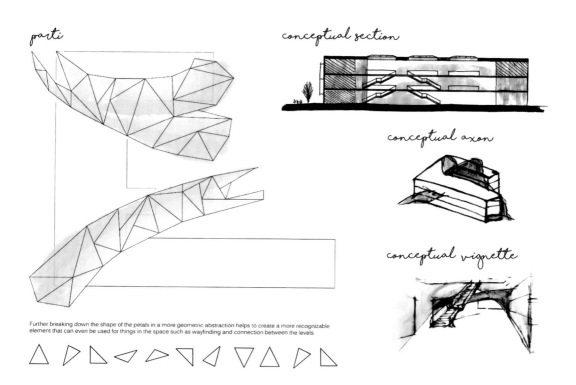

parti

conceptual section

conceptual axon

conceptual vignette

Further breaking down the shape of the petals in a more geometric abstraction helps to create a more recognizable element that can even be used for things in the space such as wayfinding and connection between the levels.

Figure 9.26
Conceptual sketches

Figures 9.27 and 9.28
Schematic plans with code markups

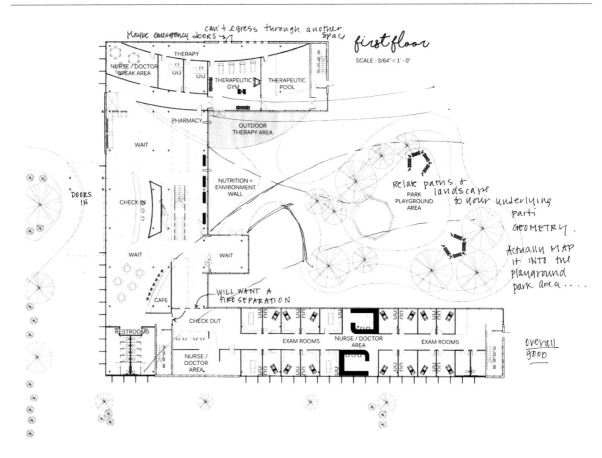

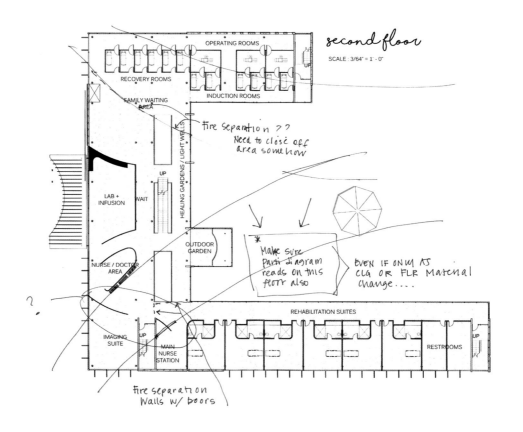

Table 9.4 IBC 2018 Table 1020.2: Corridor Widths

TABLE 1020.2
MINIMUM CORRIDOR WIDTH

OCCUPANCY	MINIMUM WIDTH (inches)
Any facility not listed in this table	44
Access to and utilization of mechanical, plumbing or electrical systems or equipment	24
With an occupant load of less than 50	36
Within a *dwelling unit*	36
In Group E with a *corridor* having an occupant load of 100 or more	72
In *corridors* and areas serving stretcher traffic in *ambulatory care facilities*	72
Group I-2 in areas where required for bed movement	96

For SI: 1 inch = 25.4 mm.

IBC 2018 TABLE 1020.2 CORRIDOR WIDTHS

Table 1020.2 has retained the same number. The only change is to the wording on the next to the last entry. The IBC 2018 now says "In *corridors* and areas serving stretcher traffic in *ambulatory care facilities*."

(Formerly IBC 2015 Table 1020.2 Corridor Widths)

Figure 9.29
Additional conceptual work

Figure 9.30
Three-dimensional integration of triangulated shape

Design Development

The final design concepts integrate code markups and final conceptual work to create an interior that is consistent with the design concept (Figures 9.31, 9.32).

Construction Documents

A limited set of construction documents included egress plans, showing travel distances and occupancy loads, as well as the design for ADA-compliant bathroom elevations (Figures 9.33–9.35).

In addition finish selections for particular spaces were also included, showing their sustainability criteria in support of LEED points. **Greenguard** certification was cited, as was WaterSense for the water closet selection. Greenguard provides certification for low-emitting products that contribute to healthy indoor air quality. They have recently added a LEED v.4 toolkit to their website. **WaterSense** is a US Environmental Protection Agency program that identifies plumbing fixtures that reduce water usage. The WaterSense label identifies products that are third-party certified to save water (Figures 9.36–9.38).

Figure 9.31
Final plan and RCP

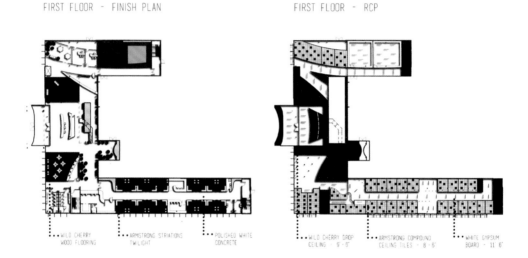

FIRST FLOOR - FINISH PLAN

FIRST FLOOR - RCP

Figure 9.32
Three-dimensional view of atrium

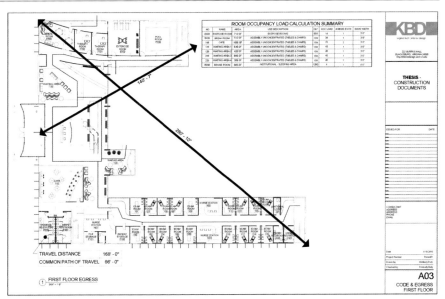

Figure 9.33
Egress plan first
floor

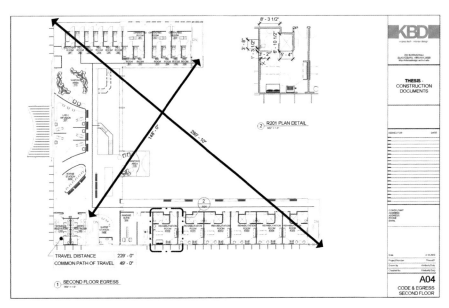

Figure 9.34
Egress plans
second floor

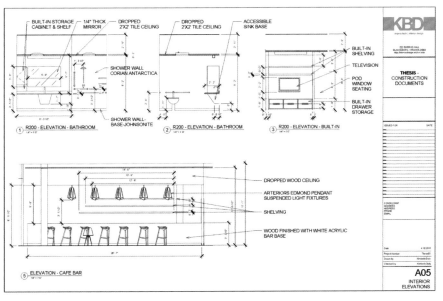

Figure 9.35
ADA elevations for
restrooms

**Figures
9.36–9.38**
Finishes and F, F
& E for various
spaces in the
project showing
sustainability
criteria met

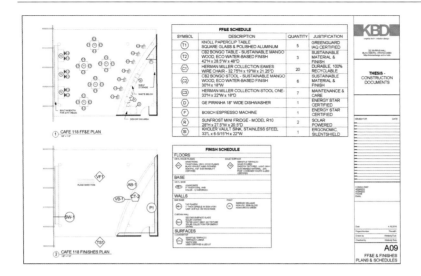

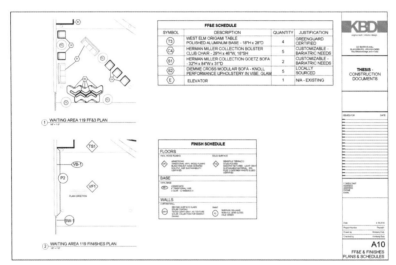

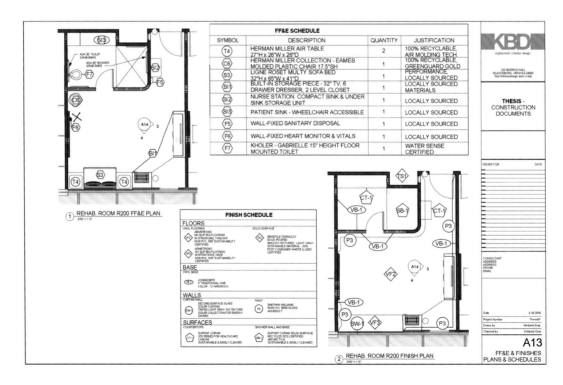

Conclusions

Healthcare projects are some of the most technical and highly regulated of the space types. In addition to building codes, the spaces will need to be accessible and meet the **Facility Guidelines Institute's (FGI)** guidelines for healthcare facilities. There are two sets of guidelines: *Guidelines for Design and Construction of Hospitals and Outpatient Facilities* and *Guidelines for Design and Construction of Residential Health, Care, and Support Facilities*. FGI guidelines are constantly updated to reflect the needs of the healthcare environment. The guidelines are divided into four sections: Part 1 addresses hospital and outpatient facilities; Part 2 provides guidance for inpatient care facilities; Part 3 also deals with outpatient facilities; and Part 4 includes ANSI/ASHE/ASHRAE Standards 170-2013.

The standards cover a variety of topics, including acoustic design, sustainable design, wayfinding design, bariatric considerations, and disaster preparation provisions. Various types of healthcare units are addressed, including areas for nurses, patients, patient support, and public and administrative use. The guidelines provide square footage allotments for different care types and support spaces, and they are an invaluable resource throughout the design process.

The relationship between **noise** (unwanted sound) and health has been well established in many studies. Thus the importance of proper acoustics in a healthcare facility is directly related to patient well-being. Noise can lead to stress that in turn can slow the healing process. **Wayfinding** in a healthcare facility is also related to stress and well-being. Healthcare environments are often experienced during times of increased stress caused by illness or other factors. The ability to clearly navigate a healthcare facility can assist in reducing or at least not increasing this stress level. Wayfinding refers to the visual cues provided in an environment to allow people to understand the interior environment and find where they need to go. This can be done through clear design planning as well as maps, signage, directions, and other visual communication. The use of landmarks by which people can reference where they are and where they are going is one example.

Bariatric design is an integral and critical part of healthcare facilities. Excess weight can lead to health problems, such as type 2 diabetes, heart disease, cancer, and increased blood pressure. As such, healthcare facilities must accommodate bariatric patients. The Centers for Disease Control has indicated that over one-third of adults in the United States are obese. Bariatric design includes the integration of furniture and fixtures that can accommodate the obese. According to *Healthcare Design Magazine*, bariatric concerns can be accommodated in three basic ways: the route (wider hallways and doorways, as well as access routes), constructability (including ceiling lifts, grab bars, and toilets), and making it feel seamless. It is critical to make all patients feel at ease without singling out anyone.

> **Key Terms**
> bariatric design
> Business (B) use group
> Facility Guidelines Institute (FGI)
> Greenguard
> Institutional (I) use group
> noise
> WaterSense
> wayfinding

Assignments

1. Find some local examples of healthcare environments. Which use group do they belong to? Why?
2. What are the various corridor widths for healthcare facilities? How do you know which one to use where?
3. Visit a healthcare facility. What do you notice about the interior? What concerns do you have as a designer? How might you improve the facility?
4. Why is wayfinding important in a healthcare facility? What might you do to make it easier for visitors and patients?

Resources

For LEED v.4 toolkit on the Greenguard website: greenguard.org/en/index.aspx
For links to WaterSense retailers: https://www.epa.gov/watersense/product-search
For FGI guidelines available to purchase: http://www.fgiguidelines.org/
For information on obesity from the CDC: https://www.cdc.gov/obesity/data/adult.html
For information about considerations in creating bariatric spaces:
http://www.healthcaredesignmagazine.com/architecture/3-design-considerations-bariatric-spaces/

10

Case Study: Mixed Use

Learning Objectives:

After reading this chapter and doing the exercises, students will be able to

- Go through the basic process of identifying occupancy type and determining construction type, occupant loads, and required exits
- Evaluate travel distance, number of exits required, and common path of travel
- Determine ADA clearances at all doors and fixtures
- Place grab bars in appropriate locations
- Calculate the number of plumbing fixtures needed for a specific use
- Identify appropriate strategies for fire separation between use groups

Introduction

The four case studies contained within this chapter are for mixed-use occupancies. For the first three projects, a four-story brick warehouse was developed for a variety of uses. The first project converts the warehouse into a small café on the first floor with spaces for the homeless on the upper levels, including shelter spaces, job development areas, and other services. The second project contains a women and children's shelter. The third project converts the warehouse into a high-end restaurant and boutique hotel. The brick warehouse with concrete columns, floors, and roof is of Type I construction.

Scope of the Problem

The A. D. German brick warehouse (Figure 10.1) used for this project was designed between 1914 and 1917 by Frank Lloyd Wright and is located in Richland Center, Wisconsin, a small town with a Main Street community within which the warehouse is situated. The building is listed on the National Register of Historic Places and should not be altered on the exterior in any way on the two street-front facades. For the A. D. German Warehouse project, the students came up with their own program for the project.

Figure 10.1
Exterior A. D.
German
Warehouse
building

Project 1: Homeless Shelter

The concept behind this project was "stronger together." The building designer seeks to combine community cohesion with social need in Richland Center by providing a building where local needs can be addressed. Specifically, the building was designed to house a restaurant on the first floor and homeless shelter on the upper three levels.

Programming Phase

During the programming phase, sun studies were conducted to determine how daylight would impact the building throughout different times of the day and year. Overall code research was conducted as to possible use groups. As a shelter for the homeless, and the use group **Residential (R)** would apply, and the entire building would require a sprinkler system. Travel distances and other overall concerns were also addressed. This was the first attempt at understanding how codes might impact the project design (Figure 10.2).

Using the concept as a springboard, the designer studied overall parti and form studies for the building. These led to a preliminary parti (Figures 10.3–10.6).

Figure 10.2
Code research
summary

BUILDING CODE SUMMARY

OCCUPANCY GROUP

Floor 1 - Restaurant/Cafe - **A2**
Floor 2 - Gallery - **A3**
Floor 3 & 4 - Residences - **R2**

WHEELCHAIR SPACES IN AN ASSEMBLY SPACE

Floor 1 - R2
170 seats - 5 spaces

OCCUPANCY LOADS
*4233 SF per floor

Restaurant - Kitchen (40%).......................2540 SF - 169 Occupants
Gallery + Classroom - Storage (30%)........3000 SF - 600 Occupants
Residences + Lounge Spaces....................4233 SF - 21 Occupants

Total..........790 Occupants

RESTROOMS

Floor 1 - 5 stalls each, 1 lavatory
Floor 2 - 5 male, 10 female, 1 lavatory
Floor 3 & 4 - 1 per residence

EGRESS

Restaurant - 2 exits
Gallery - 3 exits
Residences - 2 exits

MINIMUM EGRESS CORRIDOR WIDTH

ASSEMBLY
44" wide

RESIDENTIAL
36" wide

SPECIAL EQUIPMENT

Water fountains - 1 per 500 ft.
Assembly floors

Service sinks - 1 per Assembly
floor

TRAVEL DISTANCE
*Building is sprinklered
ASSEMBLY
75 feet travel

RESIDENTIAL
50 feet travel
35

Figure 10.3
Concept studies

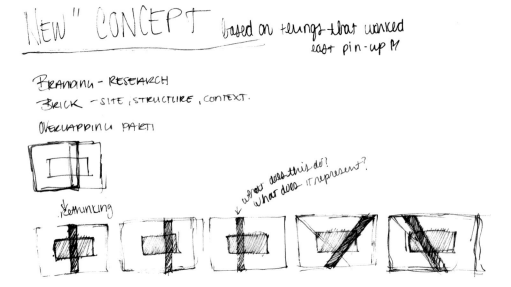

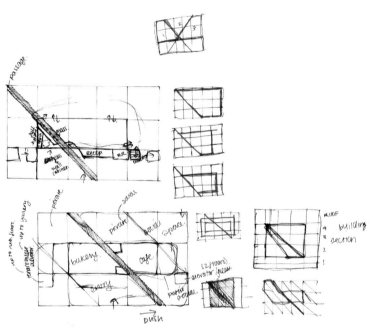

Figure 10.4
Form studies/parti
diagram

Figure 10.5
Hybrid parti/
blocking diagram

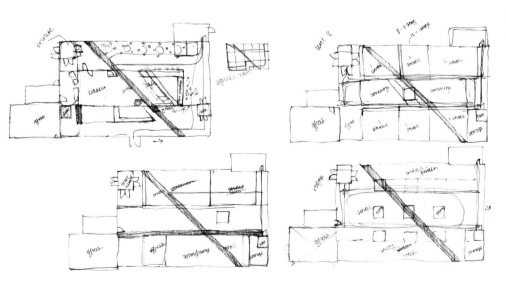

Figure 10.6
Preliminary hybrid
plan/parti diagram

Schematic Design Phase

During schematic design, a series of floor plan solutions explored possible ways to solve the design problem. Using the parti diagram as a basis combined with a series of adjacency bubble diagrams, preliminary floor plans were developed (Figures 10.7, 10.8).

Once a finalized parti diagram represented the concept, the original floor plans under consideration were revised (Figures 10.9–10.11).

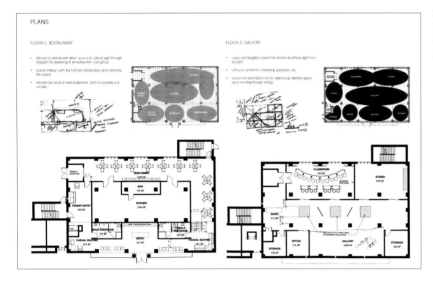

Figure 10.7
Preliminary hybrid plan/parti diagram

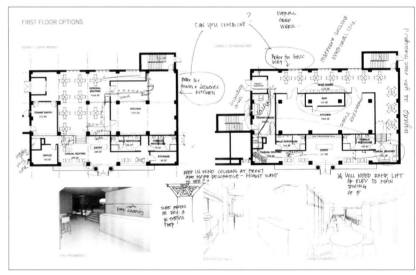

Figure 10.8
Bubble diagrams

Figure 10.9
Parti

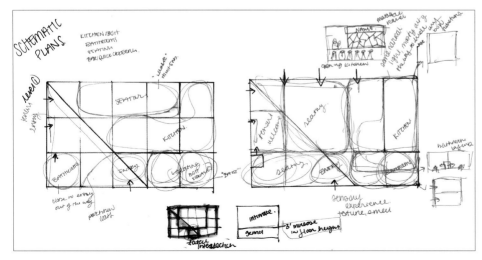

BUBBLE DIAGRAMS: RESTAURANT, FLOOR 1

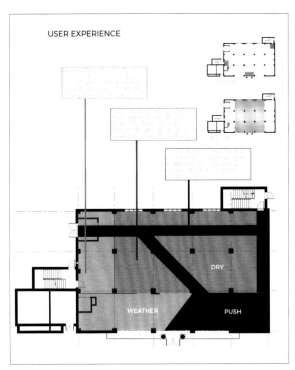

The revised plans reflect the diagonal movement evident in the parti diagram. As the plans were being developed to follow the parti, they also included several code and ADA problems (Figures 10.12–10.14).

Another round of revisions was explored in three dimensions (Figure 10.15).

Design Development

During design development, a complete code check was conducted to review the final schematic design direction. As materials were selected and egress routes were refined, another set of plan revisions was completed (Figures 10.16, 10.17).

The final design development plans reflect all necessary corrections to the plans for accessibility and egress. The code check includes information on occupancy, egress routes, fire ratings and accessibility. The drawings show how continual revisions had to be completed to fulfill the promise of the design concept and also meet pertinent codes and guidelines (Figures 10.18–10.23).

**Figures 10.12–
10.14**
Preliminary plans
with diagonals
and code problems

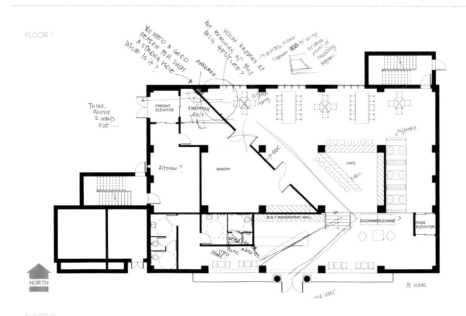

FLOOR 1

FLOOR 2

FLOORS 3 & 4

Figure 10.15
Revised plans

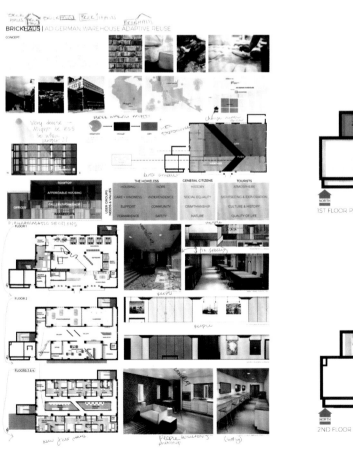

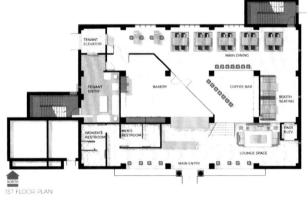

Figures 10.18–10.20
Code check drawings

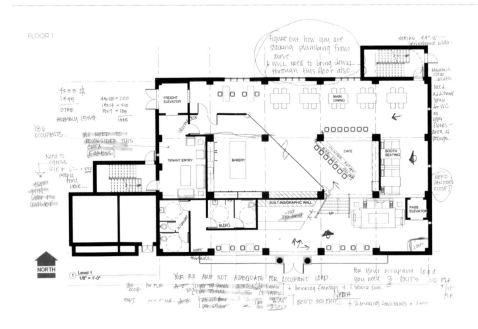

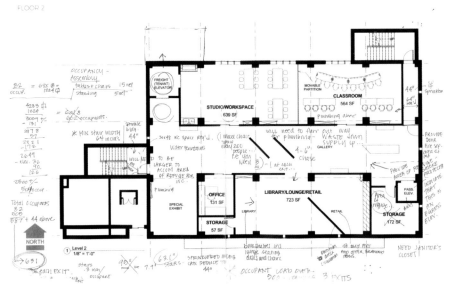

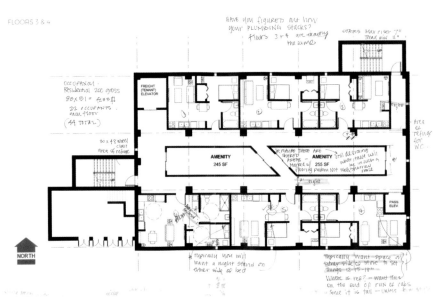

Figures 10.21–10.23
Final design
development drawings

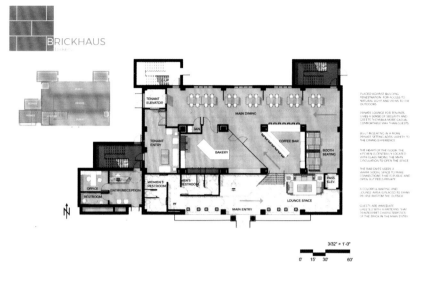

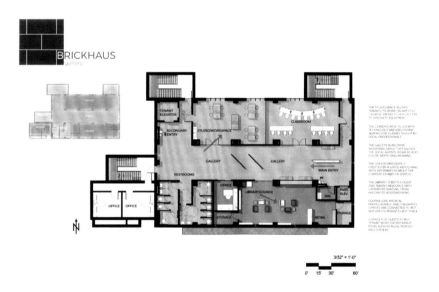

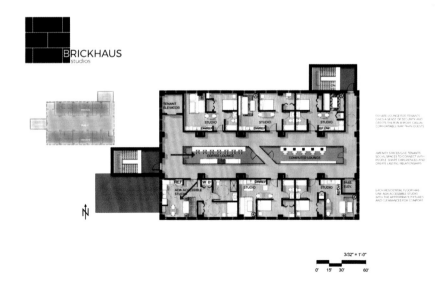

Construction Documents

A partial set of construction documents was completed and included a room occupancy calculation table, a plan with travel distance, and the common path of travel (Figures 10.24, 10.25).

The floor plan for an accessible studio apartment was also included in the set. Finishes and material notations referenced sustainability criteria (Figures 10.26, 10.27).

Figure 10.24
Room occupancy table

ROOM OCCUPANCY LOAD CALCULATION SUMMARY

Number	Name	Area	Use Description	OLF	Occupancy	Required Exits	Required Width	Level
101	ENTRY/RECEPTION	614 SF	WAITING AREAS	15 GROSS	40	1	3' - 0"	Level 1
102	LOUNGE/WAITING	331 SF	WAITING AREAS	15 GROSS	22	1	3' - 0"	Level 1
103	DINING	293 SF	ASSEMBLY, UNCONCENTRATED	15 NET	19	1	3' - 0"	Level 1
104	BAR/CAFE	231 SF	ASSEMBLY, UNCONCENTRATED	15 NET	15	1	3' - 0"	Level 1
105	MAIN DINING	1160 SF	ASSEMBLY, UNCONCENTRATED	15 NET	77	2	3' - 0"	Level 1
106	HALL	254 SF	UNOCCUPIED	0	0	0	3' - 0"	Level 1
107	BAKERY	494 SF	KITCHENS, COMMERCIAL	200 GROSS	2	1	3' - 0"	Level 1
108	TENANT ENTRY	335 SF	WAITING AREAS	15 GROSS	22	1	3' - 0"	Level 1
109	MEN'S	66 SF	UNOCCUPIED	0	0	0	3' - 0"	Level 1
110	WOMEN'S	71 SF	UNOCCUPIED	0	0	0	3' - 0"	Level 1
111	RECEPTION	192 SF	WAITING AREAS	15 GROSS	12	1	3' - 0"	Level 1
112	OFFICE	103 SF	BUSINESS AREAS	100 GROSS	1	1	3' - 0"	Level 1
113	RESTROOM	59 SF	UNOCCUPIED	0	0	0	3' - 0"	Level 1
201	MENS	65 SF	UNOCCUPIED	0	0	0	3' - 0"	Level 2
202	WOMENS	85 SF	UNOCCUPIED	0	0	0	3' - 0"	Level 2
203	STORAGE	53 SF	ACCESSORY STORAGE	300 GROSS	1	1	3' - 0"	Level 2
204	OFFICE	120 SF	BUSINESS AREAS	100 GROSS	1	1	3' - 0"	Level 2
205	LIBRARY	669 SF	LIBRARY, READING ROOMS	50 NET	13	1	3' - 0"	Level 2
206	STORAGE	61 SF	ACCESSORY STORAGE	300 GROSS	1	1	3' - 0"	Level 2
207	JAN.	41 SF	ACCESSORY STORAGE	300 GROSS	1	1	3' - 0"	Level 2
208	GALLERY	1542 SF	ASSEMBLY, EXHIBIT GALLERY	30 NET	51	2	3' - 0"	Level 2
209	CLASSROOM	551 SF	EDUCATIONAL, CLASSROOM	20 NET	27	2	3' - 0"	Level 2
210	WORKSPACE	541 SF	EDUCATIONAL, SHOPS	50 NET	10	1	3' - 0"	Level 2
211	OFFICE	139 SF	BUSINESS AREAS	100 GROSS	1	1	3' - 0"	Level 2
212	OFFICE	126 SF	BUSINESS AREAS	100 GROSS	1	1	3' - 0"	Level 2
301	ACCESSIBLE STUDIO	356 SF	RESIDENTIAL	200 GROSS	1	1	3' - 0"	Level 3 & 4
302	STUDIO	301 SF	RESIDENTIAL	200 GROSS	1	1	3' - 0"	Level 3 & 4
303	STUDIO	286 SF	RESIDENTIAL	200 GROSS	1	1	3' - 0"	Level 3 & 4
304	AMENITY LOUNGE	230 SF	ASSEMBLY, UNCONCENTRATED	15 NET	15	1	3' - 0"	Level 3 & 4
305	STUDIO	246 SF	RESIDENTIAL	200 GROSS	1	1	3' - 0"	Level 3 & 4
306	STUDIO	304 SF	RESIDENTIAL	200 GROSS	1	1	3' - 0"	Level 3 & 4
307	STUDIO	277 SF	RESIDENTIAL	200 GROSS	1	1	3' - 0"	Level 3 & 4
308	AMENITY LOUNGE	222 SF	ASSEMBLY, UNCONCENTRATED	15 NET	14	1	3' - 0"	Level 3 & 4
309	HALL	1204 SF	UNOCCUPIED	0	0	0	3' - 0"	Level 3 & 4

BRICKHAUS

CN
NADIA COLQUIETT

ISSUED FOR:

DATE:

DATE
05/05/16

PROJECT NUMBER
Project Number

DRAWN BY
NADIA COLQUIETT

CHECKED BY
LISA TUCKER

ROOM OCCUPANCY SUMMARY

A-7

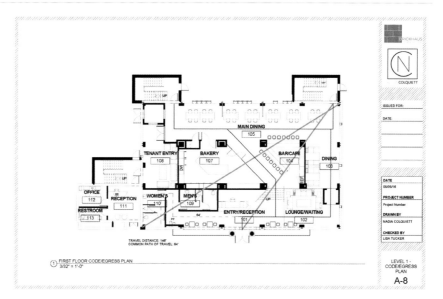

Figure 10.25
Common path of travel diagram

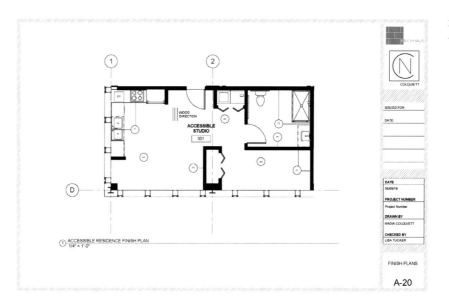

Figure 10.26
ADA apartment

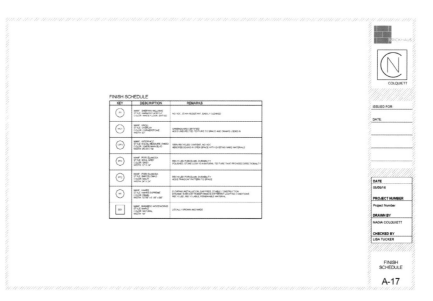

Figure 10.27
Finishes schedule

Project 2: Women and Children's Center

The second project example used the robin as inspiration and Frank Lloyd Wright's process of abstracting nature as an approach to the design. This student chose to make the building into a center for women and children escaping abusive environments. As such, the focus was on safety

and creating a comfortable home environment while also providing spaces for job training and counseling (Figure 10.28).

Programming Phase

During the programming process, overall code information was gathered for the proposed use. A site analysis revealed weather information and sun studies. This student also planned to follow the Secretary of the Interior's Standards for Preservation, since the building was listed on the National Register (Figures 10.29–10.31).

Figure 10.28
Abstraction studies of a robin

Figure 10.29
Code summary

A.D. GERMAN GERMAN WAREHOUSE CODE ASSESSMENT

OCCUPANCY TYPES:
Assembly A2 (1st Floor)
Business (2nd Floor)
Assembly A3 (3rd Floor)
Residential R2 (4th Floor)

OCCUPANT LOADS:
1st Floor- 282 people
2nd Floor- 42 people
3rd Floor- 282 people
4th Floor- 21 people
Total # of Occupants- 627

Diagonal for Egress: 10 feet
Distance Between Fire-Rated Stairs: 55 feet (minimum)
for a sprinklered building
Max. Travel Distance to the Common Path of Travel per
Floor: 1st (A2)- 250 ft; 2nd (B)- 300 ft; 3rd (A3)- 250 ft;
4th (R)- 250 ft
Minimum of 2 Exits per Floor
Minimum Egress Corridor Width: 44" (except on floors 2, 4)
Maximum Dead End Corridor Length: 50' on floors 2 and 4;
20' on floors 1 and 2)

Required Clear Distance On PUSH Side Of Door: 48"
Required Clear Distance on PULL Side of Door: 18"
Door Size to Comply with ADA Standards: 36"

Floor #	Women's Water Closets	Men's Water Closets	Men's Lavatories	Women's Lavatories	Water Fountains	Service Sinks
1	4	4	4	4	1	1
2	2	2	1	1	1	1
3	4	2	2	2	1	1
4	~9 (1/room unit)	2	2	~9 (1/room unit)	1	1

26

CODES

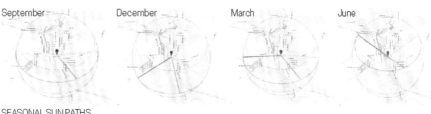

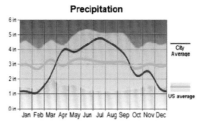
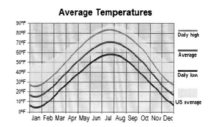

SEASONAL SUN PATHS

LOCAL CLIMATE

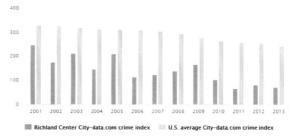

CRIME RATES

7

SITEANALYSIS

Figure 10.30
Sun and weather
studies

Figure 10.31
Secretary's
Standards
for Historic
Preservation

STANDARDS FOR REHABILITATION

A property will be used as it was historically or be given a new use that requires minimal change to its distinctive materials, features, spaces, and spatial relationships.

The historic character of a property will be retained and preserved. The removal of distinctive materials or alteration of features, spaces, and spatial relationships that characterize a property will be avoided.

Each property will be recognized as a physical record of its time, place, and use. Changes that create a false sense of historical development, such as adding conjectural features or elements from other historic properties, will not be undertaken.

Changes to a property that have acquired historic significance in their own right will be retained and preserved.

Distinctive materials, features, finishes, and construction techniques or examples of craftsmanship that characterize a property will be preserved.

Deteriorated historic features will be repaired rather than replaced. Where the severity of deterioration requires replacement of a distinctive feature, the new feature will match the old in design, color, texture, and, where possible, materials. Replacement of missing features will be substantiated by documentary and physical evidence.

Chemical or physical treatments, if appropriate, will be undertaken using the gentlest means possible. Treatments that cause damage to historic materials will not be used.

Archeological resources will be protected and preserved in place. If such resources must be disturbed, mitigation measures will be undertaken.

New additions, exterior alterations, or related new construction will not destroy historic materials, features, and spatial relationships that characterize the property. The new work will be differentiated from the old and will be compatible with the historic materials, features, size, scale and proportion, and massing to protect the integrity of the property and its environment.

New additions and adjacent or related new construction will be undertaken in such a manner that, if removed in the future, the essential form and integrity of the historic property and its environment would be unimpaired.

32

RESEARCH

Schematic Design

The schematic design process started with block and bubble diagrams (Figures 10.32, 10.33).

Using the abstracted robin parti inspiration, the designer explored the idea of nesting to create a safe-feeling environment in the preliminary floor plan (Figure 10.34).

The first schematic plan failed to reflect the parti and design concept (Figures 10.35–10.38).

This idea was refined in a subsequent version of the floor plans. These plans were then checked for building code and ADA compliance. Like the last example, as an R use group, the entire building had to be sprinklered (Figures 10.39–10.42).

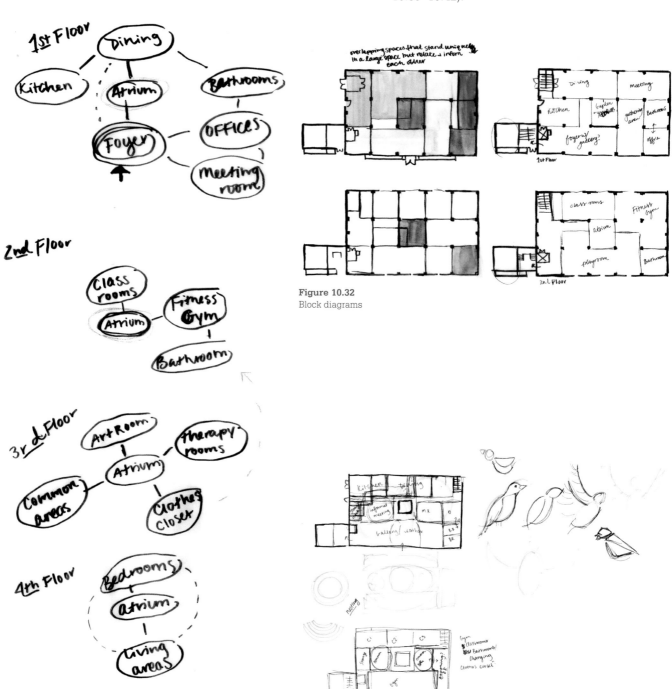

Figure 10.32
Block diagrams

Figure 10.33
Bubble diagrams

Figure 10.34
Abstracted robin and nesting for parti diagram

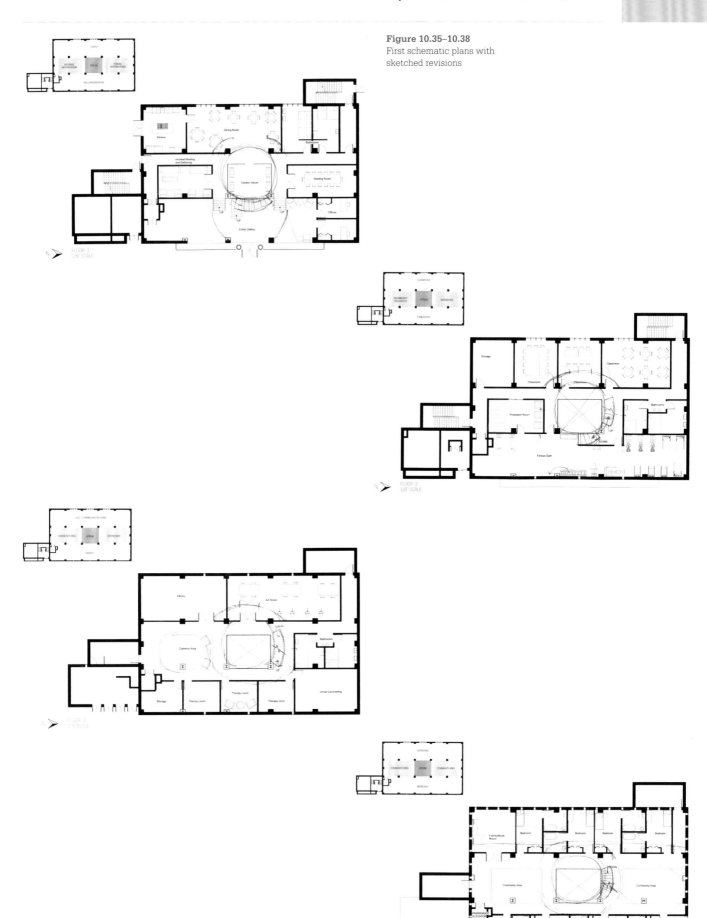

Figure 10.35–10.38
First schematic plans with
sketched revisions

Figures 10.39–10.42
Second set of
schematic plans with
sketched revisions
and code comments

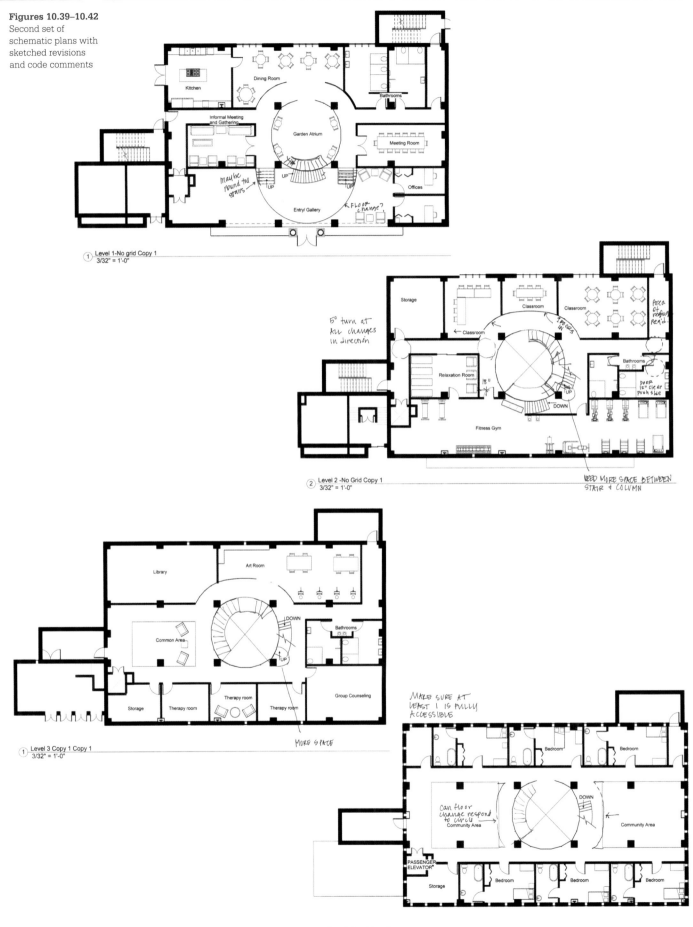

Design Development

Revisions of the schematic plans led to the design development plans (Figures 10.43–10.46).

During design development, all final material selections, finishes, and furniture and equipment were also selected, and plans were revised accordingly.

Construction Documents

The final phase of the project was a limited set of construction documents, including an occupancy load calculation table and travel distance plan with common path of travel notes (Figure 10.47).

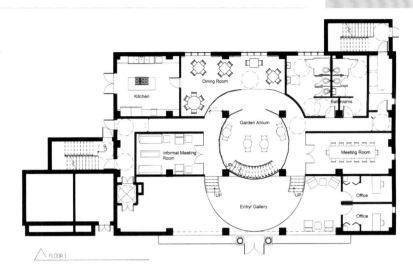

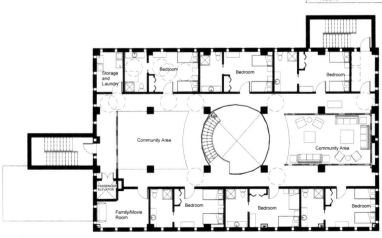

Figures 10.43–10.46
Design development plans

Figure 10.47
Occupancy load
table and common
path of travel plan

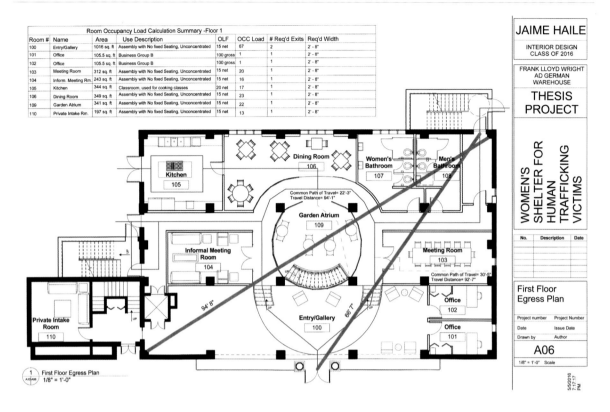

Room #	Name	Area	Use Description	OLF	OCC Load	# Req'd Exits	Req'd Width
			Room Occupancy Load Calculation Summary -Floor 1				
100	Entry/Gallery	1016 sq. ft.	Assembly with No fixed Seating, Unconcentrated	15 net	67	2	2'- 8"
101	Office	105.5 sq. ft.	Business Group B	100 gross	1	1	2'- 8"
102	Office	105.5 sq. ft.	Business Group B	100 gross	1	1	2'- 8"
103	Meeting Room	312 sq. ft.	Assembly with No fixed Seating, Unconcentrated	15 net	20	1	2'- 8"
104	Inform. Meeting Rm.	243 sq. ft.	Assembly with No fixed Seating, Unconcentrated	15 net	16	1	2'- 8"
105	Kitchen	344 sq. ft.	Classroom, used for cooking classes	20 net	17	1	2'- 8"
106	Dining Room	349 sq. ft.	Assembly with No fixed Seating, Unconcentrated	15 net	23	1	2'- 8"
109	Garden Atrium	341 sq. ft.	Assembly with No fixed Seating, Unconcentrated	15 net	22	1	2'- 8"
110	Private Intake Rm.	197 sq. ft.	Assembly with No fixed Seating, Unconcentrated	15 net	13	1	2'- 8"

JAIME HAILE

INTERIOR DESIGN
CLASS OF 2016

FRANK LLOYD WRIGHT
AD GERMAN
WAREHOUSE

THESIS
PROJECT

WOMEN'S
SHELTER FOR
HUMAN
TRAFFICKING
VICTIMS

No.	Description	Date

First Floor
Egress Plan

Project number	Project Number
Date	Issue Date
Drawn by	Author

A06

1/8" = 1'-0"   Scale

Project 3: Boutique Hotel

The third project for the conversion of the A. D. German Warehouse converted the existing warehouse into a boutique hotel and restaurant. Inspired by the hearth and Frank Lloyd Wright's use of it as the center of the home, the parti diagram used the flame as inspiration.

Programming Phase

Just as a flame has three layers of heat, the designer applied three zones to the planning of the hotel: sharing a meal, gathering in community, and resting in comfort (Figure 10.48).

Figure 10.48
Parti and concept
page

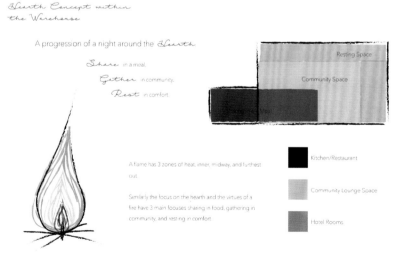

Schematic Design and Design Development

Once the concept and plan went through several iterations (as with the projects previously reviewed), the final design development plan was then evaluated for code and ADA compliance (Figures 10.49–10.52).

These changes were made prior to the construction documents phase.

Construction Documents

The limited set of final construction documents included a life-safety plan with occupancy load calculations (Figure 10.53).

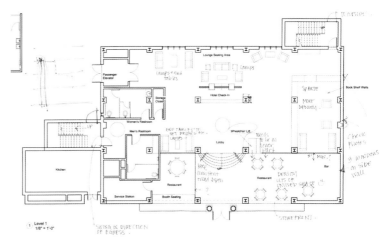

Figures 10.49–10.52
Marked-up plans with code and ADA corrections

Figure 10.53
Plan with
occupancy loads

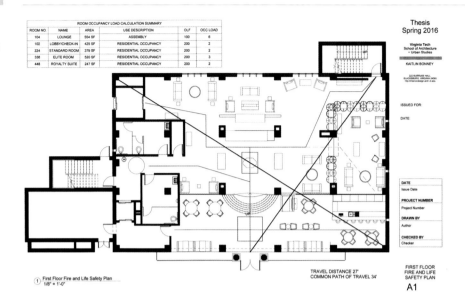

Conclusions

The initial code analysis of the A. D. German Warehouse revealed that two egress stairs would be required based on the square footage and potential occupancy loads. As a historic building these egress stairs were appended to the exterior on the non-street facing facades, so they would not change the character of the building. They are distinguishable as new construction but blend with the existing brick of the building (Figure 10.54).

Project 4: Skybox

The final project is for the design of a luxury skybox at a football stadium complex for a recording executive. The skybox contains areas for entertaining as well as a residential suite. The first thing each student had to do was select the type of music the studio produced.

Code Evaluation

The two-story skybox included an internal elevator and had two exits on each floor. As a skybox, the use group was identified as **Assembly** (A-5), with a residential component on the upper

Figure 10.54
Building diagram
with new egress
stairs

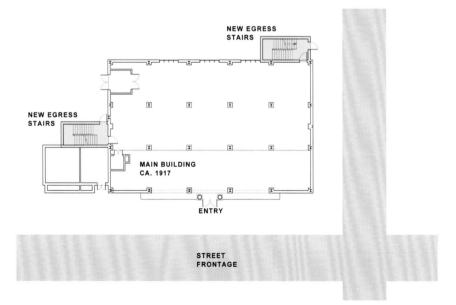

level containing a bedroom and bathroom. Each student completed a worksheet to figure out the occupant load, number of plumbing fixtures, and fire-separation requirements (Figure 10.55).

Occupancy calculations confirm the need for two exits per floor. Although the program only calls for two restrooms—one in the residence and one in the entertainment area, the entertainment area contains 1,770 square feet plus the stepped seating. Programmatically, the bleacher platform seating is for only twenty people. To use an occupancy factor of 15 net for unconcentrated tables and chairs, the kitchen, storage, circulation and other spaces listed in the design program are deducted. The remaining square footage is then divided by fifteen for the total number of occupants, which is then added to the twenty seated in the bleacher platforms.

For maximum floor area allowances per occupant, please refer to Table 4.2 and its accompanying Box 4.1, which summarizes the primary changes to the table.

The entertainment area is 1,168 square feet after deductions. Dividing 1,168 by 15 net results in seventy-eight people, plus twenty additional from the seated platforms equals a total of ninety-eight people. This indicates the following required plumbing fixtures. For A-5, one water closet is required for every seventy-five people and one lavatory for every two hundred. Since there is a second floor bathroom as well, the required numbers have been met (Table 10.1).

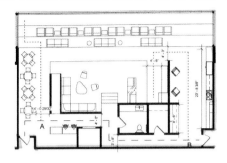

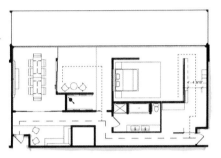

1029.7 Travel distance.

Exits and aisles shall be so located that the travel distance to an exit door shall be not greater than 200 feet measured along the line of travel in non-sprinklered buildings. Travel distance shall be not more than 250 feet in sprinklered buildings. Where aisles are provided for seating, the distance shall be measured along the aisles and aisle accessway without travel over or on the seats.

	1st Floor	2nd Floor
— — Common Path of Travel	42' - 6"	61' - 10"
······ Travel Distance	35' - 4" (A)	33' - 1" (A)
	50' - 9" (B)	45' - 1" (B)

 Separation needed at corridor

Table 10.1 IBC 2018 Table 2902.1: Plumbing Fixture Requirements

[P] TABLE 2902.1
MINIMUM NUMBER OF REQUIRED PLUMBING FIXTURES[a]
(See Sections 2902.1.1 and 2902.2)

No.	CLASSIFICATION	DESCRIPTION	WATER CLOSETS (URINALS SEE SECTION 424.2 OF THE *INTERNATIONAL PLUMBING CODE*)		LAVATORIES		BATHTUBS/ SHOWERS	DRINKING FOUNTAINS (SEE SECTION 410 OF THE *INTERNATIONAL PLUMBING CODE*)	OTHER
			Male	Female	Male	Female			
1	Assembly	Theaters and other buildings for the performing arts and motion pictures[d]	1 per 125	1 per 65	1 per 200		—	1 per 500	1 service sink
		Nightclubs, bars, taverns, dance halls and buildings for similar purposes[d]	1 per 40	1 per 40	1 per 75		—	1 per 500	1 service sink
		Restaurants, banquet halls and food courts[d]	1 per 75	1 per 75	1 per 200		—	1 per 500	1 service sink
		Casino gaming areas	1 per 100 for the first 400 and 1 per 250 for the remainder exceeding 400	1 per 50 for the first 400 and 1 per 150 for the remainder exceeding 400	1 per 250 for the first 750 and 1 per 500 for the remainder exceeding 750		—	1 per 1,000	1 service sink

(continued)

Table 10.1 IBC 2018 Table 2902.1: Plumbing Fixture Requirements *(continued)*

PLUMBING SYSTEMS

[P] TABLE 2902.1—(continued)
MINIMUM NUMBER OF REQUIRED PLUMBING FIXTURES[a]
(See Sections 2902.1.1 and 2902.2)

No.	CLASSIFICATION	DESCRIPTION	WATER CLOSETS (URINALS SEE SECTION 424.2 OF THE *INTERNATIONAL PLUMBING CODE*) Male	Female	LAVATORIES Male	Female	BATHTUBS/ SHOWERS	DRINKING FOUNTAINS (SEE SECTION 410 OF THE *INTERNATIONAL PLUMBING CODE*)	OTHER
1	Assembly	Auditoriums without permanent seating, art galleries, exhibition halls, museums, lecture halls, libraries, arcades and gymnasiums[d]	1 per 125	1 per 65	1 per 200		—	1 per 500	1 service sink
		Passenger terminals and transportation facilities[d]	1 per 500	1 per 500	1 per 750		—	1 per 1,000	1 service sink
		Places of worship and other religious services[d]	1 per 150	1 per 75	1 per 200		—	1 per 1,000	1 service sink
		Coliseums, arenas, skating rinks, pools and tennis courts for indoor sporting events and activities	1 per 75 for the first 1,500 and 1 per 120 for the remainder exceeding 1,500	1 per 40 for the first 1,520 and 1 per 60 for the remainder exceeding 1,520	1 per 200	1 per 150	—	1 per 1,000	1 service sink
		Stadiums, amusement parks, bleachers and grandstands for outdoor sporting events and activities[f]	1 per 75 for the first 1,500 and 1 per 120 for the remainder exceeding 1,500	1 per 40 for the first 1,520 and 1 per 60 for the remainder exceeding 1,520	1 per 200	1 per 150	—	1 per 1,000	1 service sink
2	Business	Buildings for the transaction of business, professional services, other services involving merchandise, office buildings, banks, light industrial, ambulatory care and similar uses	1 per 25 for the first 50 and 1 per 50 for the remainder exceeding 50		1 per 40 for the first 80 and 1 per 80 for the remainder exceeding 80		—	1 per 100	1 service sink[e]
3	Educational	Educational facilities	1 per 50		1 per 50		—	1 per 100	1 service sink
4	Factory and industrial	Structures in which occupants are engaged in work fabricating, assembly or processing of products or materials	1 per 100		1 per 100		—	1 per 400	1 service sink
5	Institutional	Custodial care facilities	1 per 10		1 per 10		1 per 8	1 per 100	1 service sink
		Medical care recipients in hospitals and nursing homes[b]	1 per room[c]		1 per room[c]		1 per 15	1 per 100	1 service sink
		Employees in hospitals and nursing homes[b]	1 per 25		1 per 35		—	1 per 100	—
		Visitors in hospitals and nursing homes	1 per 75		1 per 100		—	1 per 500	—
		Prisons[b]	1 per cell		1 per cell		1 per 15	1 per 100	1 service sink

(continued)

Table 10.1 IBC 2018 Table 2902.1: Plumbing Fixture Requirements *(continued)*

[P] TABLE 2902.1—continued
MINIMUM NUMBER OF REQUIRED PLUMBING FIXTURES[a]
(See Sections 2902.1.1 and 2902.2)

No.	CLASSIFICATION	DESCRIPTION	WATER CLOSETS (URINALS SEE SECTION 424.2 OF THE *INTERNATIONAL PLUMBING CODE*)		LAVATORIES		BATHTUBS OR SHOWERS	DRINKING FOUNTAINS (SEE SECTION 410 OF THE *INTERNATIONAL PLUMBING CODE*)	OTHER
			Male	Female	Male	Female			
5	Institutional	Reformatories, detention centers and correctional centers[b]	1 per 15		1 per 15		1 per 15	1 per 100	1 service sink
		Employees in reformitories, detention centers and correctional centers[b]	1 per 25		1 per 35		—	1 per 100	—
		Adult day care and child day care	1 per 15		1 per 15		1	1 per 100	1 service sink
6	Mercantile	Retail stores, service stations, shops, salesrooms, markets and shopping centers	1 per 500		1 per 750		—	1 per 1,000	1 service sink[e]
7	Residential	Hotels, motels, boarding houses (transient)	1 per sleeping unit		1 per sleeping unit		1 per sleeping unit	—	1 service sink
		Dormitories, fraternities, sororities and boarding houses (not transient)	1 per 10		1 per 10		1 per 8	1 per 100	1 service sink
		Apartment house	1 per dwelling unit		1 per dwelling unit		1 per dwelling unit	—	1 kitchen sink per dwelling unit; 1 automatic clothes washer connection per 20 dwelling units
		One- and two-family dwellings and lodging houses with five or fewer guestrooms	1 per dwelling unit		1 per 10		1 per dwelling unit	—	1 kitchen sink per dwelling unit; 1 automatic clothes washer connection per dwelling unit
		Congregate living facilities with 16 or fewer persons	1 per 10		1 per 10		1 per 8	1 per 100	1 service sink
8	Storage	Structures for the storage of goods, warehouses, storehouses and freight depots, low and moderate hazard	1 per 100		1 per 100		—	1 per 1,000	1 service sink

a. The fixtures shown are based on one fixture being the minimum required for the number of persons indicated or any fraction of the number of persons indicated. The number of occupants shall be determined by this code.

b. Toilet facilities for employees shall be separate from facilities for inmates or care recipients.

c. A single-occupant toilet room with one water closet and one lavatory serving not more than two adjacent patient sleeping units shall be permitted, provided that each patient sleeping unit has direct access to the toilet room and provisions for privacy for the toilet room user are provided.

d. The occupant load for seasonal outdoor seating and entertainment areas shall be included when determining the minimum number of facilities required.

e. For business and mercantile classifications with an occupant load of 15 or fewer, a service sink shall not be required.

f. The required number and type of plumbing fixtures for outdoor swimming pools shall be in accordance with Section 609 of the *International Swimming Pool and Spa Code*.

Figure 10.56
Adjacency and
bubble diagrams

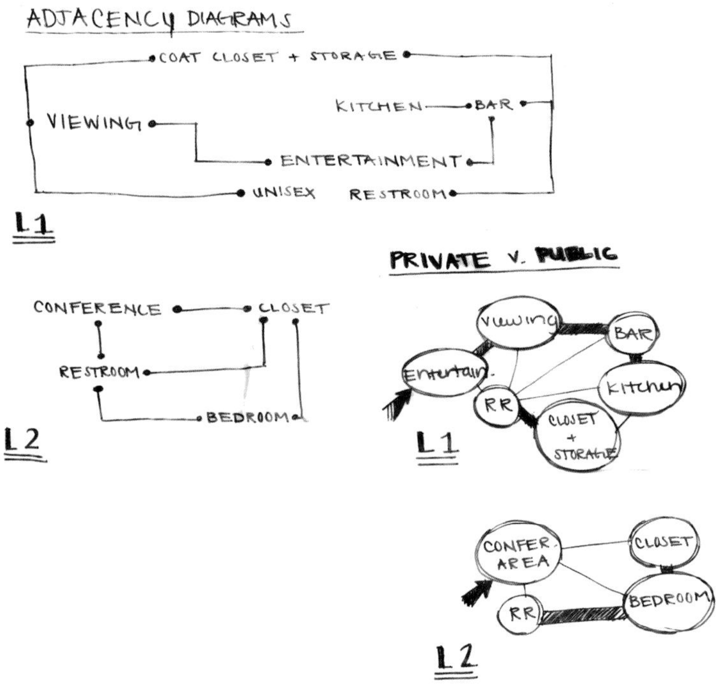

ADJACENCY DIAGRAMS

COAT CLOSET + STORAGE
VIEWING
KITCHEN — BAR
ENTERTAINMENT
UNISEX   RESTROOM

L 1

CONFERENCE — CLOSET
RESTROOM
BEDROOM

L 2

PRIVATE v. PUBLIC

Viewing   BAR
Entertain.   Kitchen
RR
CLOSET + STORAGE

L 1

CONFER AREA   CLOSET
RR   BEDROOM

L 2

Example: R&B

The interior for this project reflects the concept of linear progression as found within the rhythm of R&B. An adjacency diagram and bubble diagrams divided the private from public spaces as required in the design program (Figure 10.56).

A conceptual rhythm and repetition diagram reinforced the use of the design concept in the space planning (Figure 10.57).

The resulting design integrates all code concerns within the approach outlined by the design concept (Figures 10.58–10.64).

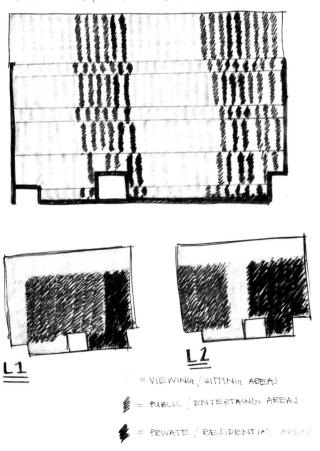

REPETION / RHYTHM / BALANCE

L 1   **L 2**

= VIEWING / SITTING AREAS

= PUBLIC / ENTERTAINING AREAS

= PRIVATE / RESIDENTIAL AREAS

Figure 10.57
Rhythm diagram

Figures 10.58–10.64
Final project pages

Inspired by R&B, formally known as Rhythm and Blues. R&B is influenced by a combination of jazz, blues, rock and roll, soul, funk, pop, hip-hop and dance. It's an immensely diverse genre that has many different contrasting elements that flow together seamlessly. The music has rich melodies, paired with a strong rhythmic component, basic blues structure, and prominent bass lines.

The interior should reflect a **concept of linear progression** of R&B through the years, and how each artist is unique but is reminiscent of the past generations of R&B music. The linear progression will **manifest through repetition of elements, geometric forms, and positive and negative voids** that pulls the eye into the various transitions within the space. To balance the seamless transitions, **moments of strong contrast** will occur throughout the space to further distinguish the area, much like how artists set themselves apart from others in the industry. The strong presence of the beat within the music is embodied in the repetition, and how it **creates a rhythm within the interior**. The linear motif further reinforces this rhythm, and introduces structure and order into the design. Since R&B is a collective assortment of diverse influences, the furniture and finishes should reiterate that. The finishes will consist of many different textures that work together seamlessly, and the furniture will mesh timeless and contemporary pieces that will result in a luxuriously curated design. The various colors aiding in way-finding by allowing occupants to feel the progression through the space.

The materials will mirror the way artists recycle and transforms old music into something new and unique. In addition, special consideration will go towards the creating a layout that will conserve both energy and water by maximizing natural light and placing plumbing fixtures adjacent to each other.

LINEAR PROGESSION

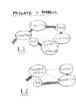

PARTI DIAGRAM

This diagram illustrates how the colors progress and blend into each other, while still maintaining contrast. This also embodies how R&B artists are similar, but are unique individuals with varying styles and sounds.

The color scheme is analogous to help enforce this visual transition through music. The occupants will be able to feel the progression through the space by the slight change in hue. Colors used are pinks, magentas, purples, and blues. In addition to black and white for contrast.

□ PUBLIC
■ PRIVATE

Public and private spaces are distinctly separated vertically. And there is a linear progression into the different zones.

Strategically positioned walls, so the linear transition is able to be seen from the outside facade, creating a pattern that compliments the existing geometries.

KITCHEN 1/4"-1'-0"

19   41
24   18
14   23   22

SUSTAINABILITY:

FAGERHULT LED LIGHTING was used exclusively within the space to provide optimum energy efficiency. **MOSA TILES** are Cradle to Cradle Silver Certified, while still being aesthetically pleasing. **FELZ FELT,** is a very innovative and eco-friendly material since its a 100% wool. In addition it has great acoustical properties. **CONCRETE,** is economic and locally sourced. **BAMBOO WOOD FLOORING,** was used which is a very resilient renewable resource. **CARNEGIE XOREL WALLCOVERING,** was used throughout the space to bring in an element of texture and its also Cradle to Cradle Gold Certified. **DAVIS FURNITURE,** was also consistently used throughout and they are Gold Certified for Indoor Air Quality for most of their lounge furniture.

9   1   51
15

ENTERTAINMENT // LOUNGE // BAR

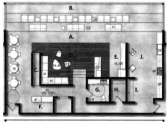

1ST FLOOR 1/8" = 1' - 0"

2ND FLOOR 1/8" = 1' - 0"

A.	ENTERTAINMENT AREA 745 SQ. FT.
B.	VIEWING PLATFORM 600 SQ. FT.
C.	RAMP
D.	SUNK-IN LOUNGE 363 SQ. FT.
E.	BUILT-IN COUNTER
F.	BAR + MOBILE BAR 77 SQ. FT.
G.	UNISEX RESTROOM 72 SQ. FT.
H.	STORAGE 51 SQ. FT.
I.	CLOSET 26 SQ. FT.
J.	KITCHEN 316 SQ. FT.

K.	CONFERENCE ROOM 266 SQ. FT. + L.
L.	*ADDIT. SEATING/BREAK OUT SPACE* 150 SQ. FT.
M.	INFORMAL SITTING NOOK 76 SQ. FT.
N.	BATHROOM 120 SQ. FT.
O.	BEDROOM 661 SQ. FT. + L.
O1.	STUDIO
P.	CLOSET 70 SQ. FT.

Figures 10.58–10.64 (continued)
Final project pages

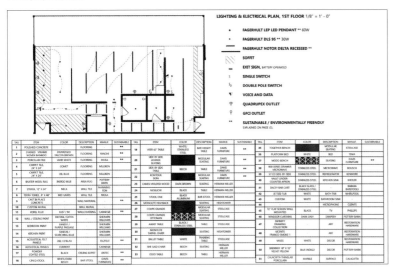

As can be seen in the finishes schedule, sustainability was a key part of the project. Universal design was also a focus of this project. Each principle was specifically addressed.

Assignments

1. How do you know what use group to use when you have more than one use in your building?

2. How might the use of a historic building impact your project?

   a. Which of the Secretary's Standards most impact your work? Why?

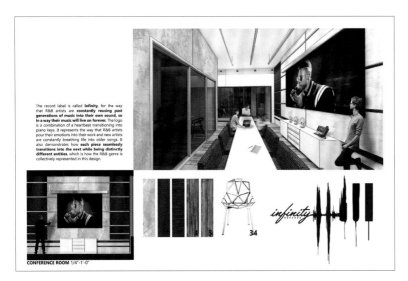

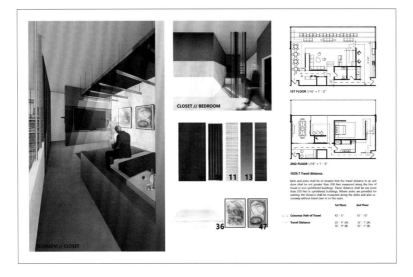

11

Post-Occupancy Evaluation

Learning Objectives:

After reading this chapter and doing the exercises, students will be able to

- Define post-occupancy evaluation
- Understand the use of post-occupancy surveys to determine the effectiveness of LEED Certification
- Understand the use of post-occupancy surveys to determine the effectiveness of WELL Building Certification
- Define building commissioning and flush out
- Describe methods used in POEs

Introduction

One of the most important phases of a project is the **post-occupancy evaluation (POE)**. Following the completion of the construction and once occupants have moved into the space, the design team visits the site to see if the building is working as intended. Several components comprise a POE. Although the POE is not a standard service in American Institute of Architects (AIA), International Interior Design Association (IIDA), or American Society of Interior Design (ASID) contracts, it is an important part of the design process. Even if a client does not wish to pay for this service, a design team benefits from the feedback and can use this information to guide future projects as well as to improve customer relations.

The POE Process

According to a study conducted by faculty at the University of Westminster, the POE involves several steps. First, the person or team conducting the evaluation must determine the goals; second, the team must decide the scope of the study and whether it is a quick look or an in-depth analysis; third, the team defines the objectives, timing, and who should be included in the study as well as how (interview, survey, and other methods); and finally, the POE preparation work is completed (preparing schedules, writing surveys, and other preparatory activities). Once the preparation is complete, the actual POE is conducted. This step is followed by the preparation of a report summarizing the results and finally a proposed action plan that might inform future projects as well as policies.

A recent report produced by Skidmore Owings and Merrill (SOM) synthesized the results gathered from twenty-nine design leaders of mid-sized firms (forty or more employees) from the United States and Canada and indicated that over half of the firms conduct POEs on most projects. In this summary report, the writers identify key reasons for why firms do not conduct POEs. Heading up the list of reasons is liability concerns—if something is not working the way it should, the designer might be open

to lawsuits. Additional reasons include client privacy concerns, lack of desire on the part of the client, the client's desire to control feedback, timing of the POE, limited site access, and that this is a lower priority for designers and a non-billable task. SOM found that higher education clients have the most interest in POE results, and European clients are far more interested in the POE than those in North America. The top results that firms hoped to obtain with a POE were as follows:

1. Solicit feedback on design and performance aspects of projects
2. Learn from previous experiences to enhance future designs
3. Extend client relationships and exposure, with potential to generate new business
4. Promote evidence-based design
5. Identify cost-savings measures
6. Demonstrate your firm's mission
7. Mitigate risk
8. Compliance with regulatory requirements

Quantitative Data

The scope of the POE is divided into quantitative and qualitative metrics. Quantitative measures include information such as lighting levels (daylight and electric), acoustics, air infiltration, wet and dry bulb temperatures, **volatile organic compounds (VOC)** measurements, air speed, carbon monoxide, relative humidity, carbon dioxide, lead, particulate matter (PM) 2.5, PM 10, water quality, and other measurable aspects of the interior environment. The top three items measured used light meters, professional decibel meters, and thermal imaging cameras.

Common Chemicals

The common chemicals that firms said they would like to measure in an interior are carbon monoxide, formaldehyde, lead, nitrogen dioxide, odors, ozone, sulfur dioxide, radon, VOCs, and **total volatile organic compounds (TVOCs)**.

Spatial Observations

In addition to the quantitative measurements, POEs also did spatial observations of density, utilization, tenant efficiency ratio, and differences from actual use versus designed use. Use of individual controls, actual energy use, and actual water use also comprised part of the POE. In addition, the POE helped to establish baseline measures for future surveys. Human resources data, such as absenteeism and productivity measures, helped support the impact of the new environment on human behavior.

Qualitative Data

In addition to quantitative measure, qualitative surveys and observations contribute to the POE. Surveys can address issues, such as happiness, energy level, perceived health impact, inspiration, beauty, likes, dislikes, overall comfort, and other impacts of the interior. Looking for patterns in the data can provide valuable information. Owner provided project requirements are evaluated against employee and occupant experiences. Conducting the POE engages the client and users. The building stakeholders potentially included in the POE process include building users and occupants, facility managers, clients, the building staff, design team consultants, as well as sometimes the construction teams and real estate brokers.

Methods

The methods used to gather the onsite data can include online interactive surveys (the most popular method), interviews, emailed or paper surveys, surveys conducted by the Human Resources department, and onsite observations. Questions include open-ended fill in the blank, ratings scales, or multiple choice.

Timing

Following building commissioning and occupancy, most POEs are conducted within twelve to twenty-four months after the building is occupied. In the majority of cases, the design team does not bill the client for this service. The average POE using a survey-based method can be completed in forty hours.

Types of POE Components

The POE can address process variables, functional performance, or technical performance. In a process evaluation, the POE focuses on the processes associated with procurement, design, construction, commissioning, and occupation of the building. A functional performance evaluation might evaluate the strategic value of a project, the aesthetics and image of the design, space, comfort, amenities, serviceability, operational and life-cycle costs, and operational management. A more technical POE would address physical systems, environmental systems, adaptability, and durability. An operational review typically takes place three to six months after occupation;

a performance review twelve to eighteen months after move-in, and a strategic review three to five years after project completion.

Established POE Methods

The University of Westminster has summarized the most widely accepted methods for POEs in the United Kingdom. These include the DeMontfort Method, Design Quality Indicators, Overall Liking Score, PROBE, BUS Occupant Survey, Energy Assessment and Reporting Methodology, and Learning from Experience (Table 11.1).

Evaluation Techniques

Various methods used to gather information for the POE range from visiting the site and making observations to in-depth interviews and focus groups.

Walk-Through and Observations

Walking through the building allows designers to see how spaces are actually being used following move-in. Few staff resources are required for this method, however how observations are made must be consistent to provide valuable information. As a part of this process, a standardized form can be used to record what activities are taking place, as well as evaluation of finishes and other interior items for durability, suitability, maintenance, and aesthetics. Light quality, air quality, and other interior conditions might also be recorded.

Interviews

In the interview process, researchers can ask occupants and building users to expand on answers in a way that might not be possible in an online survey, thus providing the team with rich data. One drawback to interviews is that people are not anonymous and might not respond in a completely candid manner. Interviews tend to be easier with groups than individuals.

Focus Groups

The primary drawback of the focus group is the need for an expert facilitator; however, this method requires only a few people and can help clarify data from surveys. Like interviews, there is a lack of anonymity.

Workshops

For workshops, a variety of users can be asked to attend. This type of group can be used to identify potential issues and solutions in a group format.

Table 11.1 From HEFSE Study

Method	Format	Focus	How long?	When?	Reference
DeMontfort Method	Forum walk-through	Board review process and functional performance	1 day	A year after occupancy	www.architecture. com (client forums)
CIC DQIs (Design Quality Indicators)	Questionnaire	Covers functionality of building quality and impact	Online 20–30 minutes	At design state and after completion	www.dqi.org.uk
Overall Liking Score	Questionnaire (hard copy and web) 7-point scale	Occupant survey diagnostic tool	10 minutes each occupant	About 12 months	www.obsconsulting. uk.com
PROBE	Questionnaire Focus groups Visual survey Energy assessment Environmental performance of systems	User satisfaction/ occupant survey Productivity Systems performance Benchmarks	Overall process time varies—2 days to several months	Any time recommended within 12 months	www. usablebuildings. co.uk
BUS Occupant Survey	Building walk-throughs Questionnaire backed by focus groups	Occupant satisfaction Productivity	10–15 minutes	On its own or in conjunction with other methods anytime but often after 12 months	www. usablebuildings. co.uk
Energy Assessment and Reporting Methodology	Energy use survey data collection	Energy use and potential savings	Full assessment up to one person week	Once building is completed on its own or with PROBE	www.cibse.org
Learning from Experience	Facilitated group discussion or interviews	Team learning from its experience	Ranges from single seminar to continuous evaluation	Can be used before, during, or after project	

Questionnaires: Operational Review Stage

Questionnaires are used to collect data from many people, and they can be administered using either hard copy or web-based methods. This type of method usually generates quantitative data, often using a rating scale, although open-ended questions might also be included.

Benchmarking

Benchmarking building data can be used to assess a building overtime. This can include user questionnaires, as well as energy and water use data. Environmental benchmarks include energy use over time, carbon dioxide emission, and water consumption. Tracking building materials and systems over time can provide life-cycle cost information for the building.

Building Commissioning

Once construction is completed and before people move in, all building systems should undergo **commissioning**. Commissioning involves making sure all systems are working as intended. This process can help make sure that no energy is wasted and that all systems are operating at peak efficiency. The LEED Green Building Rating

Systems require fundamental commissioning and verification of all building systems (prerequisite), and it awards additional points for enhanced building commissioning under the Energy and Atmosphere category. The WELL Building Standard includes Preconditions for Air Quality Standards, Water Quality Standards, and Visual Lighting Design that exceed those of the LEED Green Building Rating Systems Commissioning requirements in many cases. The ICC has also published a commissioning guideline ICC G4-2012 that addresses various aspects of building commissioning.

Building Flush Out

Prior to occupation, a **building flush out** should be conducted; flushing the building with fresh air helps remove potentially harmful environmental toxins, such as VOCs and TVOCs. Both LEED and WELL have provisions for indoor air quality to be managed during the construction process to prevent the introduction of harmful chemicals and VOCs into the indoor environment as a part of the construction process, and they also require that all filters be changed, ducts vacuumed, and other measures be taken prior to move-in. Under LEED, a minimum level of indoor air quality is required as a prerequisite, and credit can be obtained for a Construction Indoor Air Quality Management Plan. Under the WELL Building Standard, Construction Pollution Management is a required precondition and Air Flush is an optimization.

WELL Building Standard: Post-Occupancy Surveys

Post-occupancy surveys are a required precondition of both the New and Existing Interiors and New and Existing Buildings Standards under WELL. In buildings with ten or more occupants, an Indoor Environmental Quality (IEQ) Survey, as designed by the Center for the Built Environment at Berkeley (or an approved

alternate survey) must be administered to at least 30 percent of all employees at least once a year. The survey topics must include acoustics, thermal comfort, furnishings, workspace lighting, odors and other air quality concerns, cleanliness and maintenance, and layout of the space. The results must then be reported to the International WELL Building Institute, building occupants (if asked for), and building owners and managers within thirty days.

General Services Administration

In the United States, the General Services Administration (GSA) is the single biggest property owner. It has also recently adopted an agency-wide POE process. The GSA POE process is used six months to two years after a building is occupied to evaluate how the building is actually performing. The GSA's POE includes information on acoustics, air quality, lighting and thermal comfort, space utilization and floor plan analysis, social networking analysis, building metrics such as energy and water use, and occupant satisfaction surveys (Table 11.2). A report completed in 2008 assessed the performance of twelve GSA green buildings. The primary findings of the POE were that sustainably designed building cost less to operate, had excellent energy performance, and more satisfied building occupants than typical commercial buildings. Of the twelve buildings, eight were LEED certified, two others were registered, and the final two met LEED criteria.

Table 11.2 GSA Occupant Survey

Appendix E: Occupant Satisfaction Key Survey Questions

This appendix includes the key questions included in the GSA adaptation of the CBE survey, which was named the Sustainable Places and Organizational Trends "SPOT" survey.

Part 1 - Background Information
1. How would you describe the work you do?
2. Which organization do you work for?
3. How many years have you worked in this building?
4. How long have you been working at your present workspace?

Part 2 - Commute
1. On average, how many days per week do you travel to the office (i.e., commute)?

2. How far is your typical daily commute to and from this building?___ Miles Roundtrip

3. Please indicate the *number of days* per week you commute to and from this building for each mode of transportation that applies.

Walk	Bicycle
Car, truck or van - single occupant	Car, truck or van - multiple occupants (e.g., carpool, vanpool or rideshare)
Bus	Train (including light rail)
Combination of multiple modes (e.g., driving to rideshare locations then taking mass transit)	
Other	

4. Please describe any other issues related to your commute to and from this building that are important to you; and/or provide additional detail on your modes of transportation as you see fit.

Part 3 - Personal Workspace Location
1. On which floor is your workspace located?
2. In which area of the building is your workspace located?
3. Are you near a window (within 15 feet)?
4. Describe your personal workspace.

Table 11.2 GSA Occupant Survey *(continued)*

Part 4 - Your Workstation

In this section, please note your level of satisfaction with features and attributes of your workstation.

If any of these aspects are not important to you, please indicate so instead of answering with a level of satisfaction.

1. How satisfied are you with the comfort of your office furnishings (chair, desk, computer, equipment, etc.)?

This is not important to me _____

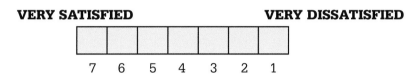

2. How satisfied are you with your ability to adjust your furniture to meet your needs?

This is not important to me _____

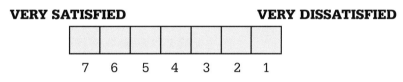

3. How satisfied are you with the colors and textures of flooring, furniture, and surface finishes?

This is not important to me _____

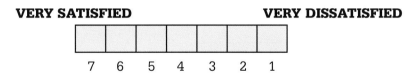

4. How satisfied are you with the amount of space available for individual work?

This is not important to me _____

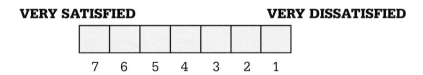

Table 11.2 GSA Occupant Survey *(continued)*

5. How satisfied are you with the level of visual privacy in your workspace?

This is not important to me _____

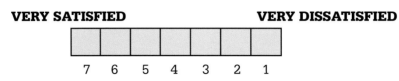

6. Please describe any other issues related to your personal workspace that are of importance to you.

Part 5 - Communication

1. How satisfied are you with your ability to communicate with co-workers in person (face to face)?

This is not important to me _____

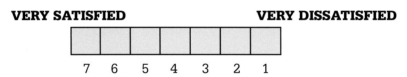

2. How satisfied are you with the ease of interaction with co-workers?

This is not important to me _____

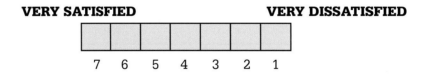

3. How satisfied are you with your ability to communicate in privacy?

This is not important to me _____

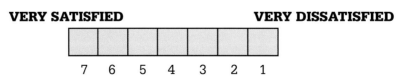

Table 11.2 GSA Occupant Survey *(continued)*

4. How satisfied are you with the availability of space where you and your colleagues can talk into a speaker phone together?

This is not important to me _____

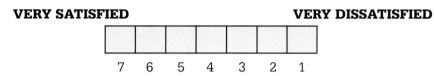

VERY SATISFIED   **VERY DISSATISFIED**

7   6   5   4   3   2   1

5. Please describe any other issues related to communication with others that are important to you.

Part 6 - Meeting Facilities

1. How satisfied are you with the availability of meeting rooms on short notice?

This is not important to me _____

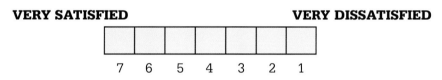

VERY SATISFIED   **VERY DISSATISFIED**

7   6   5   4   3   2   1

2. How satisfied are you with the availability of equipment in meeting rooms? (white boards, speaker phone, computer access, LCD projectors, etc.)

This is not important to me _____

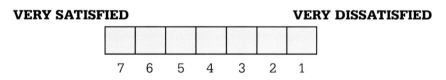

VERY SATISFIED   **VERY DISSATISFIED**

7   6   5   4   3   2   1

3. How satisfied are you with the temperature of meeting rooms?

This is not important to me _____

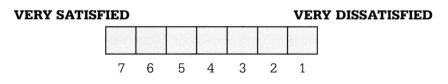

VERY SATISFIED   **VERY DISSATISFIED**

7   6   5   4   3   2   1

Table 11.2 GSA Occupant Survey *(continued)*

4. How satisfied are you with the acoustic quality of meeting rooms?

This is not important to me _____

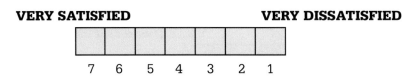

5. How satisfied are you with the variety of meeting rooms available to you?

This is not important to me _____

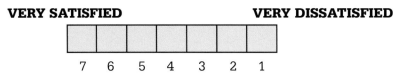

6. Please describe any other issues related to meeting facilities that are important to you.

Part 7 - Work Experiences

In this section, please rate your level of agreement with the following statements about experiences at work.

1. I look forward to working in the building.

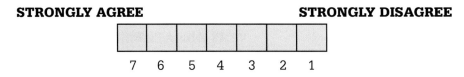

2. I am proud to show the office to visitors.

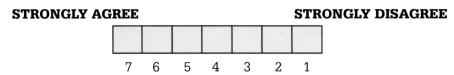

Table 11.2 GSA Occupant Survey *(continued)*

3. The overall appearance of the workplace is consistent with the mission of the agency.

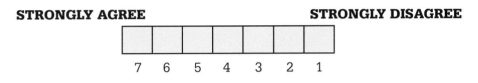

4. There is a good sense of connection to the outdoors from inside the building.

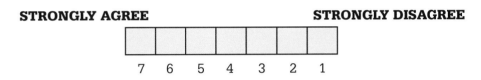

5. There is a definite space that is the 'heart' of the workplace.

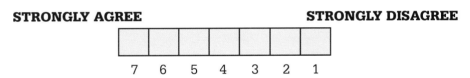

6. It is easy to locate other people and spaces (offices, meeting rooms, etc.) even when I have not been there before.

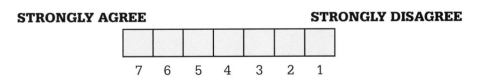

7. Communication within my group is good.

8. I learn a lot about what is going on by seeing and hearing others.

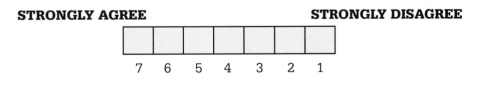

Table 11.2 GSA Occupant Survey *(continued)*

9. I often stop and talk to others in corridors or break areas.

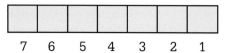

10. The security features of our building are adequate.

11. I feel safe walking to and from the building.

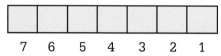

12. We have comfortable spaces to have lunch or take breaks inside the building.

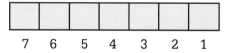

13. We have adequate restroom facilities in our offices.

14. I use the building stairs rather than the elevator at least once a day.

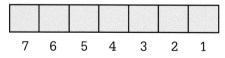

Table 11.2 GSA Occupant Survey *(continued)*

Part 8 - Indoor Environmental Quality

The following section of the survey focuses on your satisfaction with indoor environmental quality in your workplace. How important is each of the following items to doing your job well?

Thermal Comfort

1. Which of the following do you personally adjust or control in your workspace? (check all that apply)

☐ Window blinds or shades	☐ Operable window
☐ Thermostat	☐ Portable heater
☐ Permanent heater	☐ Room air-conditioning unit
☐ Portable fan	☐ Ceiling fan
☐ Adjustable air vent in wall or ceiling	☐ Adjustable air vent in floor (diffuser)
☐ Door to interior space	☐ Door to exterior space
☐ None of the above	☐ Other

2. How satisfied are you with the temperature in your workspace?

VERY SATISFIED   **VERY DISSATISFIED**

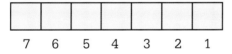

7   6   5   4   3   2   1

Air Quality

1. How satisfied are you with the air quality in your workspace (i.e., stuffy/stale air, cleanliness, odors)?

VERY SATISFIED   **VERY DISSATISFIED**

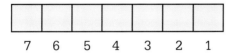

7   6   5   4   3   2   1

Table 11.2 GSA Occupant Survey *(continued)*

Lighting

1. Which of the following controls do you have over the lighting in your workspace? (check all that apply)

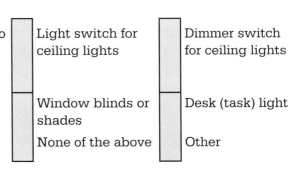

☐ Light switch for ceiling lights		☐ Dimmer switch for ceiling lights
☐ Window blinds or shades		☐ Desk (task) light
☐ None of the above		☐ Other

2. How satisfied are you with the amount of light in your workspace?

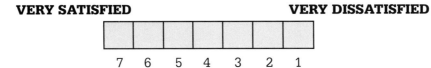

VERY SATISFIED   **VERY DISSATISFIED**

7   6   5   4   3   2   1

3. How satisfied are you with the visual comfort of the lighting (e.g., glare, reflections, contrast)?

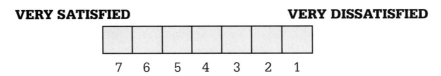

VERY SATISFIED   **VERY DISSATISFIED**

7   6   5   4   3   2   1

4. How satisfied are you with the degree of control you have over the lighting in your workspace?

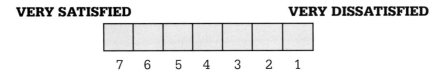

VERY SATISFIED   **VERY DISSATISFIED**

7   6   5   4   3   2   1

Windows and Daylight

1. How satisfied are you with the amount of daylight in your general office area?

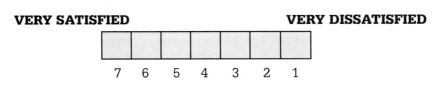

VERY SATISFIED   **VERY DISSATISFIED**

7   6   5   4   3   2   1

Table 11.2 GSA Occupant Survey *(continued)*

2. How satisfied are you with your access to a window view?

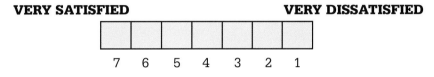

Acoustic Quality

1. How satisfied are you with the noise level in your workspace?

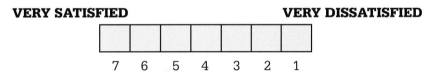

2. How satisfied are you with the speech privacy in your workspace (ability to have conversations without your neighbors overhearing and vice versa)?

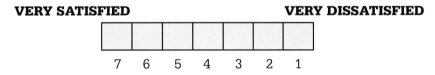

Cleanliness and Maintenance

1. How satisfied are you with the cleanliness and maintenance of the building?

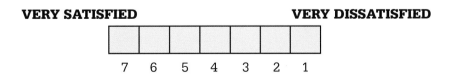

Please describe any other issues related to indoor environmental quality that are important to you.

Part 9 - General Comments

1. All things considered, how satisfied are you with your personal workspace?

VERY SATISFIED   VERY DISSATISFIED

7   6   5   4   3   2   1

Table 11.2 GSA Occupant Survey *(continued)*

2. How satisfied are you with the building overall?

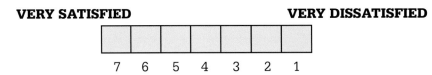

VERY SATISFIED   **VERY DISSATISFIED**

7   6   5   4   3   2   1

3. To what extent does your workplace enhance or interfere with your <u>individual work effectiveness?</u>

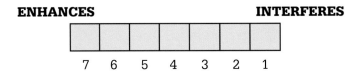

ENHANCES   **INTERFERES**

7   6   5   4   3   2   1

4. To what extent does your workplace enhance or interfere with your ability to <u>work effectively with others?</u>

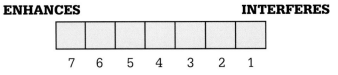

ENHANCES   **INTERFERES**

7   6   5   4   3   2   1

5. If you wanted to show a visitor around the building, but could only show one space, which space would you show?

6. Any additional comments or recommendations about your personal workspace or building overall?

Conclusions

While it is likely not billable in many cases, conducting a POE is a required part of some rating systems, such as WELL, and is the best way for firms to learn from project to project how to best provide interior spaces that work for building occupants. Using the methods described above can provide a design team with valuable information to help improve future designs, as well as to remediate any potential immediate issues in a building that will improve client–designer relationships.

Key Terms

benchmarking
building flush out
commissioning
post-occupancy evaluation (POE)
total volatile organic compounds (TVOCs)
volatile organic compounds (VOCs)

Assignments

1. In teams of two to four people, write a series of questions that might be used to interview building occupants. (Use the GSA survey questions as a launching point for further inquiry.)

2. Describe the similarities and differences between the LEED Rating Systems and the WELL Building Standard. How does each one relate to POE?

3. Why might designers avoid conducting POEs?

Resources

Center for the Built Environment (2017, March 22), *Occupant Indoor Environmental Quality (IEQ) Survey and Building Benchmarking*. Available online: http://www.cbe.berkeley.edu/research/briefs-survey.htm

Fowler, Kim and Rauch, Emily, (2008), *Assessing Green Building Performance: A Post Occupancy Evaluation of 12 GSA Buildings*, GSA: Pacific Northwest National Laboratory, Contract DE-AC05-76RLO1830. Retrieved 7/20/16 from http://www.gsa.gov/portal/mediaId/214299/fileName/GSA_Assessing_Green_Full_Report.action

GSA, (2017), "Post Occupancy Evaluation," GSA. Retrieved from http://www.gsa.gov/portal/content/103959

Hiromoto, Julie, (2015), *Architect & Design Sustainable Design Leaders Post Occupancy Evaluation Survey Report*, prepared for SOM, NY, NY. Retrieved 7/19/16 from https://www.som.com/ideas/research/post_occupancy_evaluation_survey_report

HEFC, (2006), *Guide to Post Occupancy Evaluation*. University of Westminster. Retrieved 7/19/16 from http://www.smg.ac.uk/documents/POEBrochureFinal06.pdf

12

Check Sheets—Code Information for All Phases of the Project

Introduction

At the beginning of the project, some basic building code information should be collected to ensure that overall space planning will meet future code requirements as the design is refined.

Programming

During the programming phase, the following information is determined:

1. Use group(s) or occupancy classification(s)
2. Identify the base building construction
    a. Construction type
    b. Number of stories and height in feet

3. Is the building going to be equipped with a fire sprinkler system?
4. Will there be an atrium?
5. Based on the initial program, are there assembly spaces?
6. If mixed occupancy, where are fire separations likely to be needed and what is the fire-resistance rating of these separations?
7. What is the strategy for fire safety?
8. What interior wall assemblies will be explored to ensure fire separations?

Adjacency Matrix

Also during programming, the first iteration of an adjacency matrix can be completed. This can then be used for some basic code analysis (Table 12.1).

Table 12.1 Check Sheet for Building Codes: Schematic Design

As the actual design begins to take shape, it is important to recheck all the building code and ADA assumptions made during the programming stage of the project.

Code used:
Year:

Proposed occupancy type(s):
Proposed building square footage:
stories:

Revised programmed uses of spaces:

Space Name	Quantity	Square Footage	Is There Plumbing?	Natural Light	Other

Table 12.1 a Revised occupant load calculations from IBC 2018 Table 1004.5

MEANS OF EGRESS

TABLE 1004.5
MAXIMUM FLOOR AREA ALLOWANCES PER OCCUPANT

FUNCTION OF SPACE	OCCUPANT LOAD FACTOR[a]
Accessory storage areas, mechanical equipment room	300 gross
Agricultural building	300 gross
Aircraft hangars	500 gross

Airport terminal
   Baggage claim
   Baggage handling
   Concourse
   Waiting areas
	
	20 gross
	300 gross
	100 gross
	15 gross

Assembly
   Gaming floors (keno, slots, etc.)
   Exhibit gallery and museum
	
	11 gross
	30 net

Assembly with fixed seats	See Section 1004.6

Assembly without fixed seats
   Concentrated
      (chairs only—not fixed)
   Standing space
   Unconcentrated (tables and chairs)
	
	7 net
	
	5 net
	15 net

Bowling centers, allow 5 persons for each lane including 15 feet of runway, and for additional areas	7 net
Business areas Concentrated business use areas	150 gross See Section 1004.8
Courtrooms—other than fixed seating areas	40 net
Day care	35 net
Dormitories	50 gross

Educational
   Classroom area
   Shops and other vocational room areas
	
	20 net
	50 net

Exercise rooms	50 gross
Group H-5 fabrication and manufacturing areas	200 gross
Industrial areas	100 gross

Institutional areas
   Inpatient treatment areas
   Outpatient areas
   Sleeping areas
	
	240 gross
	100 gross
	120 gross

Kitchens, commercial	200 gross

Library
   Reading rooms
   Stack area
	
	50 net
	100 gross

Locker rooms	50 gross
Mall buildings—covered and open	See Section 402.8.2
Mercantile Storage, stock, shipping areas	60 gross 300 gross
Parking garages	200 gross
Residential	200 gross

Skating rinks, swimming pools
   Rink and pool
   Decks
	
	50 gross
	15 gross

Stages and platforms	15 net
Warehouses	500 gross

For SI: 1 foot = 304.8 mm, 1 square foot = 0.0929 m².

a. Floor area in square feet per occupant.

Table 12.1 b Common path of travel from IBC 2018 Table 1006.2.1

TABLE 1006.2.1
SPACES WITH ONE EXIT OR EXIT ACCESS DOORWAY

OCCUPANCY	MAXIMUM OCCUPANT LOAD OF SPACE	MAXIMUM COMMON PATH OF EGRESS TRAVEL DISTANCE (feet)		With Sprinkler System (feet)
		Without Sprinkler System (feet)		
		Occupant Load		
		OL ≤ 30	OL >30	
A[c], E, M	49	75	75	75[a]
B	49	100	75	100[a]
F	49	75	75	100[a]
H-1, H-2, H-3	3	NP	NP	25[b]
H-4, H-5	10	NP	NP	75[b]
I-1, I-2[d], I-4	10	NP	NP	75[a]
I-3	10	NP	NP	100[a]
R-1	10	NP	NP	75[a]
R-2	20	NP	NP	125[a]
R-3[e]	20	NP	NP	125[a, g]
R-4[e]	20	NP	NP	125[a, g]
S[f]	29	100	75	100[a]
U	49	100	75	75[a]

For SI: 1 foot = 304.8 mm.

NP = Not Permitted.

a. Buildings equipped throughout with an automatic sprinkler system in accordance with Section 903.3.1.1 or 903.3.1.2. See Section 903 for occupancies where automatic sprinkler systems are permitted in accordance with Section 903.3.1.2.

b. Group H occupancies equipped throughout with an automatic sprinkler system in accordance with Section 903.2.5.

c. For a room or space used for assembly purposes having fixed seating, see Section 1029.8.

d. For the travel distance limitations in Group I-2, see Section 407.4.

e. The common path of egress travel distance shall only apply in a Group R-3 occupancy located in a mixed occupancy building.

f. The length of common path of egress travel distance in a Group S-2 open parking garage shall be not more than 100 feet.

g. For the travel distance limitations in Groups R-3 and R-4 equipped throughout with an automatic sprinkler system in accordance with Section 903.3.1.3, see Section 1006.2.2.6.

Table 12.1 c Number of exits required from IBC 2018 Table 1006.3.2

TABLE 1006.3.2
MINIMUM NUMBER OF EXITS OR
ACCESS TO EXITS PER STORY

OCCUPANT LOAD PER STORY	MINIMUM NUMBER OF EXITS OR ACCESS TO EXITS FROM STORY
1-500	2
501-1,000	3
More than 1,000	4

Table 12.1 d Plumbing Fixture Calculations from IBC 2018 Table 2902.1

[P] TABLE 2902.1
MINIMUM NUMBER OF REQUIRED PLUMBING FIXTURES[a]
(See Sections 2902.1.1 and 2902.2)

No.	CLASSIFICATION	DESCRIPTION	WATER CLOSETS (URINALS SEE SECTION 424.2 OF THE *INTERNATIONAL PLUMBING CODE*)		LAVATORIES		BATHTUBS/ SHOWERS	DRINKING FOUNTAINS (SEE SECTION 410 OF THE *INTERNATIONAL PLUMBING CODE*)	OTHER
			Male	Female	Male	Female			
1	Assembly	Theaters and other buildings for the performing arts and motion pictures[d]	1 per 125	1 per 65	1 per 200		—	1 per 500	1 service sink
		Nightclubs, bars, taverns, dance halls and buildings for similar purposes[d]	1 per 40	1 per 40	1 per 75		—	1 per 500	1 service sink
		Restaurants, banquet halls and food courts[d]	1 per 75	1 per 75	1 per 200		—	1 per 500	1 service sink
		Casino gaming areas	1 per 100 for the first 400 and 1 per 250 for the remainder exceeding 400	1 per 50 for the first 400 and 1 per 150 for the remainder exceeding 400	1 per 250 for the first 750 and 1 per 500 for the remainder exceeding 750		—	1 per 1,000	1 service sink

Table 12.1 d *(continued)*

PLUMBING SYSTEMS

[P] TABLE 2902.1—(continued)
MINIMUM NUMBER OF REQUIRED PLUMBING FIXTURES[a]
(See Sections 2902.1.1 and 2902.2)

No.	CLASSIFICATION	DESCRIPTION	WATER CLOSETS (URINALS SEE SECTION 424.2 OF THE *INTERNATIONAL PLUMBING CODE*) Male	Female	LAVATORIES Male	Female	BATHTUBS/ SHOWERS	DRINKING FOUNTAINS (SEE SECTION 410 OF THE *INTERNATIONAL PLUMBING CODE*)	OTHER
1	Assembly	Auditoriums without permanent seating, art galleries, exhibition halls, museums, lecture halls, libraries, arcades and gymnasiums[d]	1 per 125	1 per 65	1 per 200		—	1 per 500	1 service sink
		Passenger terminals and transportation facilities[d]	1 per 500	1 per 500	1 per 750		—	1 per 1,000	1 service sink
		Places of worship and other religious services[d]	1 per 150	1 per 75	1 per 200		—	1 per 1,000	1 service sink
		Coliseums, arenas, skating rinks, pools and tennis courts for indoor sporting events and activities	1 per 75 for the first 1,500 and 1 per 120 for the remainder exceeding 1,500	1 per 40 for the first 1,520 and 1 per 60 for the remainder exceeding 1,520	1 per 200	1 per 150	—	1 per 1,000	1 service sink
		Stadiums, amusement parks, bleachers and grandstands for outdoor sporting events and activities[f]	1 per 75 for the first 1,500 and 1 per 120 for the remainder exceeding 1,500	1 per 40 for the first 1,520 and 1 per 60 for the remainder exceeding 1,520	1 per 200	1 per 150	—	1 per 1,000	1 service sink
2	Business	Buildings for the transaction of business, professional services, other services involving merchandise, office buildings, banks, light industrial, ambulatory care and similar uses	1 per 25 for the first 50 and 1 per 50 for the remainder exceeding 50		1 per 40 for the first 80 and 1 per 80 for the remainder exceeding 80		—	1 per 100	1 service sink[e]
3	Educational	Educational facilities	1 per 50		1 per 50		—	1 per 100	1 service sink
4	Factory and industrial	Structures in which occupants are engaged in work fabricating, assembly or processing of products or materials	1 per 100		1 per 100		—	1 per 400	1 service sink
5	Institutional	Custodial care facilities	1 per 10		1 per 10		1 per 8	1 per 100	1 service sink
		Medical care recipients in hospitals and nursing homes[b]	1 per room[c]		1 per room[c]		1 per 15	1 per 100	1 service sink
		Employees in hospitals and nursing homes[b]	1 per 25		1 per 35		—	1 per 100	—
		Visitors in hospitals and nursing homes	1 per 75		1 per 100		—	1 per 500	—
		Prisons[b]	1 per cell		1 per cell		1 per 15	1 per 100	1 service sink

(continued)

Table 12.1 d *(continued)*

[P] TABLE 2902.1—continued
MINIMUM NUMBER OF REQUIRED PLUMBING FIXTURES[a]
(See Sections 2902.1.1 and 2902.2)

No.	CLASSIFICATION	DESCRIPTION	WATER CLOSETS (URINALS SEE SECTION 424.2 OF THE *INTERNATIONAL PLUMBING CODE*) Male	Female	LAVATORIES Male	Female	BATHTUBS OR SHOWERS	DRINKING FOUNTAINS (SEE SECTION 410 OF THE *INTERNATIONAL PLUMBING CODE*)	OTHER
5	Institutional	Reformatories, detention centers and correctional centers[b]	1 per 15		1 per 15		1 per 15	1 per 100	1 service sink
		Employees in reformitories, detention centers and correctional centers[b]	1 per 25		1 per 35		—	1 per 100	—
		Adult day care and child day care	1 per 15		1 per 15		1	1 per 100	1 service sink
6	Mercantile	Retail stores, service stations, shops, salesrooms, markets and shopping centers	1 per 500		1 per 750		—	1 per 1,000	1 service sink[c]
7	Residential	Hotels, motels, boarding houses (transient)	1 per sleeping unit		1 per sleeping unit		1 per sleeping unit	—	1 service sink
		Dormitories, fraternities, sororities and boarding houses (not transient)	1 per 10		1 per 10		1 per 8	1 per 100	1 service sink
		Apartment house	1 per dwelling unit		1 per dwelling unit		1 per dwelling unit	—	1 kitchen sink per dwelling unit; 1 automatic clothes washer connection per 20 dwelling units
		One- and two-family dwellings and lodging houses with five or fewer guestrooms	1 per dwelling unit		1 per 10		1 per dwelling unit	—	1 kitchen sink per dwelling unit; 1 automatic clothes washer connection per dwelling unit
		Congregate living facilities with 16 or fewer persons	1 per 10		1 per 10		1 per 8	1 per 100	1 service sink
8	Storage	Structures for the storage of goods, warehouses, storehouses and freight depots, low and moderate hazard	1 per 100		1 per 100		—	1 per 1,000	1 service sink

a. The fixtures shown are based on one fixture being the minimum required for the number of persons indicated or any fraction of the number of persons indicated. The number of occupants shall be determined by this code.
b. Toilet facilities for employees shall be separate from facilities for inmates or care recipients.
c. A single-occupant toilet room with one water closet and one lavatory serving not more than two adjacent patient sleeping units shall be permitted, provided that each patient sleeping unit has direct access to the toilet room and provisions for privacy for the toilet room user are provided.
d. The occupant load for seasonal outdoor seating and entertainment areas shall be included when determining the minimum number of facilities required.
e. For business and mercantile classifications with an occupant load of 15 or fewer, a service sink shall not be required.
f. The required number and type of plumbing fixtures for outdoor swimming pools shall be in accordance with Section 609 of the *International Swimming Pool and Spa Code*.

Table 12.1 e Required finishes based on space from IBC 2018 Table 803.13

INTERIOR FINISHES

TABLE 803.13
INTERIOR WALL AND CEILING FINISH REQUIREMENTS BY OCCUPANCY[k]

GROUP	SPRINKLERED[l]			NONSPRINKLERED		
	Interior exit stairways and ramps and exit passageways[a, b]	Corridors and enclosure for exit access stairways and ramps	Rooms and enclosed spaces[c]	Interior exit stairways and ramps and exit passageways[a, b]	Corridors and enclosure for exit access stairways and ramps	Rooms and enclosed spaces[c]
A-1 & A-2	B	B	C	A	A[d]	B[e]
A-3[f], A-4, A-5	B	B	C	A	A[d]	C
B, E, M, R-1	B	C[m]	C	A	B	C
R-4	B	C	C	A	B	B
F	C	C	C	B	C	C
H	B	B	C[g]	A	A	B
I-1	B	C	C	A	B	B
I-2	B	B	B[h, i]	A	A	B
I-3	A	A[j]	C	A	A	B
I-4	B	B	B[h, i]	A	A	B
R-2	C	C	C	B	B	C
R-3	C	C	C	C	C	C
S	C	C	C	B	B	C
U	No restrictions			No restrictions		

For SI: 1 inch = 25.4 mm, 1 square foot = 0.0929 m².

a. Class C interior finish materials shall be permitted for wainscotting or paneling of not more than 1,000 square feet of applied surface area in the grade lobby where applied directly to a noncombustible base or over furring strips applied to a noncombustible base and fireblocked as required by Section 803.15.1.

b. In other than Group I-3 occupancies in buildings less than three stories above grade plane, Class B interior finish for nonsprinklered buildings and Class C interior finish for sprinklered buildings shall be permitted in interior exit stairways and ramps.

c. Requirements for rooms and enclosed spaces shall be based on spaces enclosed by partitions. Where a fire-resistance rating is required for structural elements, the enclosing partitions shall extend from the floor to the ceiling. Partitions that do not comply with this shall be considered to be enclosing spaces and the rooms or spaces on both sides shall be considered to be one room or space. In determining the applicable requirements for rooms and enclosed spaces, the specific occupancy thereof shall be the governing factor regardless of the group classification of the building or structure.

d. Lobby areas in Group A-1, A-2 and A-3 occupancies shall be not less than Class B materials.

e. Class C interior finish materials shall be permitted in places of assembly with an occupant load of 300 persons or less.

f. For places of religious worship, wood used for ornamental purposes, trusses, paneling or chancel furnishing shall be permitted.

g. Class B material is required where the building exceeds two stories.

h. Class C interior finish materials shall be permitted in administrative spaces.

i. Class C interior finish materials shall be permitted in rooms with a capacity of four persons or less.

j. Class B materials shall be permitted as wainscotting extending not more than 48 inches above the finished floor in corridors and exit access stairways and ramps.

k. Finish materials as provided for in other sections of this code.

l. Applies when protected by an automatic sprinkler system installed in accordance with Section 903.3.1.1 or 903.3.1.2.

m. Corridors in ambulatory care facilities shall be provided with Class A or B materials.

Table 12.1 f Required fire separations of spaces with mixed uses from IBC 2018 Table 508.4

GENERAL BUILDING HEIGHTS AND AREAS

TABLE 508.4
REQUIRED SEPARATION OF OCCUPANCIES (HOURS)[f]

OCCUPANCY	A, E		I-1[a], I-3, I-4		I-2		R[a]		F-2, S-2[b], U		B[e], F-1, M, S-1		H-1		H-2		H-3, H-4		H-5	
	S	NS	S	NS	S	NS	S	NS	S	NS	S	NS	S	NS	S	NS	S	NS	S	NS
A, E	N	N	1	2	2	NP	1	2	N	1	1	2	NP	NP	3	4	2	3	2	NP
I-1[a], I-3, I-4	—	—	N	N	2	NP	1	NP	1	2	1	2	NP	NP	3	NP	2	NP	2	NP
I-2	—	—	—	—	N	N	2	NP	2	NP	2	NP	NP	NP	3	NP	2	NP	2	NP
R[a]	—	—	—	—	—	—	N	N	1[c]	2[c]	1	2	NP	NP	3	NP	2	NP	2	NP
F-2, S-2[b], U	—	—	—	—	—	—	—	—	N	N	1	2	NP	NP	3	4	2	3	2	NP
B[e], F-1, M, S-1	—	—	—	—	—	—	—	—	—	—	N	N	NP	NP	2	3	1	2	1	NP
H-1	—	—	—	—	—	—	—	—	—	—	—	—	N	NP	NP	NP	NP	NP	NP	NP
H-2	—	—	—	—	—	—	—	—	—	—	—	—	—	—	N	NP	1	NP	1	NP
H-3, H-4	—	—	—	—	—	—	—	—	—	—	—	—	—	—	—	—	1[d]	NP	1	NP
H-5	—	—	—	—	—	—	—	—	—	—	—	—	—	—	—	—	—	—	N	NP

S = Buildings equipped throughout with an automatic sprinkler system installed in accordance with Section 903.3.1.1.

NS = Buildings not equipped throughout with an automatic sprinkler system installed in accordance with Section 903.3.1.1.

N = No separation requirement.

NP = Not Permitted.

a. See Section 420.

b. The required separation from areas used only for private or pleasure vehicles shall be reduced by 1 hour but not to less than 1 hour.

c. See Section 406.3.2.

d. Separation is not required between occupancies of the same classification.

e. See Section 422.2 for ambulatory care facilities.

f. Occupancy separations that serve to define fire area limits established in Chapter 9 for requiring fire protection systems shall also comply with Section 707.3.10 and Table 707.3.10 in accordance with Section 901.7.

Table 12.1 g For individual occupancies, fire enclosures from IBC 2018 Table 707.3.10

TABLE 707.3.10
FIRE-RESISTANCE RATING REQUIREMENTS FOR
FIRE BARRIERS, FIRE WALLS OR HORIZONTAL
ASSEMBLIES BETWEEN FIRE AREAS

OCCUPANCY GROUP	FIRE-RESISTANCE RATING (hours)
H-1, H-2	4
F-1, H-3, S-1	3
A, B, E, F-2, H-4, H-5, I, M, R, S-2	2
U	1

707.4 Exterior walls. Where exterior walls serve as a part of a required fire-resistance-rated shaft or stairway or ramp enclosure, or separation, such walls shall comply with the requirements of Section 705 for exterior walls and the fire-

Sustainability concerns, such as LEED, the Living Building Challenge or Green Globes and WELL Building criteria, can and should also be addressed as a part of this initial planning. Sun studies can be used to inform initial space-planning decisions as well as passive solar strategies, daylight harvesting, and other integrated approaches. If the jurisdiction where the project is located has adopted the IgCC, then IgCC green and sustainability provisions must be considered.

Diagramming

Once some basic information has been collected, and the adjacency matrix completed with some preliminary occupancy load information, a fire-separation diagram can be done in plan and section. The diagrams can be used to identify existing exits, as well as the placement of remote egressing strategies that meet both diagonal separation requirements and travel distance limitations.

Schematic Design

As the project moves into the schematic design phase, the design concept and inspiration are identified, as well as the overall conceptual approach for the design (Table 12.2).

Table 12.2 Check Sheet Occupancy Loads

Occupancy Load Calculation Summary

Room Number	Room Name	Area Use Description	OLF Occ. Load	Req'd Exits	Req'd Width

Occupancy load calculations should be done for all spaces in each level of the building. The information is then provided as a part of the life-safety plan that also includes common path of travel and travel distances, as well as other key life-safety information.

OLF = Occupancy Load Factor from Table 1004.1.2 (indicate gross or net)

Occ. Load = Occupancy Load

Req'd Exits = Required Exits

Req'd Width = Required Width

The following should be identified:

CONCEPT

COLOR PALETTE
Color scheme used:
Justification for colors used (symbolic, behavioral, cultural, based on research, etc.)

CODE RESEARCH
Additional code research is conducted as the plans are developed:
Diagonal: _____
Sprinklered: Y   N
Distance exits must be apart from one another:

_____

Specific fire-separation requirements based on occupancies: _____

UNIVERSAL DESIGN

Universal design consideration might also be addressed during the programming and schematic design stages of the project. Although we often think of universal design as applying only to residential applications, designing for all people of all sizes and abilities is relevant for all project types (Table 12.3).

Table 12.3 Check Sheet Universal Design

PRINCIPLE ONE: Equitable Use

The design is useful and marketable to people with diverse abilities.

Guidelines:
1a. Provide the same means of use for all users: identical whenever possible; equivalent when not.
1b. Avoid segregating or stigmatizing any users.
1c. Provisions for privacy, security, and safety should be equally available to all users.
1d. Make the design appealing to all users.

PRINCIPLE TWO: Flexibility in Use

The design accommodates a wide range of individual preferences and abilities.

Guidelines:
2a. Provide choice in methods of use.
2b. Accommodate right- or left-handed access and use.
2c. Facilitate the user's accuracy and precision.
2d. Provide adaptability to the user's pace.

PRINCIPLE THREE: Simple and Intuitive Use

Use of the design is easy to understand, regardless of the user's experience, knowledge, language skills, or current concentration level.

Guidelines:
3a. Eliminate unnecessary complexity.
3b. Be consistent with user expectations and intuition.
3c. Accommodate a wide range of literacy and language skills.
3d. Arrange information consistent with its importance.
3e. Provide effective prompting and feedback during and after task completion.

PRINCIPLE FOUR: Perceptible Information

The design communicates necessary information effectively to the user, regardless of ambient conditions or the user's sensory abilities.

Guidelines:
4a. Use different modes (pictorial, verbal, tactile) for redundant presentation of essential information.
4b. Provide adequate contrast between essential information and its surroundings.
4c. Maximize "legibility" of essential information.
4d. Differentiate elements in ways that can be described (i.e., make it easy to give instructions or directions).
4e. Provide compatibility with a variety of techniques or devices used by people with sensory limitations.

PRINCIPLE FIVE: Tolerance for Error

The design minimizes hazards and the adverse consequences of accidental or unintended actions.

Guidelines:
5a. Arrange elements to minimize hazards and errors: most used elements, most accessible; hazardous elements eliminated, isolated, or shielded.
5b. Provide warnings of hazards and errors.
5c. Provide fail-safe features.
5d. Discourage unconscious action in tasks that require vigilance.

PRINCIPLE SIX: Low Physical Effort

The design can be used efficiently and comfortably and with a minimum of fatigue.

Guidelines:
6a. Allow user to maintain a neutral body position.
6b. Use reasonable operating forces.
6c. Minimize repetitive actions.
6d. Minimize sustained physical effort.

PRINCIPLE SEVEN: Size and Space for Approach and Use

Appropriate size and space is provided for approach, reach, manipulation, and use regardless of user's body size, posture, or mobility.

Guidelines:
7a. Provide a clear line of sight to important elements for any seated or standing user.
7b. Make reach to all components comfortable for any seated or standing user.
7c. Accommodate variations in hand and grip size.
7d. Provide adequate space for the use of assistive devices or personal assistance.
Please note that the Principles of Universal Design address only universally usable design, while the practice of design involves more than consideration for usability. Designers must also incorporate other considerations such as economic, engineering, cultural, gender, and environmental concerns in their design processes. These principles offer designers guidance to better integrate features that meet the needs of as many users as possible.

Source: Copyright 1997, NC State University, The Center for Universal Design

Design Development

Once all code concerns have been integrated into the space planning and the schematic design has been approved, the project moves into design development. During design development, as actual furniture, fixtures and equipment, and finishes are selected, the design drawings are altered to accommodate the actual selections.

As a part of this process, all code information should be rechecked and refined. A complete fire safety approach should be established, including use of fire sprinklers, type and placement, locations for fire alarms, smoke alarms, fire extinguishers, stand pipes, and other fire-safety equipment. During this stage, egress plans must also be completed to establish common path of travel and over all travel distances; double check for dead-end corridors, areas of refuge, and other features related to safe egress (Table 12.4).

In addition, the reflected ceiling plan should integrate all exits signs, emergency lights, sprinklers, fire alarms, and smoke detectors (Table 12.5 and Figures 12.1–12.8).

During design development, the LEED checklist, Green Globes checklist, the Living Building Challenge Petals worksheet, or WELL checklists should be consulted for final point selections (as applicable). IgCC requirements must be considered if it has been adopted by the jurisdiction (Table 12.6).

Table 12.4 Design Development Code Check Sheet

1. Determine your occupancy classification(s) and list in the space provided:

2. Determine your occupancy factor (gross or net) for each of the above occupancy classifications:

Occupancy	Factor	Gross/Net?

3. Calculate your occupant load for each space:

Occupancy	Factor	Sq. Footage	# occupants permitted

TOTAL number of occupants

4. What is the diagonal for egress? _____

5. How far apart must your fire-rated stair towers/exits be (minimum)? _____

6. Is your building sprinklered?

7. What is the maximum travel distance to an exit (common path of travel) for each floor
   a. First _____
   b. Second _____
   c. Third _____
   d. Fourth _____

8. How many of each of the following do you need for your design?
   a. WC   M_____ F _____
   b. Lavatory   M _____ F_____
   c. Water fountains   _____
   d. Service sinks   _____

9. According to your use group, what is the minimum egress corridor width you can use? _____

10. What is the maximum dead-end corridor width you are permitted for this use group? _____

11. What is the required clear distance on the PUSH side of an accessible door? ____

12. What is the required clear distance on the PULL side of an accessible door? ____

13. What size door is required to comply with ADA requirements? _____

14. Where should exit signs be placed in your reflected ceiling plan? Describe in the space provided below:

Table 12.5 Reflected Ceiling Plans and Life Safety

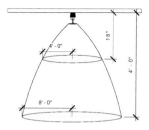

Figure 12.1
Sprinkler
distribution
pattern

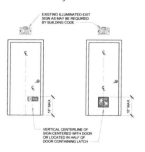

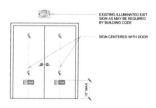

Figure 12.2
Exit sign
placement above
door

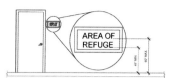

Figure 12.3
Area of Refuge
sign placement

Sprinklers
Ceiling mounted—spread 16 feet distribution in diameter
Must be aligned—plumbing supply (water)

Exit Signs
Visible from all occupied spaces
At every change in direction
Above each exit door

HVAC
All spaces must have a supply and a return
In large spaces, one supply every 200 square feet or so and one return for every 400 to 500 square feet
If using exposed ceiling you will see duct work connecting supplies and returns

Exposed Ceilings
If you are using an exposed ceiling, you will see the underside of the structure above
This means you will see . . .
A metal pan, a concrete slab, a waffle slab, a coffered ceiling (concrete) or other similar structural ceiling . . .
Electrical conduit going to all lights and smoke detectors . . .
All mechanical ducts and supply and return . . .
Water pipes connecting all sprinkler heads which are also visible . . .

Table 12.5 Reflected Ceiling Plans and Life Safety *(continued)*

Legends

You must have a legend, and it needs to include information on the fixture and lamps you use in your space (use only LED or fluorescent); HID Metal halide (color corrected) is also a possible lamp type to use

You should include exit signs, smoke detectors, supply and return and ceiling finishes on your legend AND all light fixtures

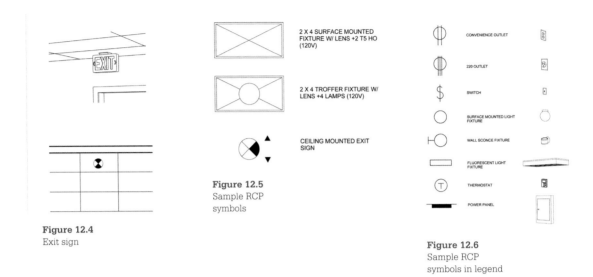

Figure 12.4
Exit sign

Figure 12.5
Sample RCP symbols

Figure 12.6
Sample RCP symbols in legend

Dimensions

RCPs should include ceiling heights of all ceilings, dropped soffits, and other design details

Special features need to be dimensioned

Materials

Materials should be indicated and differentiated

Other Life-Safety Items

Smoke alarm in all corridors and open office spaces

Fire alarm with visible strobe and sound in each enclosed space with multiple occupants

Figure 12.7
Smoke detector

Figure 12.8
Fire alarm

Table 12.6 LEED v.4 ID + C Checklist

LEED v4 for ID+C: Commercial Interiors
Project Checklist

Project Name:
Date:

Y	?	N		Credit / Prereq	Item	Possible Points
			Credit	Integrative Process		2
0	**0**	**0**		**Location and Transportation**		**18**
			Credit	LEED for Neighborhood Development Location		18
			Credit	Surrounding Density and Diverse Uses		8
			Credit	Access to Quality Transit		7
			Credit	Bicycle Facilities		1
			Credit	Reduced Parking Footprint		2
0	**0**	**0**		**Water Efficiency**		**12**
Y			Prereq	Indoor Water Use Reduction		Required
			Credit	Indoor Water Use Reduction		12
0	**0**	**0**		**Energy and Atmosphere**		**38**
Y			Prereq	Fundamental Commissioning and Verification		Required
Y			Prereq	Minimum Energy Performance		Required
Y			Prereq	Fundamental Refrigerant Management		Required
			Credit	Enhanced Commissioning		5
			Credit	Optimize Energy Performance		25
			Credit	Advanced Energy Metering		2
			Credit	Renewable Energy Production		3
			Credit	Enhanced Refrigerant Management		1
			Credit	Green Power and Carbon Offsets		2
0	**0**	**0**		**Materials and Resources**		**13**
Y			Prereq	Storage and Collection of Recyclables		Required
Y			Prereq	Construction and Demolition Waste Management Planning		Required
			Credit	Long-Term Commitment		1
			Credit	Interiors Life-Cycle Impact Reduction		4
			Credit	Building Product Disclosure and Optimization - Environmental Product Declarations		2
			Credit	Building Product Disclosure and Optimization - Sourcing of Raw Materials		2
			Credit	Building Product Disclosure and Optimization - Material Ingredients		2
			Credit	Construction and Demolition Waste Management		2
0	**0**	**0**		**Indoor Environmental Quality**		**18**
Y			Prereq	Minimum Indoor Air Quality Performance		18
Y			Prereq	Environmental Tobacco Smoke Control		8
			Credit	Enhanced Indoor Air Quality Strategies		7
			Credit	Low-Emitting Materials		1
			Credit	Construction Indoor Air Quality Management Plan		2
			Credit	Indoor Air Quality Assessment		
			Credit	Thermal Comfort		
			Credit	Interior Lighting		
			Credit	Daylight		
			Credit	Quality Views		
			Credit	Acoustic Performance		
0	**0**	**0**		**Innovation**		
			Credit	Innovation		
			Credit	LEED Accredited Professional		
0	**0**	**0**		**Regional Priority**		
			Credit	Regional Priority: Specific Credit		
			Credit	Regional Priority: Specific Credit		
			Credit	Regional Priority: Specific Credit		
			Credit	Regional Priority: Specific Credit		
0	**0**	**0**		**TOTALS**		**Possible Points:**

Certified: 40 to 49 points,   **Silver:** 50 to 59 points,   **Gold:** 60 to 79 points,   **Platinum:** 80+

Table 12.6 LEED v.4 ID + C Checklist *(continued)*

LEED v4 for ID+C: Hospitality
Project Checklist

Project Name:
Date:

Y	?	N			Possible Points
			Credit	Integrative Process	2

Y	?	N	**Location and Transportation**		18
0	0	0			
			Credit	LEED for Neighborhood Development Location	18
			Credit	Surrounding Density and Diverse Uses	8
			Credit	Access to Quality Transit	7
			Credit	Bicycle Facilities	1
			Credit	Reduced Parking Footprint	2

Y	?	N	**Water Efficiency**		12
0	0	0			
Y			Prereq	Indoor Water Use Reduction	Required
			Credit	Indoor Water Use Reduction	12

Y	?	N	**Energy and Atmosphere**		38
0	0	0			
Y			Prereq	Fundamental Commissioning and Verification	Required
Y			Prereq	Minimum Energy Performance	Required
Y			Prereq	Fundamental Refrigerant Management	Required
			Credit	Enhanced Commissioning	5
			Credit	Optimize Energy Performance	25
			Credit	Advanced Energy Metering	2
			Credit	Renewable Energy Production	3
			Credit	Enhanced Refrigerant Management	1
			Credit	Green Power and Carbon Offsets	2

Y	?	N	**Materials and Resources**		13
0	0	0			
Y			Prereq	Storage and Collection of Recyclables	Required
Y			Prereq	Construction and Demolition Waste Management Planning	Required
			Credit	Long-Term Commitment	1
			Credit	Interiors Life-Cycle Impact Reduction	4
			Credit	Building Product Disclosure and Optimization - Environmental Product Declarations	2
			Credit	Building Product Disclosure and Optimization - Sourcing of Raw Materials	2
			Credit	Building Product Disclosure and Optimization - Material Ingredients	2
			Credit	Construction and Demolition Waste Management	2

Y	?	N	**Indoor Environmental Quality**	
0	0	0		
Y			Prereq	Minimum Indoor Air Quality Performance
Y			Prereq	Environmental Tobacco Smoke Control
			Credit	Enhanced Indoor Air Quality Strategies
			Credit	Low-Emitting Materials
			Credit	Construction Indoor Air Quality Management Plan
			Credit	Indoor Air Quality Assessment
			Credit	Thermal Comfort
			Credit	Interior Lighting
			Credit	Daylight
			Credit	Quality Views
			Credit	Acoustic Performance

Y	?	N	**Innovation**	
0	0	0		
			Credit	Innovation
			Credit	LEED Accredited Professional

Y	?	N	**Regional Priority**	
0	0	0		
			Credit	Regional Priority: Specific Credit
			Credit	Regional Priority: Specific Credit
			Credit	Regional Priority: Specific Credit
			Credit	Regional Priority: Specific Credit

Y	?	N	**TOTALS**	Possible Points
0	0	0		

Certified: 40 to 49 points, **Silver:** 50 to 59 points, **Gold:** 60 to 79 points, **Platinum:** 80 to 110

Table 12.6 LEED v.4 ID + C Checklist *(continued)*

LEED v4 for ID+C: Retail
Project Checklist

Project Name:
Date:

Y	?	N				
			Credit	Integrative Process		2

0	0	0	**Location and Transportation**		**18**
			Credit	LEED for Neighborhood Development Location	18
			Credit	Surrounding Density and Diverse Uses	8
			Credit	Access to Quality Transit	7
			Credit	Bicycle Facilities	1
			Credit	Reduced Parking Footprint	2

0	0	0	**Water Efficiency**		**12**
Y			Prereq	Indoor Water Use Reduction	Required
			Credit	Indoor Water Use Reduction	12

0	0	0	**Energy and Atmosphere**		**38**
Y			Prereq	Fundamental Commissioning and Verification	Required
Y			Prereq	Minimum Energy Performance	Required
Y			Prereq	Fundamental Refrigerant Management	Required
			Credit	Enhanced Commissioning	5
			Credit	Optimize Energy Performance	25
			Credit	Advanced Energy Metering	2
			Credit	Renewable Energy Production	3
			Credit	Enhanced Refrigerant Management	1
			Credit	Green Power and Carbon Offsets	2

0	0	0	**Materials and Resources**		**14**
Y			Prereq	Storage and Collection of Recyclables	Required
Y			Prereq	Construction and Demolition Waste Management Planning	Required
			Credit	Long-Term Commitment	1
			Credit	Interiors Life-Cycle Impact Reduction	5
			Credit	Building Product Disclosure and Optimization - Environmental Product Declarations	2
			Credit	Building Product Disclosure and Optimization - Sourcing of Raw Materials	2
			Credit	Building Product Disclosure and Optimization - Material Ingredients	2
			Credit	Construction and Demolition Waste Management	2

0	0	0	**Indoor Environmental Quality**		**18**
Y			Prereq	Minimum Indoor Air Quality Performance	18
Y			Prereq	Environmental Tobacco Smoke Control	8
			Credit	Enhanced Indoor Air Quality Strategies	7
			Credit	Low-Emitting Materials	1
			Credit	Construction Indoor Air Quality Management Plan	2
			Credit	Indoor Air Quality Assessment	
			Credit	Thermal Comfort	
			Credit	Interior Lighting	
			Credit	Daylight	
			Credit	Quality Views	

0	0	0	**Innovation**		
			Credit	Innovation	
			Credit	LEED Accredited Professional	

0	0	0	**Regional Priority**		
			Credit	Regional Priority: Specific Credit	
			Credit	Regional Priority: Specific Credit	
			Credit	Regional Priority: Specific Credit	
			Credit	Regional Priority: Specific Credit	

0	0	0	**TOTALS**	**Possible Points**

Certified: 40 to 49 points, **Silver:** 50 to 59 points, **Gold:** 60 to 79 points, **Platinum:** 80+

Table 12.7 Construction Documents Code Check Sheet

❏ Cover sheet
  ❏ Codes used listed with year
  ❏ Site/building location information

❏ Life-safety plan included
  ❏ Diagonal identified
  ❏ Travel distance and common path of travel included
  ❏ Occupancy load tables provided

❏ Accessibility detail drawings
  ❏ Reception desk detailed according to ADA
  ❏ Restrooms detailed in accordance with ADA
  ❏ Water fountains in accordance with ADA
  ❏ Turning radius indicated where required

❏ Reflected ceiling plan
  ❏ All exit signs located
  ❏ Sprinklers included (if applicable)
  ❏ Emergency lights
  ❏ Smoke detectors
  ❏ Fire alarms
  ❏ Additional Items
    __ Fire extinguishers located
    __ Corridor clearances dimensioned
    __ No dead-end corridors
    __ No exits through intervening spaces
    __ Doors swing in direction of egress
    __ Areas of refuge indicated
    __ Fire-rated assembly details including wall types

Construction Documents

During construction documents, all drawings and specifications for the project are produced. The construction documents will include a cover page that outlines all codes, standards, and other guidelines, as well as which version was used for the enclosed set of drawings and specifications (Table 12.7).

Conclusions

During the phases of a design project, the building code and other guidelines will need to continue to be complied with as decisions are made and finalized. This is an integral part of the design process. As the project details are refined, small changes will necessitate constant review to make sure all applicable codes, guidelines, and standards are still being met.

Credits

Front Matter
0.1   Fairchild Books

Chapter 1
1.1   Rendered by Yelena Safronova
1.2   LEED
1.3   USBGC
1.4   WELL Building Institute
1.5–8   Concept by author, drawn by Meagan Kelley

Chapter 2
2.1   Horydczak Collection/Library of Congress
2.2   Bridgeman-Giraudon/Art Resource, NY
2.3   Museum of London/HIP/Art Resource, NY
2.4   Chicago History Museum/Getty Images
2.5   ScienceSource
2.6   Robert Gauthier/Los Angeles Times via
          Getty Images
2.7   International Green Construction Code/
          International Code Council
2.8   US Government
2.9   © 2014 NFPA; Life Safety Code® and 101®
          are registered trademarks of the National
          Fire Protection Association, Quincy, MA
2.10   The Facilities Guidelines Institute
2.11   US Government

Chapter 3
3.1   Author

Chapter 4
4.1   Concept by author, drawn by Andrea Bonilla
4.2   Amy Groome

Chapter 5
5.1–5   Concept by author, drawn by Meagan Kelley
5.6–10   Leigh Ann Soistma
5.11–16   Janey Green
5.17–21   Kela Bogaard
5.22–25   Concept by author, drawn by Meagan Kelley

Chapter 6
6.1–4   Concept by author, drawn by Meagan Kelley
6.5–19   L. Soistmann, J. Green
6.20–30   Meagan Kelley
6.31–44   Jill Tucker

Chapter 7
7.1–9   Nadia Colquiett
7.10–15   Jill Tucker
7.16–35   Joevannah Harris
7.36–54   Amy Groome
7.55–62   WELL Building Institute

Chapter 8
8.1–10a   Julia Sakowitz
8.10b   Leemage/Corbis via Getty Images
8.11a   Julia Sakowitz
8.11b   DeAgostini/Getty Images
8.12–15   Leigh Ann Soistmann
8.16   Annie Gusler
8.17–20   Shannon Myers

Chapter 9
9.1–5   Savannah Mills
9.6–25   Leigh Ann Soistmann
9.26–38   Kimberly Duty

Chapter 10
10.1   Drawing by Frank Lloyd Wright, from the
          collection of Harvey Glanzer, photographed
          by author
10.2–27   Nadia Colquiett
10.28–47 Jaime Haile
10.48–53 Kaitlin Bonney
10.54   Concept by author, drawn by Meagan Kelley
10.55–64 Joevannah Harris

Chapter 12
12.1–6   Concept by author, drawn by Meagan Kelley
12.7–8   Author

Index

People Helping People Build a Safer World®

Count on ICC to help you get Up-to-Code

Building Code Essentials: Based on the 2018 International Building Code®

Achieve a more complete understanding of the code's requirements and the intent and application behind its provisions.

This helpful resource explores the most important concepts of the 2018 IBC® and the most commonly encountered building practices in a straightforward, easy-to-understand manner. Developed for all code user levels, from first-timers to veterans, Essentials can help to build a solid foundation for learning and applying the code's requirements. This valuable publication is an up-to-date, step-by-step guide to understanding and applying the 2018 IBC provisions. Features:

✓ Updated content accurately reflects the requirements of the IBC.

✓ Detailed, full-color illustrations and tables enhance the reader's comprehension and help them visualize and understand the code requirements.

✓ "Code Essentials" and "You Should Know" topics reinforce the content and offer helpful snapshots of the code basics.

✓ A glossary of code and construction terms clarifies critical terminology, explaining it in the context of the code.

✓ Detailed, real-world examples facilitate the user's comprehension of code application and methods of determining code compliance.

Soft Cover #4031S18   **PDF Download** #8951P009

Significant Changes to the International Building Code, 2018 Edition

This must-have guide provides comprehensive, yet practical, analysis of the critical changes made between the 2015 and 2018 editions of the IBC. Key changes are identified then followed by in-depth discussion of how the change affects real-world application. Features:

✓ A quick summary, color illustration, and discussion accompanies each change

✓ Key insights into the IBC's content, meaning and implications

✓ Includes changes to the 2018 IEBC®

Soft Cover #7024S18   **PDF Download** #8950P785

Get your 2018 IBC resources today!
1-800-786-4452 | www.iccsafe.org/books